# PALEFACE

# PALEFACE

## THE PHILOSOPHY OF THE
## ' MELTING-POT '

*By*

# WYNDHAM
# LEWIS

LONDON

## CHATTO & WINDUS

## 1929

Republished 1971
Scholarly Press, Inc., 22929 Industrial Drive East
St. Clair Shores, Michigan 48080

Library of Congress Catalog Card Number:  70-145142
ISBN  0-403-01073-X

HT
1521
L 455
1971

# PREFACE

PART II of this essay was written during a visit to the United States (summer 1927): since its first appearance in *Enemy No. 2* it has been somewhat modified and other material has been incorporated in it. The part entitled 'A Moral Situation' and the passages coming beneath the heading 'A Model Melting-pot' have been written during the last few months, and are published here for the first time.

For what our white skin is worth, symbolically or otherwise, it is in America that its destinies are to-day most clearly foreshadowed: the essential universality of the problems provided for the Palefaces of America by the indian factor in Latin America, by the Negro in North America and the West Indies, and by the proximity of Asia to the western shores of the United States, makes their attitudes in face of them of some moment to Europeans. And though there is no White Man's Burden in Europe at present, the isolation of Europe is rather artificial; and so, politically, even, the questions lightly touched upon in this book are not insignificant. In other respects, humanly, and artistically, there is an inexhaustible fund of simple amusement in consciousness of pigment. Colour is not perhaps so fundamental a thing as form, but it is, beyond dispute, in many respects of more immediate importance to men. Gentlemen prefer blondes, for instance—that was a question of *pigment*, and what a popular subject it proved! But gentlemen prefer, as far as their own persons are concerned, sunburn and a certain swarthiness. How brunette, however, would the masculine mind suffer gentlemen to become, in a search for the virile?—is it possible for gentlemen to be too 'dago' and too 'dark'? And then there must be a certain number of blond gentlemen.

But ultimately whiteness is, in a pigmentary sense, aristocratic, perhaps—the proper colour for a 'gentleman': and blackness irretrievably proletarian. May not this be an absolute, established in our senses? Then the dispute about cuticles would be seen to be another facet of the general assault upon privilege. Whiteness of skin if, like ermine, it is a symbol of rank, must be suspect to the democrat. The most humble Babbitt possesses something enviable, to which, besides, intellectually and socially, he has no right—namely his 'pale' face. But I need not insist: colour is not only controversial, it is for the human being of symbolical importance—it is able to dwarf stature, put intelligence in the shade, challenge quarterings: pallor and divinity are quite possibly in some way associated in our human eyes.

WYNDHAM LEWIS.

*March* 1929.

# CONTENTS

# PALEFACE

## PART II

## PALEFACE

viii

# CONTENTS

# CONTENTS

# PART I

## A 'MORAL SITUATION'

A

# A 'MORAL SITUATION'

## § 1. *The Future of the Paleface Position.*

NOW that my essay *Paleface* is to appear almost intact as part of this book, I hope by what I shall say in the opening pages to make it impossible to misinterpret its drift too much. I have been denounced as a 'champion' or 'saviour,' and that charge I must deal with once and for all, if only to be able to prosecute my function of 'impartial observer.' After a couple of years or eighteen months more of intense anti-Paleface propaganda, such champions will in fact arise. That I regard as fairly obvious. A variety of either astute or indignant men (persons actually *pale* with rage, or else persons reflecting that they might as well get *something* out of the possession of our traditional hue, since up to the present it has not exactly been an asset) are at this moment, upon that we can depend, preparing to assume that rôle.

To all these bolivars I wish a prosperous outcome to their spirited endeavours. At first their lot will be a hard one. They will have to idealize us a little, I expect—our pale faces have been so systematically blackened. And it will of course be difficult to prove that the Paleface is *better* than his Black or Yellow brother, not only because it is not true, but also because it is so unpopular a notion.

My position is that I am ready and most anxious to assist all those who suffer from *paleness* of complexion and all those under a cloud because their grandfathers exterminated the Redskins, or bought

and sold cargoes of Blacks.    My sense of what is just
suffers when I observe some poor honest little palefaced three-pound-a-week clerk or mechanic being
bullied by the literary Borzoi big-guns of Mr. Knopf,
and told to go and kiss the toe of the nearest Negress,
and ask her *humbly* (as befits the pallid and unpig-
mented) to be his bride.    I also am convulsed with
a little laughter at the solemnity with which so often
these discussions are pursued—the measurements of
cranial index, of lip brain and eye, in which the
Borzoi 'investigator' will indulge, the high scientific
plane in short upon which so much of this matter
is gushed forth.    But there are strict limits to my
ability to help, and these I must now define.

Meantime· I again publish and foretell that the
time will come (and that immediately) when, upon
the daily 'starred and red-billed' appearance before
the footlights of some indignant righteous figure (his
face corked to look black) despatched by Mr. Knopf
or Mr. Mencken or Mr. Plomer to abuse and ridicule
the audience (squatting beneath him, *pale* both with
natural pigment and with equally understandable
alarm), and to tell them what a lousy lot they
are, an extremely *pale* figure will either arise from
among the spectators and dramatically approach the
stage, or else will appear out of a trap, or descend
from the ceiling, or merely stalk from the wings, and
we shall hear what we shall hear.


§ 2. *If the Redskin were in our Position.*

THIS first essay, entitled *A 'moral situation,'* is
devoted to showing the part played by the puritan

morality in the present situation. I do not of course mean that without that harsh, double-faced and double-edged, deeply sentimental code the world-scene would not have changed drastically. What I do mean is that the transformation of our society, consequent upon the technical triumphs of science, would have been conducted perhaps in a more rational atmosphere—not, as at present, thick with a medieval gloom of bloodshot righteousness.

Historically, the mischief that resides in unbridled moral righteousness can be described as follows.—Having wiped out or subjugated all peoples who had not had the advantages of a christian training in gentleness, humility, and other-worldliness, the puritan Palefaces of America and Europe naturally were very contrite and tried to make up for it to those who were left. Quantities of edifying books (which were translated into all languages) were produced, pointing out what a beast the Paleface was. There were just a few Palefaces who tried to bluff it out and announced roundly that they were ' blond beasts '—but such sectaries abused both their brother Palefaces and their imported 'Pale Galilean' God into the bargain, so that made no difference.

There is no especially sentimental or even mis-guided movement of emancipation today, anywhere in the world, that the typical protestant moralist can oppose, on any logical ground. For *logically* he is committed to every sentimental moral value what-ever. I do not of course mean that we should behave like Redskins, but it is not quite pointless to note that were the Redskins where today the Whites are, technically paramount in a mixed population,

5

no 'Colour Question' could possibly have arisen. The supreme beauty significance and limitless *superiority* of the copper skin, that of Choctaw or Blackfoot, over skins of all other colours, would be a settled axiom and doctrine: no hint of any other point of view would ever pass the severe red lips of the Red legislators and their fellow Redskins. Also, the Redskin being notoriously taciturn, there would not be much even of that: there would be no need of palaver, of course, whatever.—In short, it is *conscience* that makes cowards, or saints, or just sentimental pinky-pinky little *Palefaces* of us, that is the truth of the matter: and yet we are as harsh as ever with each other, in business and in private life, and there is some chance that we may wipe each other completely out—where, with the disappearance of the White skin, the Colour question would automatically cease.

A question is lying in wait for me: 'Are you not then upon the side of conscience—you despise the christian ethic?' But it is to that I wished to lead, and I answer promptly—'Oh no—you have quite mistaken my meaning. You expect too much of me, or too little, according to the point of view. The "principle of an absolute value in the human person as such," of whatever race or order, I am eager to advance. But you? I only question if you fully understood the nature of your christian sacrifice. If you do not understand it, then it is useless and you are merely a fool. When a person as it were *selfishly* immolates himself, in response to some very tawdry emotional appeal, we call it a sentimentality. Are you sure that your asceticism (or

6

humanitarianism, radicalism, or liberalism) is not of that kind?'

If you want to know the answer to these questions of mine, see whether my further analysis outrages or annoys you or not. Then you will know.

## § 3. *The Ethics at the Basis of the Colour Question.*

THE european political leaders have been almost fantastically sensitive to ethical considerations in their policies from time to time—they have seldom acted too brutally without afterwards acting too gently, to restore the christian balance. This hyper-sensitive condition induced by their protestant christian training, of kirk and sunday-school, has had its good and bad side, in the sequel: but as statesmanship, upon the old jingo basis, it was indefensible.

So having isolated in the present situation in which our society finds itself the principal motive power, that which gives it the colour that it has though not the form, we can proceed to an examination of those ethical principles at their source. For this purpose I will take the very useful *Prolegomena to Ethics* of T. H. Green. (Green was a celebrated Oxford moral philosopher, issuing from the revolutionary philosophy of Hegel, rather earlier than Bradley and Bosanquet.) I had better say at once that it is a book that appears to me almost typically unintelligent. It is indeed representative of that blight that morals have insinuated under the skin of most Europeans. The sheer sentimentalism of this revolutionary protestant moralist is nevertheless a

7

very interesting medium through which to look at the objects of our present concern. One reason for this is that it was the characteristic atmosphere of anglo-saxon life, during many years, during which the events of today were being prepared, throughout the world.

## § 4. *The Cause of 'God and the People.'*

In speaking of the conscientious perplexities of the religious mind, when it finds the teaching of its dogma in conflict with the interest of the State, Green writes:

'the same difficulty . . . in earlier days must have occurred to Quakers and Anabaptists, where the law derived from Scripture seemed contradictory to that of the state, and to those early Christians for whom the law which they disobeyed in refusing to sacrifice retained any authority. In still earlier times it may have arisen in the form of that conflict between the laws of the family and the law of the State, presented in the *Antigone*. Nor is the case really different when the modern citizen, in his capacity as an official or as a soldier, is called upon to help in putting down some revolutionary movement which yet presents itself to his inmost conviction as the cause of "God and the People!"'

Green goes on to consider what must be the attitude of the philosopher in this painful situation—in which God, or conscience, is upon one side, apparently, and the State, or the organized authority at any given moment, upon the other. He concludes that the philosopher, by the effect of his teaching beforehand upon the minds of the effective minority, may have some useful influence in the moment of crisis.

'In preparation for the times when conscience is thus liable to be divided against itself, much practical service may be rendered by a philosophy which, without depreciating the authority of conscience as such, can explain the origin of its conflicting deliverances, and, without pronouncing unconditionally for either, can direct the soul to the true end. . . .'

The counsel of such a philosopher as he has been considering might 'have its effect upon the few who lead the many, in preparing the mind through years of meditation for the days when prompt practical decision is required': that is the point.

In any 'conflict between private opinion and authority,' Green's counsel would always be on the side of the individual and his independent conscience. And indeed to the full-blooded claims of such a 'conscience' to make a waste-land of our life, Green would set positively no bounds at all. Every year 'conscience' must weigh more heavily upon us, as christian men, he affirms. Every fresh star that swims into our ken is a fresh burden—never a new delight, always an added nightmare. Reflection upon the load *we* have to carry in comparison with the lighthearted Hellene of Antiquity, provides Green with a long series of dismal reflections, inviting us to an ideal of mechanical and colourless asceticism.

9

## § 5. *Passing 'the point beyond which there seems no longer to be either good or evil.'*

To pass the barrier described above by Aristotle into a non-ethical region is not part of the asceticism of this particular kind of moralist, for his 'willingness to endure even unto complete self-renunciation, even to the point of forsaking all possibility of pleasure,' is envisaged by Green in the most cheerless manner, in a kind of paroxysm of middleclass nineteenth-century christian-duty, that is calculated to make the flesh creep far more thoroughly than could any self-imposed rigours of the gymnosophist.

'To an ancient Greek a society composed of a small group of freemen, having recognized claims upon each other and using a much larger body of men with no such recognized claims as instruments in their service, seemed the only possible society. In such an order of things those calls could not be heard which evoke the sacrifices constantly witnessed in the nobler lives of Christendom, sacrifices which would be quite other than they are, if they did not involve the renunciation of those "pleasures of the soul" and "unmixed pleasures," as they were reckoned in the Platonic psychology, which it did not occur to the philosophers that there could be any occasion in the exercise of the highest virtue to forgo. The calls for such sacrifices arise from that enfranchisement of all men which, though in itself but negative in its nature, carries with it for the responsive conscience a claim on the part of all men to such positive help from all men as is needed to make

10

their freedom real. Where the Greek saw a supply
of possibly serviceable labour, . . . the Christian
citizen sees a multitude of persons, who in their
actual present condition may have no advantage
over the slaves of an ancient state, but who in
undeveloped possibility, and in the claims which
arise out of that possibility, are all that he himself is. Seeing this, he finds a necessity laid upon
him. It is no time to enjoy the pleasures of eye
and ear, of search for knowledge, of friendly inter-
course, of applauded speech or writing, while the
mass of men . . . whom we declare to be meant
with us for eternal destinies, are left without the
chance . . . of making themselves in act what
in possibility we believe them to be. Interest in
the problem of social deliverance . . . forbids a
surrender to enjoyments which are not incidental
to that work of deliverance, whatever the value
which they, or the activities to which they belong,
might otherwise have.'

As to this progressive renunciation of every ves-
tige of pleasure, on behalf of this 'principle of an
abstract value in the human person as such,' Green
says that with 'every advance towards its universal
application comes a complication of the necessity,
under which the conscientious man feels himself
placed, of sacrificing personal pleasure in satisfaction
of the claims of human brotherhood. On the one
side the freedom of everyone to shift for himself . . .
on the other, the responsibility of everyone for
everyone, acknowledged by the awakened conscience: *these together form a moral situation in which*

11

*the good citizen has no leisure to think of developing in due proportion his own faculties of enjoyment.'* (I have italicized the last sentence.)

The 'good citizen's' lot, having to forgo more and more enjoyment, even 'the pleasures of the soul' (which it did not so much as occur to a Greek to sacrifice), is indeed a melancholy one, it seems, as the number of people in the world increases and as the newspapers or cinemas inform him, or put visibly before him, more and more creatures for whom he is 'responsible.' This is surely the very madness of morality, for there is no compensating beauty such as you get in the great catholic mystics; there is nothing but this cold and ever growing, dutiful, quantitative, *responsibility.*

### § 6. *'Every man both by law and common sentiment is recognized as having a "suum."'*

ACCORDING to Green's expanding principle of 'the common good' there is no limit to such expansion, or to the corresponding depression and ascetic continence of the conscientious Christian. As 'men' we call a halt, however, before 'animals and things.' This at least, for Green, confines the question to the surface of this globe and to two-legged animals: no inhabitant of another world, or a mere horse or cat in this one, can make us unhappy. But to every 'man' we should not only postpone our own interest, but in his behalf, though we may never have seen him but only heard of him, we should abstain from any pleasure, *even of the mind.* (The abstaining from the 'pleasures of the mind' may be a compliment to our neighbour in his capacity of 'man,' in contradistinction to 'animal.')

In quoting the definition of Justice from the *Institutes* ('Justicia est constans et perpetua voluntas suum cuique tribuendi') he writes 'every man both by law and common sentiment is recognized as having a "suum"—that is the typical abstract expression of the notion that there is something due from every man to every man.' (The mere principle, of course, that everyone, of whatever caste, creed or race, has a 'suum,' is not sufficient to base our moral conduct upon, as we must first know what 'suum' is.)

But in Green's view 'there is no necessary limit of numbers or space beyond which the spiritual principle of social relations becomes ineffective.' His expansiveness is really infinite, that is to say.

'In the whole view of life which [philanthropic work] implies, in the objects which inspire it, . . . a view of life [is implied] in which the maintenance of any form of political society scarcely holds a place: in which lives that would be contemptible and valueless, if estimated with reference to the purposes of the State, are invested with a value of their own in virtue of capabilities of some society not seen as yet.'

This readiness of the fanatical moralist to ignore the claims of 'any form of political society' and to give up his life for the publicans and sinners, who are peculiarly adapted to 'some society not seen as yet,' gives him an unquestionable advantage over the Greek, contemporary with Plato: he proves

13

PALEFACE

that the 'progress of the species' is not a phantasy. —Yet of course, to the superficial eye, the Greek might be supposed to have the best of it. This is an absolute mistake.

'Now, when we compare the life of service to mankind, involving so much sacrifice of pure pleasure, which is lived by men whom in our consciences we think best, and which they reproach themselves for not making one of more complete self-denial, with the life of free activity in bodily and intellectual exercises, in friendly converse, in civil debate, in the enjoyment of beautiful sights and sounds, which we commonly ascribe to the Greeks . . . we might be apt, in the first view, to think that, even though measured not merely by the quantity of pleasure incidental to it but by the fulness of the realization of human capabilities implied in it, the latter kind of life was the higher of the two. Man for man, the Greek . . . might seem to be intrinsically a nobler being— one of more fully developed powers—than the self-mortifying Christian, upon whom the sense of duty to a suffering world weighs too heavily to allow of his giving free-play to enjoyable activities. . . .'

'On the first view' you would fall perhaps into that mistake, and as far as this philosopher's account of the situation is concerned no one could find it in his heart, or conscience, to blame you, I believe. I find it impossible to rescue myself from that initial error.

§ 7. *Our World has become an almost purely* Ethical
    *Place.*

THE 'moral situation' which in these quotations
from Green I have, I hope, brought clearly before
you, is the *moral situation* that underlies all the
questions that are agitating us today.—The funda-
mentals of this situation are clearly explained to
you by these quotations from Green.  It is 'a moral
situation,' that is the essential point: our world
has become an almost purely *ethical* place.  But
since the time of Green much progress has been
made—he would scarcely recognize it.  (If he came
to life again I shudder to think of the sheer avoirdu-
pois of miserable duty that would be added to his
already staggering load.)   There is the same 'moral
situation,' but men's capacity to harm and interfere
with each other has immensely increased, and they
have not been slow to take advantage of this.   So
side by side we have an ever-increasing *ethical* pressure—more and more strenuous streams of moral
persuasiveness—and a darker and darker cloud of
poison-gas always gathering upon the horizon, and
larger and larger birds of prey—in the form of aero-
planes pregnant with colossal bombs—hovering over
us: also war-films and war-books multiply at a
dumbfounding rate.—So it is an intensely 'moral
situation': soon any 'ascetic' worth his salt will
sink immediately beneath the burden, as he steps
out of his cradle and looks round—already several
are mere spectres in our midst, from whose lips
issue a few sepulchral words at rare intervals.

Discussing a remark of Matthew Arnold's regard-

15

ing *righteousness,* Samuel Butler made some comments worth considering in this connection. Among
other things he wrote as follows:

'I would join issue with Mr. Matthew Arnold
on yet another point. I understand him to imply
that righteousness should be a man's highest aim
in life. I do not like setting up righteousness,
nor yet anything else, as the highest aim in life:
a man should have any number of little aims about
which he should be conscious and for which he
should have names, but he should have neither
name for, nor consciousness concerning, the main
aim of his life. Whatever we do we must try and
do rightly—this is obvious—but *righteousness*
implies something much more than this: it con-
veys to our minds not only the desire to get whatever we have taken in hand as nearly *right* as
possible, but also the general reference of our lives
to the supposed will of an unseen but supreme
power. Granted that there is such a power, and
granted that we should obey its will, we are the
more likely to do this the less we concern ourselves about the matter and the more we confine
our attention to the things immediately round
about us.'

That has a most agreeable sound after Green: the
'desire to dogmatise about matters whereon the
Greek and Roman held certainty to be at once unimportant and unattainable' (again Butler's words)
grows upon a person or upon a community: and
though I should not be able to agree with all of
Butler's text, the passion for tolerance, at least,

which was such a feature of that light-hearted and penetrating philosopher, is surely today a thing of which we cannot have enough, as we find ourselves hemmed in more and more by righteousness and intolerance.

## § 8. *Esprit de Peau.*

PLAINLY if no obligation of any sort were recognized, we should not be discussing these things at all and the man with the money and the gun would do as he liked.   It is true that such an event as the Civil War has been accounted for on the ground of the existence of certain economic factors; and from what we know of such events, unadulterated altruism is unlikely to have been the sole incentive.   But however impure the motives that can be smelt out— and that is seldom difficult—the brutal physical subjection of one race to another could not co-exist with such conditions as at present obtain throughout the world.   And, once that first radical emancipation effected, the race-prejudice or traditional superstition of some absolute or mystical 'superiority' could not be maintained, either.   Step by step the sensation that he was dealing with a being of a lower order was bound to be wormed or beaten out of the average White, for the simple reason that the average White has the same master as the average Black; and although that master's skin is more or less White, he is not a man of sentiment and he *s'en moque pas mal*, as far as the question of *skins* is concerned: what interests him is what he has to pay the hands he employs, naturally, and not their

B                    17

colour. And this applies both in Africa and America, or wherever else you get that situation— of a master (who happens usually to be White, but that is neither here nor there) and a mixed population of Black and White wage-slaves, of all shades of race and creed.

A belief in racial superiority (such as was entertained by the White Brahmin in India for the negritic population of the Dekkan, or such as is still felt by the average uninstructed White American for a Negro) is a political factor of great effectiveness, of course, but only on condition that the political power be jealously invested in the hands of a minority of a certain skin, and with a flourishing esprit de corps or *esprit de peau*, as it might be called, and provided real inalienable privileges go with the pigment. That is only possible in the closed political systems represented by Greece, India, China, or, as regards America, in the earlier history of the United States.

Where privilege disappears and a pigmentation or a racial descent takes with it no artificial advantages, these formal beliefs wither at once. For take another racial superstition, the most intense and inveterate that the world has ever known—namely that of the *inferiority* of the Jew. A 'superiority complex' has, until recently, been enjoyed by everybody at the expense of that kind of religious outcast, almost 'untouchable,' of the West. With their immense intellectual resources, the lustre of their theologic past, the Jews themselves were lifted above this superstition, no doubt. But today that particular superstition has little chance of survival in the bosom of some very average European, left to him-self, and confronted in the mechanical jungle of a modern city by some jewish competitor, who prob-ably possesses twice as much intelligence as he does, and whose industry or even mania for work puts what is quite likely his very moderate zeal in the shade. And when you add to this the fact of the admirable organization of the jewish consciousness, and that the poor little non-jewish protagonist will have nothing behind him but our untidy, selfish, chaotic political systems, and about as much esprit de corps or *esprit de peau* to support him as would be found in a family of guinea-pigs, it is difficult to see how *that* particular sense of superiority could have survived in present conditions. And indeed it has not. That 'superiority' superstition is, of course, the extreme case: but there is no other top-dog-feeling either, based on tribal or national self-feeling, or prestige of skin, which can survive in the heart of a wage-slave or economic under-dog, in touch with men technically of 'inferior' races, in the same situation as himself, competing with him, when no favour of an artificial sort, but indeed rather the contrary, is extended to him.

§ 9. *How you must beware of too much 'esprit de peau.'*

UNABLE to ignore in my analysis of what under-lies the literary and pictorial expression of the pre-sent time, the political factors so busily at work, I find myself with some surprise writing about human skins. And under more normal conditions I should probably be ranged upon the other side of the argument. I am really driven into the position of the Devil's Advocate to some extent (the devil or villain-of-the-piece being now of course the overbearing, stupid, wicked *Paleface* as seen by the conventional revolutionary tract) by the excesses of the anti-Whites—not, I am afraid, from what I have called *esprit de peau*. But flung violently into that diabolical position, I did I must say at first find myself developing what was a sort of *esprit de peau*, of a quite respectable dimension. I detected myself looking with a new complacency upon the White skin: there was something about a *Paleface*, was there not? that I had overlooked in my zeal for a non-national consciousness: I could scarcely understand how it had escaped my attention that all these familiar lightish masks held something for my eye, nevertheless (blunted by familiarity), that the varnished countenance of a quadroon or a 'high yaller,' or the sickly liverish ambers of an Hawaian belle, did not contain.

As a consequence of these personal experiences of mine (to which I have had to call a halt, but which I shall not forget) I really believe that we could, if we wanted to, get up quite a fellow-feeling for our fellow *Palefaces*. What I fear is that as things stand at present it would immediately result in our looking askance at our Black and Yellow brothers: for everybody has been so long indoctrinated with intolerant attitudes of mind, that dogmatical mechanical reversals have become the only way that the average Paleface is now able to express himself at all. So when it suddenly became plain to the enlightened Paleface what admirable people the White Europeans, his brothers and sisters, were (how far more significant to an unprejudiced and romantically-unrotted outlook the Paleface girl was than the average coloured lady), he would turn with an unsocial or even anti-social animosity upon the simple-hearted African, who is in no way responsible for all these 'Dark Princesses' or the Colour phantasies indulged in by the Borzoi big-guns and some others.

As far as I am concerned I would rather have things as they are than provoke in any way a re-action of intolerance. But there is no fear of that for the moment: and when the reaction comes, as it must, I hope that what I shall have had to say will serve to make its manifestations less ridiculous, and to offer some resistance to the colour-blind fanatic who can only see one colour at a time, as it were, and not simultaneously embrace a walnut brown and an ivory white, as we all should be able to do with ease and conviction.

If these reactionary dangers could be conjured, then I believe that some sort of *esprit de peau* might be cultivated with advantage: for the intensive propagation of *inferiority-complexes* (in the present revolutionary reversals—and all Whites are suspect to some extent on account of their privileged position over against the Coloured Peoples) is not good for the morale of our communities and so affects all of us indirectly. Assuredly there are limits beyond which Green's counsel of depression and 'self-mortification' can be consummated in nothing but self-death : and self-death or suicide is not a step to which we should allow ourselves too tamely to be led—if only upon grounds of conscience. We have a responsibility of an order unguessed at by Green. For, if all *Palefaces* in the world were so truly righteous that we as one man succumbed, consequent upon the impossible burdens laid upon us by our puritan consciences (and I am perfectly ready to admit that if we sat down and thought comprehensively enough of all our sins and those of all our ancestors we should see no alternative but to succumb in that manner), why then all the Blacks, after us (who are even more emotional than we are and if anything better evangelists) would follow suit as one man, unable to bear the spectacle of this wholesale Tragedy of Conscience, of which they had been the innocent cause. No no! the example we have set already to all other peoples of the world has been unfortunate enough, in its mechanical sterility, and its agressive philistinism, without taking that further sin upon ourselves. Let us draw back in time. Let us keep our noses well in the air. It is the White Man's Burden!

§ 10. *The White in the same Boat as the Black.*

In § 7 I was dealing with what is the most powerful argument against the extension of an anti-White campaign—namely that the great majority of *Palefaces* are now in the same boat as their Coloured friends—that obviously they are in the position of fellow-slaves, and not of a 'White Conqueror' at all. It is even amazing that this should not be at once recognized. It is on account of what the communist would call the 'bourgeois' state of mind of the West that this simple fact is never noticed. But the whole situation (the 'moral situation'), as it stands, appears to me on the face of it exceedingly false, even laughable. One would almost think, while reading a typical propagandist book, of the Plomer or Du Bois variety, that their authors had never considered (apart from giving their assent or not) the message of the communist, nor were familiar with the picture the latter delights to draw of the Capitalist System and its inhuman results. Yet they are communists, for the most part. But they are *bourgeois* communists, of our pink Western variety.

I will assemble for your inspection a few of the contradictions of this particular 'moral' situation. First, there are vociferous advocates or 'champions' for every description of man in the world today *except* for the White Man. If any one announced his intention of becoming that, the Paleface World would be amazed. It would be as though a man had proclaimed himself a 'Champion of the Kaiser' —before the Kaiser's fall! Everybody assumes that the White Man (and that I take it does not mean a handful of magnates but the White Average) is an oppressive, overbearing, unintelligent, cruel, conceited top-dog—obviously not in need, there-fore, of a 'champion,' in the way that a poor down-trodden Mexican Peon, American Negro, Chinaman or Bantu, is. This may be so: but there are hundreds of thousands of miners and their families in England today who are out of work and without the proper requirements for animal life. Against the

London parks at night penniless people lie huddled in their hundreds. Our streets both day and night swarm with every variety of beggar. All these are White People, and they rule the world, suffering to a man from 'superiority' complexes. It is a paradox: for they have a strange way of testifying to their superiority!

By turning to the more prosperous levels of the community, you will find equally many evidences of overweening mastery—only there the tyrannous Paleface is merely more restrained—he does not fling himself down upon the pavement to sleep on a winter night to show his 'mastery,' he has other and subtler ways.

If there is mastery, at all events, let us confess that it is very skin-deep: employment is obtained and held under more exacting conditions than before, there is everywhere more anxiety and less freedom. On this last head let me quote from the *Daily Telegraph*, a paper that cannot be accused of 'bolshevist' propensities, surely.

### 'MOST GOVERNED NATION
#### 'THIRTY YEARS' CHANGE

' OTTAWA, *Monday*

'Sir William Clark, British High Commissioner, addressing the Institute of Professional Men and Civil Servants of Canada, went on to say:

'"It is fairly safe to say that thirty years ago Great Britain was less governed than almost any country in Europe, but now its inhabitants are more thoroughly inspected, controlled, and administered from the cradle to the grave than those, perhaps, of any other nation." '

It is nothing, of course, to be 'inspected and controlled.' But *masters* are not overlooked, numbered like sheep, inspected and hectored for minor disobedience.

We are in Europe barely ten years away from an unexampled War (both in losses, duration and in aimlessness) of the most consummate barbarity; and we are told on all hands in our 'capitalist' Press that we are well on the way to another one, which will be far worse. In the last war (Mr. Citizen is informed) the noble airmen of the various countries were only able to bomb to bits a mere handful of citizens (owing to the regrettable backwardness of the man of science—after all an air-force officer or a munition magnate cannot be expected to know anything about chemicals himself—*he* cannot make the bombs, nor improve the planes to carry them!) —but in the next jolly old flare-up (the next 'Great Adventure' in other words) millions of people, it is confidently expected, will be wiped out in a single night of fairly successful bombing.

Now as very few people today are thoroughly taken in by jingo cries and sudden accounts of the detestable characters possessed by all Frenchmen, or Germans, or Russians or whatever it may be (followed by a peremptory order to massacre all these villains and devils), it is not easy for them to feel very perfectly top-doggy or to enjoy as fully as they might wish the sensation that they are 'the roof and crown of things.' The gilded palaces in which

the Million drinks its tea or sees Ramon Novarro or
Dolores Costello, give them a little that feeling, but
not altogether.  And not being quite irrational, they
do see beneath this luxurious gilding, for which they
pay their sixpences, in glimpses (between the cracks
of some foolish film, between the lines of some drivelling article), a 'moral situation' that has little enough
comfort to satisfy the philosopher from whom I
have quoted.  May not, you ask yourself as you
watch him, this Master of the World find himself in
the end, abject and leaderless, a herd whose pale
skin is a standing reproach—an emblem of tyranny
instead of an emblem of privilege—driven madly
hither and thither in gigantic wars that have at
length become completely meaningless?  If this
apocalyptic picture sounds to your ears sensational
or far-fetched, I can only say that you forget very
quickly what was called at the time 'Armageddon.'

With these circumstances (of enormous disaster
so close behind us and of a most uncertain future—
to judge by Naval-Pacts and the rest of what we are
told in our papers) featured for once properly, as
they deserve, well in the forefront of our mind, is it
possible to listen very patiently to tales of 'our'
oppression of the Black, the Yellow or the Red?
They are doubtless 'oppressed,' all of them, just as
we are—if you must talk about oppression: but
that *we* is a thing that today sticks deeper and
deeper in our throats.  'Our Indian Possessions' is
not a phrase that even the stupidest Englishman
would employ today: and whoever Indians have
to deal with—and no doubt they have to deal with
somebody—it is not with *us*.

I have been accused, for my *Paleface*, of a desire to keep under *my* heel the population of Bengal, by my friend Paul and my friend Sage (as I have been accused for my remarks on *Mother India* of a desire to rescue India from Paleface dominion and its abuses). I have answered those gentlemen elsewhere, however. In addressing my brother Palefaces, at the start, and in using, possibly, an *us* or a *we* (as one Paleface to another), it may really have been assumed, of course, that I was implying that 'our' interests, if there are such things, possess a beautiful coherence and simplicity that in fact is far from the case. Were there readers who assumed that I intended to say that the 'Palefaces' should be given for ever and for ever softer beds, nicer and warmer clothes, better roofs over their heads, and more pocket-money than their Black, Yellow, and Red brothers? I hope at all events that now I shall have succeeded in disabusing any one of such a belief. But in a further section I will be engaged in eradicating even more thoroughly such a misconception from the casual mind.

§ 11. *The Paleface, that 'negation of colour,' as seen by Du Bois.*

To the European who has not followed at all the sociological controversy peculiar to the Publics of America, some of the point of what I have written may quite well be lost, for the 'problem' that certainly exists as between the inhabitants of Europe (that 'small cape' tacked on to Asia) and the great continents inhabited by the 'coloured' peoples, or

27

shared with the Whites, is not a matter of everyday interest. The european Press resounds with the disputes of the alsatian Separatists, the roumanian or tyrolean minorities, the frontier squabbles of Fascist Italy with France or Switzerland, and of course with dog-racing and the explosion of gas-mains, but it is strictly the european scene of the moment that is reflected, and all other parts of the world are shut out, they have no news-value. This is far more so today than when what happened in America or Asia mattered immeasurably less to the average European.

It may under these circumstances be as well to select a book or two, and by means of a few extracts show that this 'problem' is at least an extremely exciting one to many people, and that books dealing with it are able to command a wide public. The books of Mr. Plomer the South African novelist are no doubt known to all South Africans, and in England they have received some attention, so I will not take them, but rather make my selection from american lists.

'The Negro in Borzoi Books' (as the Knopf advertisement runs) is very prominent, and it is Mr. Knopf, the New York publisher, who in his sponsoring of the *American Mercury* and his constant featuring of Negro subjects has done more than any one else to bring this sort of agitation to a head. In *The Autobiography of an ex-coloured Man,* in *The Fire in the Flint, Flight, Wooings of Jezebel, Pettyfer, The Weary Blues, Fine Clothes for the Jew, Negro Drawings, Fo'melsaday, Lily, Lady Luck, The Wildcat, The American Negro, Quicksand,* and *The Sailor's*

*Return*, you have throughout the theme of Black *versus* White as a *leit motiv*—or at all events that of the sad lot of the Negro in the White World.

It has never been my privilege to meet Mr. Knopf, and I can hazard no opinion as to what actuates him in this matter: but I have no reason to suppose that it has been anything but a compassionate sense of the Negro's sufferings, coupled with an intelligent dislike of that certain shallow cocksureness shown by many Palefaces, both of which feelings, if they are his, I share with him. He has certainly been instrumental, however that may be, in improving the Negro's position a great deal in the North, and in reducing on all sides the cocksureness I have just mentioned. But both the important *Review* that has had his support, and the books he has published, have adopted often an exceedingly partisan and bellicose attitude. And it is that which must in the end, if persisted in, call out the White Hopes, to whom I referred at the commencement of this book.

There is however a volume entitled *Dark Princess*, by W. E. B. Du Bois, published by Harcourt Brace, which suggests itself to me as the best thing of the sort to quote from of any, in order to provide the uninitiated White reader with some idea of the character and intensity of this movement. *Dark Princess* is a novel: it describes the adventures of a negro doctor, named Matthew Towns. It is a novel of the best-seller type, from that point of view in the same category as say Van Vechten. It is written I believe by a Negro, which is of course to start with better for a book than being written

29

by Van Vechten (the author of *Nigger Heaven*—so
well known that there could be no object in quoting
from it). A rather fiery political purpose informs
the *Dark Princess*, and it combines the characteristics of one of the cheaper films with a violent
political tract, but in this case, I believe, quite a
sincere political tract.

Matthew Towns is a negro medical student in
New York. After two years at a medical school he
wishes to register for obstetrics. The 'Dean' refuses
to allow him to do this. In the course of an alterca-
tion the Dean remarks, 'Well, what did you expect?
Juniors must have obstetrical work. Do you think
white women patients are going to have a nigger
doctor delivering their babies?' Towns throws his
certificate and other documents in the face of the
Dean: after that he leaves America, naturally in a
very savage state of mind.

In a Berlin Café, where he is sitting very home-
sick for the Dark World from which he has become
exiled, his eyes suddenly fall upon a beautiful and
romantic figure—a *dark* figure—in short, upon one
of his own kind. This event is described as follows.

'First and above all came that sense of color:
into this world of pale yellowish and pinkish
parchment, that absence or negation of color,
came suddenly a glow of golden brown skin.'

(This World 'of pale yellowish and pinkish parchment' is *our* World, the White World; in language
of this sort in fact our poor World is always described—in a most disrespectful and wounding
manner.)

The eyes of the dark, the 'colorful' apparition are 'pools of night,' they have 'beautiful depths' (you could imagine yourself in the midst of a story by D. H. Lawrence, almost).   Matthew pulls himself together.   'Here—here in Berlin, and a few tables away, actually sat a radiantly beautiful woman, *and she was colored.*'

But out of that circumambient world of 'pale yellowish and pinkish parchment' comes a figure, one with a pinkish parchment face—in short, White —an american White.   This pasty 'negation of color' attempts to thrust himself upon the beautiful dark apparition.   Towns follows them outside, and as the dark lady is about to enter a taxi, he hits the pinkish parchment mask 'right between the smile and the ear.'   Exit the White World.   Matthew Towns springs into the taxi.   After a little conversation he finds he is in the presence of an Indian Princess.

'H.R.H. The Princess Kautilya of Bwodpur, India,' it transpires, is one of the leaders of an organization for arming all the Coloured Peoples, in Asia, America, and Africa, against the Whites.   He is invited to a dinner, at which Coloured leaders from all parts of the world are present.   Here is the description of the guests.

'Ten of them sat at the table.   On the Princess' left was a Japanese, faultless in dress and manner, evidently a man of importance, as the deference shown him and the orders on his breast indicated. He was quite yellow, short and stocky, with a face which was a delicately handled but perfect mask. There were two Indians, one a man grave,

31

haughty, and old, dressed richly in turban and embroidered tunic, the other, in conventional dress and turban, a young man, handsome and alert, whose eyes were ever on the Princess. There were two Chinese, a young man and a young woman, he in a plain but becoming Chinese costume of heavy blue silk, she in a pretty dress, half Chinese, half European in effect. An Egyptian and his wife came next, he suave, talkative, and polite—just a shade too talkative and a bit too polite, Matthew thought; his wife a big, handsome, silent woman, elegantly jeweled and gowned, with much bare flesh. Beyond them was a cold and rather stiff Arab who spoke seldom, and then abruptly.'

These were the guests of the Princess Kautilya— who turns to Towns and remarks, '"You will note, Mr. Towns, that we represent here much of the Darker World. Indeed, when all our circle is present, we represent all of it, save your world of Black Folk." "All the darker world except the darkest," said the Egyptian.'

As to the deportment of this Dark, conspiratorial company, it left nothing to be desired, from the standpoint of the most exacting Paleface traditions. Indeed, after they 'had eaten some delicious tidbits of meat and vegetables' and been 'served with a delicate soup' (the service and cuisine are thoroughly european, only more magnificent, of course, than anything known to the Gourmets Club in Paris— there are 'des trous normandes' at the right moment in the 'collation,' only deeper holes than any Paleface ever dug, and as to the caviare—!!)—but after the first 'tidbits of meat' Towns becomes more and more thunderstruck at 'the ease and fluency with which most of this company used languages, so easily, without groping or hesitation, and with light sure shading,' and the manner in which 'they talked art in French, literature in Italian, politics in German, and everything in clear English.'

For my own part I must confess that, in reading *Dark Princess*, I was somewhat abashed, myself, to remark that these Dark plotters were as familiar with 'Vorticism'—my invention—as with chopsticks. But I was flattered, too, of course: whereas Towns grows less and less elated as the meal goes on.

' "Pan-Africa," says the Princess, "belongs logically with Pan-Asia; and for that reason Mr. Towns is welcomed tonight by you, I am sure, and by me especially. He did me a service as I was returning from the New Palace.'

'They all looked interested, but the Egyptian broke out:

' "Ah, Your Highness, the New Palace, and what is the fad today? What has followed expressionism, cubism, futurism, vorticism? I confess myself at sea. Picasso alarms me. Matisse sets me aflame. But I do not understand them. I prefer the classics."

' "The Congo," said the Princess, "is flooding the Acropolis. There is a beautiful Kandinsky on exhibit, and some lovely and startling things by unknown newcomers."

' "*Mais*," replied the Egyptian, dropping into French—and they were all off to the discussion,

c           33

save the silent Egyptian woman and the taciturn Arab.

'Here again Matthew was puzzled. These persons easily penetrated worlds where he was a stranger. Frankly, but for the context he would not have known whether Picasso was a man, a city, or a vegetable. He had never heard of Matisse. Lightly, almost carelessly, as he thought, his companions leapt to unknown subjects. Yet they knew. They knew art, books, and literature, politics of all nations, and not newspaper politics merely, but inner currents and whisperings, unpublished facts.'

The european culture of this gathering of dusky principals is in brief nothing short of staggering— they can mix Picasso with a 'tidbit of meat' and impale 'Futurism' on the way to a potato: but at a certain point in the ceremony Matthew Towns 'left the piquant salad and laid down his fork slowly.' For he detected what is described as 'a color line within a color line.' It was the Japanese who had made him leave 'the piquant salad.'

The Japanese has cast a doubt upon the honourable capacity of the american Negro. But the Princess says that in Moscow she has heard such accounts of the Negro as to make her in fact sit up.

' "You see, Moscow has reports," she says, "careful reports of the world's masses. And the report on the Negroes of America was astonishing. At the time, I doubted its truth: their education, their work, their property, their organizations; and the odds, the terrible, crushing odds against

which, inch by inch and heartbreak by heartbreak, they have forged their unfaltering way
upward.   If the report is true, they are a nation
today, a modern nation worthy to stand beside
any nation here."

' "But can we put any faith in Moscow?" asked
the Egyptian.   "Are we not keeping dangerous
company and leaning on broken reeds?"

' "Well," said Matthew, "if they are as sound in
everything as in this report from America, they'll
bear listening to."

'The young Indian spoke gently and evenly,
but with bright eyes.

' "Naturally," he said, "one can see Mr. Towns
needs must agree with the Bolshevik estimate of
the lower classes."

It is in this manner that Towns meets with 'a
prejudice within a prejudice.'   The 'lower classes'
amongst Coloured people are, it seems, the Negroes.
The Negro is racially a sort of *Proletariat*, it becomes
evident, and is treated a little 'de haut en bas' by
these brilliant asiatic conversationalists, plotting
world-war by the side of the Spree, in the heart of
a White capital.   'The Congo is flooding the Acropolis'—even the Princess had said that, indicating
that the Congo Black was considered by her in some
way a come-down for the White Overlord, in whose
blood symbolically was that of Praxiteles—a very
different thing from a Congo Black.   Still, the Princess is a bit of a Bolshie—it is evident from the start
that she does not share with her fellow-Asiatics
that inveterate aristocratism of the Hindu, which

makes him such an uncomfortable customer in some ways.

' "We American Blacks," said Matthew Towns, "are very common people. My grandfather was a whipped and driven slave; my father was never really free and died in jail. My mother plows and washes for a living. We come out of the depths—the blood and mud of battle. And from just such depths, I take it, came most of the worth-while things in this old world. If they didn't—God help us."

'The table was very still, save for the very faint clink of china as the servants brought in the creamed and iced fruit.

'The Princess turned, and he could feel her dark eyes full upon him.

' "I wonder—I wonder," she murmured, almost catching her breath.

'The Indian frowned. The Japanese smiled, and the Egyptian whispered to the Arab.'

The party does not break up till after midnight.

'It started on lines so familiar to Matthew that he had to shut his eyes and stare again at their swarthy faces: Superior races—the right to rule —born to command—inferior breeds—the lower classes—the rabble. How the Egyptian rolled off his tongue his contempt for the "r-r-rabble"! How contemptuous was the young Indian of inferior races! But how humorous it was to Matthew to see all tables turned; the rabble now was the white workers of Europe; the inferior races were the ruling whites of Europe and

36

America. The superior races were yellow and brown.'

Matthew at least is comforted to find 'all the tables turned.' It is pleasant to hear the White Workers of Europe and America described as the 'rabble,' and the White Rulers as the members of 'an inferior race.' But it is disagreeable to find the American Negro discriminated against by people so very little lighter than himself.

*Dark Princess* is a long book, this is only the beginning. It takes you back to America and you pass with Towns through a series of revolutionary adventures. He loses faith in the Princess, whom he loses sight of: he becomes steward on a railway and is almost lynched by members of the Ku Klux Klan, on their way to a great Clan rally at Chicago. He suffers prison, he makes reports on the revolutionary potentialities of his people, and so forth. At length he is mated with the 'Dark Princess' and all is well: he is eventually hailed as the 'Messenger and Messiah of all the Darker Worlds.' Everything ends upon a Hosanna.

A few isolated quotations will show how useful this book is to sum up all this literature, which already is so considerable in bulk, and which will of course become year by year of more importance. This first quotation is from a letter written by the 'Dark Princess' to Matthew Towns; she has told him how lucky he is really to be in America, where his

' "feet are further within the secret circle of that power that . . . rules the world. That" [she goes on] "is the advantage that your people have had. You are working within. They are standing here in this technical triumph of human power and can use it as a fulcrum to lift earth and seas and stars.

' "But to be in the center of power is not enough. You must be free and able to act. You are not free in Chicago nor New York. But here in Virginia you are at the edge of a black world. The black belt of the Congo, the Nile, and the Ganges reaches by way of Guiana, Haiti, and Jamaica, like a red arrow, up into the heart of white America. Thus I see a mighty synthesis: you can work in Africa and Asia right here in America if you work in the Black Belt. For a long time I was puzzled, as I have written you, and hesitated; but now I know. I am exalted, and with my high heart comes illumination. I have been sore bewildered by this mighty America, this ruthless, terrible, intriguing Thing. My home and heart is India. Your heart of hearts is Africa. And now I see through the cloud. You may stand here, Matthew—here, halfway between Maine and Florida, between the Atlantic and the Pacific, with Europe in your face and China at your back; with industry in your right hand and commerce in your left and the Farm beneath your steady feet: and yet be in the Land of the Blacks." '

Here are a few extracts from letters that constantly pass between Matthew and the Dark Princess.

' "Revolution must come, but it must start from within. We must strip to the ground and fight up. Not the colored Farm but the white Factory is the beginning; and the white Office and the Street stand next. The white artisan must teach technique to the colored farmer. White business men must teach him organization; the scholar must teach him how to think, and the banker how to rule."'

This third extract is from a letter of the Princess Kautilya in which she tells Matthew of the meeting of the Central Committee and the nature of their deliberations.

' "I did not—I could not tell you all, Matthew, until now. The Great Central Committee of Yellow, Brown, and Black is finally to meet. You are a member. The High Command is to be chosen. Ten years of preparation are set. Ten more years of final planning, and then five years of intensive struggle. In 1952, the Dark World goes free—whether in Peace and fostering Friendship with all men, or in Blood and Storm— it is for Them—the Pale Masters of today—to say.

' "We are, of course, in factions—that ought to be the most heartening thing in human conference —but with enemies ready to spring and spring again, it scares one.

' "One group of us, of whom I am one, believes in the path of Peace and Reason, of co-operation among the best and poorest, of gradual emancipation, self-rule, and world-wide abolition of the color line, and of poverty and war.

'"The strongest group among us believes only in Force. Nothing but bloody defeat in a world-

wide war of dark against white will, in their opin-
.ion, ever beat sense and decency into Europe and
America and Australia. They have no faith in
mere reason, in alliance with oppressed labor,
white and colored; in liberal thought, religion,
nothing! Pound their arrogance into submission,
they cry; kill them; conquer them; humiliate
them. . . . Last night twenty-five messengers
had a preliminary conference in this room, with
ancient ceremony of wine and blood and fire. I
and my Buddhist priest, a Mohammedan Mullah,
and a Hindu leader of Swaraj, were India; Japan
was represented by an artisan and the blood of
the Shoguns; young China was there and a Lama
of Thibet; Persia, Arabia, and Afghanistan;
black men from the Sudan, East, West, and South
Africa; Indians from Central and South America,
brown men from the West Indies, and—yes, Matthew, Black America was there too. Oh, you
should have heard the high song of consecration
and triumph that shook these rolling hills!

' "We came in every guise, at my command
when around the world I sent the symbol of the
rice dish; we came as laborers, as cotton pickers,
as peddlers, as fortune-tellers, as travellers and
tourists, as merchants, as servants. A month we
have been gathering. Three days we have been
awaiting you—in a single night we shall all fade
away and go, on foot, by boat, by rail, and air-
plane. The Day has dawned, Matthew—the
Great Plan is on its way." '

Have you read *Uncle Tom's Cabin*? It was a

book that was reputed to have put the spark to the gunpowder, and to have precipitated the American Civil War.  If you are disposed to dismiss the sort of Film-farrago I have been quoting, you must at the same time recall that Mrs. Beecher Stowe was as a novelist no better than Du Bois.  I do not indeed mean that any single book today could have the same effect that *Uncle Tom's Cabin* had in a simpler time, with fewer books.  But hundreds of such books as *Dark Princess*, accompanied by Films and plays, might reasonably be expected to have some such effect—a particular consciousness being evolved by this mass of books and plays, that is the point.

That the Whites, on their side, are being given a certain consciousness—this dual process is what I have been discussing: for the Coloured Peoples are urged to develop a consciousness of *superiority*, and the same book seeks to force upon the Paleface a corresponding sense of *inferiority*.  It is this that is unfortunate: the mere reversal of a superiority—a change in its *colour*, nothing more—rather than its total abolition.

So far it has been found an easier matter to make the Paleface put his tail between his legs than it has to provide the Negro or Coolie with a 'superiority complex.'  The Negro is not really interested and is much too happy-go-lucky to approach these matters with the same earnestness as his mentors. As to the people of the East, their traditions are not propitious for such a transformation, it is only indirectly that they can be worked upon, though in the end, and with the changing conditions of their life, it will be accomplished.

PALEFACE

The Negro it would seem is the despair of the propagandist.  In the book from which I have just been quoting there is a Coloured meeting in Atlanta, of local Black 'Radicals,' and one of them exclaims at the end of it—'You couldn't get one nigger in a million to fight at all, and then they'd sell each other out.'  The trouble of course is that the 'nigger' is of much the same stuff as the White, he wants to be left alone: above all, he wishes to identify himself with his Paleface neighbour as far as possible, not to be put in opposition, and so in *contrast*.  He has much more in common with Babbitt than with the Coloured Intellectual.

The moment a Negro develops any purpose and ambition in life, his one idea, it seems, is to transform himself into the nearest approach to a White member of the respectable middleclass his colour handicap will allow.  Matthew Towns, while a coloured porter on a train, found that the Coloured passengers he tried to befriend resented his zealous attentions.  Thus:

'His colored passenger did "not care" to be brushed . . . he glanced at her again.

' "Anything I can do for you?" he asked.

' "Aren't you a college man?" she asked, rather abruptly.

' "I was," he answered.

'She regarded him severely.  "I should think then you'd be ashamed to be a porter," she said.

'He bit his lips and gathered up her bags.'

It is a lip-biting business to go to the rescue of your fellow 'skin,' either Black or White.  I am sure that any one would have the same experience

42

who attempted to go to the help of the Paleface. All this is exceedingly disappointing from the standpoint of the propagandist; and indeed one cannot help sympathizing with him in this respect, for the middleclass ideal of the Paleface is not a very high one, in the first instance: and then the conversion of millions of Negroes into coffee-coloured Babbitts is not an exceedingly stimulating picture for the revolutionary mind, nor for the intelligent person of whatever political opinion.

§ 12. *The Black, and the Paleface Middleclass Democratic Ideal.*

I will next quote a few passages from *Quicksand* (Knopf, 1928) by Nella Larson. The following dialogue occurs between the Coloured girls who are teachers in a Coloured College.

'Margaret laughed. "That's just ridiculous sentiment, Helga, and you know it. But you haven't had any breakfast, yourself. Jim Vayle asked if you were sick. Of course nobody knew. You never tell anybody anything about yourself. I said I'd look in on you."

' "Thanks awfully," Helga responded, indifferently. She was watching the sunlight dissolve from thick orange into pale yellow. Slowly it crept across the room, wiping out in its path the morning shadows. She wasn't interested in what the other was saying.

' "If you don't hurry, you'll be late to your first class. Can I help you?" Margaret offered uncertainly. She was a little afraid of Helga. Nearly every one was.

PALEFACE

'"No. Thanks all the same." Then quickly in another, warmer tone: "I do mean it. Thanks, a thousand times, Margaret. I'm really awfully grateful, but—you see, it's like this, I'm not going to be late to my class. I'm not going to be there at all."

'The visiting girl, standing in relief, like old walnut against the buff-colored wall, darted a quick glance at Helga. Plainly she was curious. But she only said formally: "Oh, then you *are* sick." For something there was about Helga which discouraged questionings.

'No, Helga wasn't sick. Not physically. She was merely disgusted. Fed up with Naxos. If that could be called sickness. The truth was that she had made up her mind to leave. That very day. She could no longer abide being connected with a place of shame, lies, hypocrisy, cruelty, servility, and snobbishness. "It ought," she concluded, "to be shut down by law." '

The manner of writing here and the dialogue of Helga and Margaret is a good example of what might be called *the conversion into 'old walnut,'* as it were, of the White middleclass democratic ideal, of ladylikeness and gentlemanliness. The colour-adjustment required, to the formulas of the worst type of sentimental fiction of the Whites, ends in absurdity and pathos. The 'visiting girl, standing in relief, like old walnut, against the buff-colored wall,' is a sad, uncomfortable parody of a *Family Herald* sort of scene. It is the 'Thanks awfully' that comes from Helga, and all the rest of the orthodox Paleface technique, that makes the 'walnut' adjustment ridiculous.

But the heroine of this book is described as aware of this type of confusion, and all that is humiliating in it for the Negro. In the ensuing passage Helga is reflecting about the dress-problem as it concerns the Negro.

'Turning from the window, her gaze wandered contemptuously over the dull attire of the women workers. Drab colors, mostly navy blue, black, brown, unrelieved, save for a scrap of white or tan about the hands and necks. Fragments of a speech made by the dean of women floated through her thoughts—"Bright colors are vulgar"—"Black, gray, brown, and navy blue are the most becoming colors for colored people"—"Dark-complected people shouldn't wear yellow, or green or red."—The dean was a woman from one of the "first families"—a great "race" woman; she, Helga Crane, a despised mulatto, but something intuitive, some unanalyzed driving spirit of loyalty to the inherent racial need for gorgeousness told her that bright colors *were* fitting and that dark-complexioned people *should* wear yellow, green, and red. Black, brown, and gray were ruinous to them, actually destroyed the luminous tones lurking in their dusky skins. One of the loveliest sights Helga had ever seen had been a sooty black girl decked out in a flaming orange dress, which a horrified matron had next day consigned to the dyer. Why, she wondered, didn't some one write *A Plea for Color*?

'These people yapped loudly of race, of race

45

consciousness, of race pride, and yet suppressed its most delightful manifestations, love of color, joy of rhythmic motion, naïve, spontaneous laughter.  Harmony, radiance, and simplicity, all the essentials of spiritual beauty in the race they had marked for destruction.'

It would be easy to say to Miss Nella Larson (who is I believe not a Paleface) that in her novel she was full of 'race-consciousness' but that she had 'suppressed its most delightful manifestations' and produced too orthodoxly Palefaced an article: but I should not say that myself to that particular writer, for she seems to grasp many of the difficulties on both sides of the Colour dispute and to have suffered herself considerably.  And perhaps it may be as well to add, at this point, that all books dealing with Negroes are not purely propagandist, and that, as with other things, a small percentage are even intelligent and so useful.

## § 13.  *A German Vision of Black* versus *White.*

In England there is no equivalent at all for such a book as *Dark Princess.*  The mixture of the Oppenheim detective-story and World-Politics does not occur, in the field of station-bookstall literature in which books of that order exist;  the British Public remains imperial and parochial, Publicschool-boyish and domestic, inveterately non-political.  It would be worth no mystery-spinner's while to deal with such a theme.  In Germany it is a different matter:  *Dark Princess* would be much *goûté* by the German—it should be translated.  In France also, with certain differences, the sensational 'World'-book flourishes.

A novel almost identical with *Dark Princess* may be cited, as my germanic illustration: it is *Atlantis* by Hans Dominik. This is one of a series of adventure-novels dealing with the Future—in the first half of the next century the scene is laid. You must imagine a World-political picture of half a century hence in which Russia and Asia are treated as non-existent. It is supposed that the three principal World-Powers at that time are the United States of Europe, the United States of America, and the empire of the Negro Emperor, Augustus Salvator, whose capital is Timbuctoo. The story opens in Timbuctoo, and there is the Negro Emperor at a great Circus, adulated by the dense black masses of his 'Coloured' subjects; and there likewise are two Germans in a box, one a great industrialist, the other an engineer. The Emperor Augustus, with the object of tapping some world-shaking source of power, has driven a gigantic shaft into the earth to a depth of 6000 metres. The german engineer in the box is employed in this undertaking. These two excellent Hamburgers occupy the same box by pure chance, though of course the engineer is familiar with the name of the great industrialist, his *Landsmann*. But in another part of this vast assembly may also be observed the villain of all that is to ensue, namely Guy Rouse, the american super-capitalist, in whose 'stahlharten grauen Augen' all the most ruthless and detestable—yet admirable ('das war ein Mann, ein Mann von aussergewöhnlicher Grösse . . . die verkörperte Macht des

Goldes' ruminates romantically Augustus) characteristics of transatlantic super-capitalism can be
clearly detected.

The heroes in this german book are strangely
enough (from the standpoint of an anglo-saxon
reader) the two Germans. The villain is (as every
European today would take as a matter of course)
the American: but I am afraid that the Negro Emperor is not painted so black as he should be—indeed he turns out to be a sort of Matthew Towns,
installed as Kaiser at Timbuctoo, instead of as
Maharajah at Bwodpur—but actuated, on all occasions, by motives so noble and unusual that he is
reminiscent of one of the great saviours of humanity:
even the Whitest reader would not, I feel sure, consider that Tredrup, the german engineer, was quite
justified in destroying as he did (in defence of the
White Race) this Dark Deliverer's life-work—for
Tredrup eventually comes back and blows up the
gigantic shaft, and so saves the White Race; it is
inevitable.

Tredrup is strongly pro-White—as strongly pro-
White in fact as the hero of an anglo-saxon book is
always anti-White, or rather pro-anything that is
not the same colour as himself: but *Atlantis* is written for a public incapable of that (perhaps sentimental) detachment which is such a feature of the
english and american tradition, whether popular or
learned.—Indeed when present at the All-Black
Circus, it is as much as Tredrup, the honest Ham-
burger, can do to contain himself, when above all
called upon to witness the White lady Circus-rider
kissing her hand to the Black audience. 'Schwein-

48

erei verdammte!' he exclaims. 'Man möchte am liebsten dem ganzen Dreck den Rücken kehren! Müssen die armen Luder hier ihr weisses Fleisch zu Schau stellen . . . und dann noch mit Kusshänder dafür danken . . .!' (It is interesting to note that in this Black Metropolis the performers most favoured by the Black Public are White, just as in the greatest metropolis of the Paleface World today the performers tend more and more to be Black.)

The true goal of the Negro Emperor is laid bare in a soliloquy, which ensues upon a visit from Mr. Rouse, the american arch-villain. Augustus Salvator talks to himself first about Mr. Rouse. Mr. Rouse (though Augustus cannot help admiring him) is blind, he thinks. 'Er sieht nicht die Grenzen, die jeder Macht gezogen sind.—Die Reaktion muss kommen . . . der Zeitpunkt ist nicht mehr fern.' Then Augustus Salvator goes on to talk about himself and to compare the brutal and selfish policies of the great White emperor, Napoleon Bonaparte, with his own.

'Meine Feinde nennen mich den schwarzen Napoleon . . . den gefürchteten und gehassten. Wie wenige sind es, die mir gerecht werden!

'Was war sein Ziel?—Was ist meins?

'In unersättlicher Machtgier verschlang er ein Land nach dem anderen, bis er an Russland erstickte. Was tat ich? Ich kämpfte den Kampf meines Volkes gegen die weissen Bedrücker. Den Kampf um die Freiheit nach jahrhundertelanger Knechtschaft. Das war die erste Tat!

'Die befreiten Länder habe ich zu einem Reich

zusammengerafft, denn nur ein geeintes Volk kann sich behaupten. Das war die zweite Tat!

'Die dritte — gleichberechtigt in der ganzen Welt sollen die Schwarzen mit den Weissen sein! . . .

'Aber die Gleichberechtigung will ich—gutwillig —oder mit Gewalt!—Das ist mein letztes Ziel.'

As to 'Racial Equality,' what that 'equality' really signifies Tredrup learns from his impressive friend, the great german industrialist—who is not the dupe, of course, of such a word as *equality*—'und dann hatte Uhlenkort zu ihm gesprochen—lange, eindringlich, bis es auch ihm klar geworden. *Die Bedeutung der Frage: Gleichberechtigung der Rassen —Gleichbedeutend mit dem Abstieg der weissen Rasse. Erste Stufe eines Abstieges, der weiter und weiter zum Unterliegen führen musste.*'

The faithful Tredrup ponders these words: and it is as a consequence of this political enlightenment that he strikes his blow for the White Race, and becomes a *Nationalheld*.

As for the sentiments of the Blacks with regard to the Whites, it is the same 'dark' anger with which Du Bois and so many other writers familiarize us. Here is a typical sample of the conversation of Negro workmen within the borders of the Negro imperium.

' "Weshalb kommst du hier her?" . . .

' " . . . hab genug von den verdammten Weisshäuten. Fehlt nur noch der Shambok, dann wär's da wie früher. Schwarze—Hunde. Leute wie wir beide—Halfkasts—nicht viel mehr!'

'Der erste nickte.

' "Verflucht die weisse Bande! . . . Dieser Hochmut, dieser gottverfluchte, der alle Andersfarbigen als Vieh behandelt.—Mein Herr Vater war auch ein Weisser—." Er lachte das heisere Bellen eines Hundes. "Meine Mutter schwarz, ihm ehelich angetraut. Jefferson heiss ich—schwarz auf weiss steht's in meinen Papieren. Und doch! Die Farbe—meiner Mutter Blut war wohl besser gewesen—tats. Sie stempelte mich zum Vieh. Aber!" Er hob drohend seine Rechte. "Der Kaiser!—unser Kaiser—er wird sie lehren, er wird's ihnen beibringen, ob sie wollen oder nicht! . . . Krieg!" zischte es durch seine Lippen. "Krieg! Täglich warte ich darauf, dass es losgeht!" '

This is pure *Dark Princess*—it is the true hot Black stuff! But, luckily for the Palefaces, there is a german hero in this instance to put a spoke in the Black wheel, in the person of Tredrup.

The american magnate has still to be reckoned with, however—the sorrows of the Whites do not end with the Blacks—there is America!

Mr. Rouse blows a hole in the isthmus of Panama, the Gulf Stream is diverted, and Europe returns to polar conditions; Ireland becomes an icecap merely and a new Migration era opens, southwards—away from the polar conditions, brought upon Europe by american greed. Mr. Guy Rouse, incarnating the United States, is not only more 'ruthless,' but more difficult to circumvent, than the magnanimous Negro Superman. (As I said to start with, such things as Soviet Russia, Asia, and so forth, never appear at all: they escape the attention of Hans Dominik altogether.) The White Race is eventually saved; it is installed on a brand new Atlantis, which however has to rise out of the ocean to receive it— nothing short of a miracle can save the White Race, in this story.


§ 14. *White Phobia in France.*

FROM France an entire library of books to our purpose could be selected. The Huxley of France, M. Paul Morand, will suggest himself at once to many readers: there are his *Magic Noire* and *Bouddha Vivant.* A sensibility for all that is exotic has always been very common among Frenchmen—such figures as Baudelaire or Gauguin are not singular.— One specimen, however, is all I have space for : I will choose *Loin des Blondes,* by Thomas Raucat.

This book is a desultory account of romantic and mildly erotic *tourisme* in the Far East. Its first forty pages however is passed in descriptions of Paleface life upon an ocean liner. We do not reach those delicious regions that are *Far from the Palefaces* and all their works until we step off the japanese Packet at Yokohama. I will quote a little from what passes upon the japanese Packet, and leave it at that.

Mr. Raucat falls beneath the spell of a lovely german-american blonde. The affair is rather unfortunate; she becomes for him the symbol of all that is Paleface. At their second meeting on deck this is what takes place.

'Le lendemain matin donc, à peine eus-je vu cette dame s'allonger sur son fauteuil de pont, que

je m'approchai d'elle. Je m'assis à son côté.
Comme la veille je la trouvai belle.'

But his 'interlocutrice' is more distant: a kind of
'nonchalance aggressive' supervenes.

'Ironiquement, et par touches légères, mon
interlocutrice me plaignit d'être Français, et sur-
tout Français du midi. Dans la hiérarchie des
races humaines, à ce que je compris, je me trouvais
à un rang plus élevé que le nègre, mais tout juste.

' "L'empire terrestre," disait-elle, "doit appar-
tenir aux races supérieures. Mais, dans la race
blanche, quelle est celle dont le sang n'est pas
mêlé, et qui possède à l'état pur les qualités du
chef? C'est la race germanique, les conquérants
venus du Nord, les fiers hommes blonds au crâne
haut, ceux qui ont vaincu et rejeté les légions
romaines."

'Cette femme, d'une voix chantante, et sans
se presser, citait Nietzsche et Gobineau, les met-
tant en avant avec autant de familiarité que s'ils
eussent été des membres de sa famille.

' "Les races méditerranéennes," répétait-elle,
"sont des races de second ordre, des races mêlées.
La forme du crâne, les pommettes saillantes, tout
dénote l'apport du sang nègre." '

He retires very soon in face of this attack, and in
any case he is due at the ping-pong championship.
As he leaves the lovely but militant blonde—who
'faisait de sa blondeur un étendard'—he reflects:

'Croit-elle à la vérité de ce qu'elle m'a dit? Son
orgueil serait par trop insensé. Et je me repré-
sentais, avec tous leurs petits détails physiques

les mâles que mon interlocutrice de tout à l'heure jugeait seuls dignes de l'avoir pour compagne : des individus brutaux, aux cheveux frisés d'un rouge fauve, à la peau uniformément rose, d'un rose de foie gras.   Je n'avais pas l'impression que ces messieurs me fussent supérieurs en quoi que ce soit.'

He takes part in the ping-pong championship. There he meets another blonde.

'C'était encore une blonde qui était en face de moi, et bien qu'elle n'eût pas encore quinze ans, celle-là aussi était sûre d'elle-même, et se plaisait à me prouver sa supériorité.'

He loses the ping-pong championship.   At last the long sea trip draws to an end; all the championships—of ping-pong, swimming, deck-tennis, chess, draughts, boxing, etc. etc.—are over.   *Asia* is in sight!

'  . . . debout, et je regardais avec passion défiler la terre d'Asie.   Mes pensées bouillonnaient.

'Je me sentais rassasié des pays que j'avais jusqu'alors habités, où la vie n'est qu'un perpétuel championnat.

'Même sur ce paquebot, alors qu'il eût été si facile et agréable de n'y rien faire, les passagers poussés par leur atavisme s'étaient ingéniés à tourmenter leur et mon existences par des tournois qui n'avaient pas toujours été amicaux.

'La nausée me prenait des hommes de race blonde, et des manières de leurs compagnes. Sans lutte, j'abandonnais à leur orgueil les contrées que je quittais.   Quel soulagement tout à

l'heure, quand je foulerais le sol de l'Asie, l'immense et mystérieux continent brun, aux femmes
craintives et presque esclaves, dans la douceur
desquelles je me baignerais comme à une source
fraîche. . . . tel un plongeur symbolique . . .
j'allais me lancer dans le mystère . . .'

But before 'plunging' into the dark and 'mysterious' East he delivers himself of an anti-White
incantation.

'En mâchant le dernier cigare de Sims, je me
répétais comme un enfant qui boude:
' "J'ai assez des blondes. Je ne veux plus les
voir." '

Such is *Loin des Blondes*: unlike the impulses of
those earlier Europeans, such as Doughty, Burton,
or Livingstone, it is not with the contemporary
romantic merely a desire to 'plunge' into something
'dark' and 'mysterious': *this expansiveness is accompanied by a hostile repulsion for what is left behind.*
Arthur Rimbaud was the first European of this
newer order of exotics.

Again, whether there are such people as M. Raucat's lovely german-american blonde, who talk race-
war and Gobineau upon the slightest provocation,
it is impossible to say: but what is certain is that
there are plenty of people similar to M. Raucat, who
expect to meet, or imagine they have met, such
militant blondes—whose minds run, in short, upon
such lines of race and race-rivalry and who have a
deep prejudice against their own skin.

England, although more than any european nation
in touch, for generations, with the 'dark' world, of

Asia, Africa and America, is the least interested in
these questions, probably because it has been a
feature of these contacts, with the Englishman, to
pretend not to notice that they had occurred—
partly, too, for the reason that the sort of Englishman engaged where those contacts existed, in administration or trade, 'for thinking had no great
turn,' as Arnold put it. But France and Germany
are as full as America of such racial awareness, and
their literatures reflect it very thoroughly.

The subject that my last american quotation, to
return to Miss Larson, brought to the front will be
a very useful one to dwell upon for some moments,
and it will also serve as a natural transition to my
next and final illustration.

If you could really persuade any class of people
whatever that they were essentially *better* than all
the rest—more generous, gifted and intelligent—
then there would at least be the possibility of some
advantage to the world at large. If they should
behave consistently in such a way as to conform to
this belief, then, in effect, for the time being they
could be said to *be* 'better'—if we were agreed upon
what was ultimately desirable. On the other hand,
if it remained merely a matter of words—and in a
world given over to Advertisement we are only too
familiar with the way in which words take the place
of facts—there would clearly be no gain, but truly
a mass of fine words, and a great deal of ill-feeling
engendered in the fury of competition.

Experience has shown, in past revolutions, that
what is apt to happen is that one class—inflated by
resounding words—takes the place of another class,

which it violently dispossesses, and proceeds to behave in exactly the same way as the last. So if the
Coloured population of America or Africa is to super-
sede the White, it is essential, to start with, that
they should not secretly or openly harbour, as their
dearest wish, an approximation to the present condition of the Paleface 'master.' The Paleface at
present, owing to adverse circumstances, has fallen
so low intellectually, is socially so impotent, and his
standards of work and amusement are so mechanical,
that he cannot be taken as an ideal by any man.—
Yet I think that the most extreme propagandist for
the 'Coloured Races' would agree with me that the
trouble really is that when those races become politically 'emancipated,' as we call it, they tend at
once to approximate more and more closely to the
White world-standard. Thereby we get the same
situation that we find in the case of 'nations,' locked
up inside historical territories. The more the latter
grow like all other nations in the same situation, the
more 'nationalist,' politically, they become; the
deeper their animosity towards all 'foreigners,' the
more (through seeing the same films and submitting
to similar influences of one kind and another) they
come to resemble those 'foreign' devils, against
whom it is so easy to excite their passions.

The sort of situation you would have eventually
to anticipate is this. In such towns as New York
or Johannesburg you will get a Black quarter, where
there will be large dance-halls where nothing but
waltzes and mazurkas and possibly minuets will be
danced, by stately Negroes; and there will be a
Paleface quarter, where there will be a dance-hall

with nothing but jazz. In the Black quarter the
beauty-chorus in the revues will be All White: in the
White quarter they will be All Black. The plays in
the Black quarter will be such plays as *Hamlet*: the
plays in the White will be *All God's Chillun*. The
books the Paleface reads will be romances about the
oppressed Blacks, cast in a most sentimental anti-
christian vein: the Black, on the other hand, will
devour books about White middleclass prosperity,
where all the characters will be slightly *yellow*.

But the Black will say fiercely that he is a better
man than the White because he is more dignified in
his amusements (pointing to his waltzes, his Shakespeare Repertory Theatre, etc.). The White will insist that *he* is the better man, because he is not so
emotional and jazzy as the Black, and because he is
responsible for Shakespeare, Molière, and so on. (I
am a little indebted to Herr Dominik for this picture.)

Long before such a state of affairs as that came
to pass, the races would, in practice, have intermarried and their habits would have become identical. But it is no part of my business here to draw
pictures of a problematical future, but only to study
the problems of behaviour at the present time, as
they apply between Palefaces and 'Coloured' people.

### § 15. *The Effect of the Pictures of the White Man's World upon the East.*

INSTEAD of quoting something from Close's book,
*The Revolt of Asia*, to show how the Black *versus*
White problem is prolonged into and all over the

East, I will take a few pages from Mr. Aldous Huxley's *Jesting Pilate*. Mr. Huxley goes to an open-air Cinema in Java and these are his impressions and reflections (necessarily curtailed).

'Fifty yards away we found an open-air picture show. A crowd, as fishily dumb as the young dancers, stood or squatted in front of an illuminated screen, across which there came and went, in an epileptic silence, the human fishes of a cinema drama. And what a drama! We arrived in time to see a man in what the lady novelists call "faultless evening dress," smashing a door with an axe, shooting several other men, and then embracing against her will a distressed female, also in evening dress. Meanwhile another man was hurrying from somewhere to somewhere else, in motor-cars that tumbled over precipices, in trains that villains contrived to send full tilt into rivers—in vain, however, for the hurrying young man always jumped off the doomed vehicles in the nick of time and immediately found another and still more rapid means of locomotion. . . .

'The violent imbecilities of the story flickered in silence against the background of the equatorial night. In silence the Javanese looked on. What were they thinking? What were their private comments on this exhibition of Western civilization? . . . The crook drama at Tunis is the same as the crook drama at Madras. On the same evening, it may be, in Korea, in Sumatra, in the Sudan, they are looking at the same seven soulful reels of mother-love and adultery. The same fraudulent millionaires are swindling for the diversion of a Burmese audience in Mandalay, a Maori audience in New Zealand. Over the entire globe the producers of Hollywood are the missionaries and propagandists of white civilization. . . . What is this famous civilization of the white men which Hollywood reveals? These are questions which one is almost ashamed to answer. The world into which the cinema introduces the subject peoples is a world of silliness and criminality. When its inhabitants are not stealing, murdering, swindling or attempting to commit rape (too slowly, as we have seen, to be often completely successful), they are being maudlin about babies or dear old homes, they are being fantastically and idiotically honourable in a manner calculated to bring the greatest possible discomfort to the greatest possible number of people, they are disporting themselves in marble halls, they are aimlessly dashing about the earth's surface in fast-moving vehicles. When they make money they do it only in the most discreditable, unproductive and socially mischievous way—by speculation. Their politics are matters exclusively of personal (generally amorous) intrigue. Their science is an affair of secret recipes for making money—recipes which are always getting stolen by villains no less anxious for cash than the scientific hero himself. Their religion is all cracker mottoes, white-haired clergymen, large-hearted mothers, hard, Bible-reading, puritanical fathers, and young girls who have taken the wrong turning and been betrayed (the rapes, thank goodness, are occasionally successful) kneeling with their illegitimate babies in front of cruci fixes. As for their art—it consists in young men in overalls and large ties painting, in cock-lofts, feminine portraits worthy to figure on the covers of magazines. And their literature is the flatulent verbiage of the captions.

'Such is the white man's world as revealed by the films, a world of crooks and half-wits, morons and sharpers. A crude, immature, childish world. A world without subtlety, without the smallest intellectual interests, innocent of art, letters, philosophy, science. A world where there are plenty of motors, telephones and automatic pistols, but in which there is no trace of such a thing as a modern idea. A world where men and women have instincts, desires and emotions, but no thoughts. A world, in brief, from which all that gives the modern West its power . . . has been left out. . . . White men complain that the attitude of the members of the coloured races is not so respectful as it was. Can one be astonished?

'What astonishes me is that the attitude remains as respectful as it does. Standing in the midst of that silent crowd of Javanese picture fans, I was astonished, when the performance attained its culminating imbecility, that they did not all with one accord turn on us with hoots of derision, with mocking and murderous violence. I was astonished that they did not all rush in a body through the town crying "Why should we be ruled any longer by imbeciles?" and murdering every white man they met. The drivelling nonsense that flickered there in the darkness, under the tropical clouds, was enough to justify

61

any outburst. . . . The coloured peoples think a
great deal less of us than they did, even though
they may be too cautious to act on their opinions
. . . the share of Hollywood in lowering the white
man's prestige is by no means inconsiderable.  A
people whose own propagandists proclaim it to be
mentally and morally deficient, cannot expect to
be looked up to.  If films were really true to life,
the whole of Europe and America would deserve
to be handed over as mandated territories to the
Basutos, the Papuans and the Andaman pygmies.
Fortunately, they are not true. . . . But the untutored mind of the poor Indian does not know it.
He sees the films, he thinks they represent Western reality, he cannot see why he should be ruled
by criminal imbeciles.  As we turned disgusted
from the idiotic spectacle and threaded our way
out of the crowd, that strange aquarium silence
of the Javanese was broken by a languid snigger
of derision.  Nothing more.  Just a little laugh.
A word or two of mocking comment in Malay, and
then, once more, the silence as of fish.  A few
more years of Hollywood's propaganda, and perhaps we shall not get out of an Oriental crowd
quite so easily.'

There is more than a touch in this narrative, I
know, of the sort of conventionality you would expect from its agreeably discursive author.  But
nevertheless he has not a political axe to grind and
is a more reliable witness probably than Mr. Close.—
The sentimentality of outlook is of course apparent
in his interpretation of 'the strange aquarium sil-

ence' of the Javanese: it is unlikely that the javanese, maori, tunisian or hindu picture-goers are either equipped, or disposed, to view the 'imbecility' of the White Man's Film quite as Mr. Huxley would have us believe—for all their 'impassible oriental' fishiness and their traditional, but today quite non-existent, wisdom. It is unlikely that, unless it were repeatedly pointed out to them, they would see anything discreditable in the ethics of Hollywood, or be very critical of the abject intelligence displayed, or be averse to the violence and crudity of the action. In short, Mr. Huxley, I think, romanticises his 'Oriental'—there is a little too much turban and grease-paint, too much 'Garden of Allah,' in the picture. When however that has been discounted, and when you allow for the fact that in every corner of the East the russian agent is busy whispering against the Whites—those overbearing bourgeois interlopers—this account of a Picture-show in Java is not without its instruction. As to Mr. Huxley's account of the sort of Film in question, that, we can all agree, is accurate enough: and it is after all just from those standards that it is important to rescue the Untutored Mind of the Poor Indian, or the over-susceptible Negro. If the Negro, as dreamed of by Alain Locke, is to become a reality, he can find no better way of proving his 'cultural' qualifications than by turning his back altogether upon the White Man's World as it exists at present.

I have mentioned Alain Locke, and before terminating this section of my book I will turn to a debate which figured in the *Forum* about six months ago. Alain Locke is a negro intellectual and he

presented the case for the Negro in that debate very
ably.   Mr. Lothrop Stoddard answered, with equal
ability, for the White Man, telling his dark opponent
that White America would never depart from its
policy of the 'Colour-Line.'   I will not here enter
into the many interesting issues brought to light by
this debate, but will confine myself to a few observations upon the arguments advanced by the
Black debater.   Mr. Locke shows with excellent
pointedness how the White World is confronted with
'an increasing social dilemma and self-contradiction,'
for the simple reason that the Negro Question is not
merely the Negro Question, but is 'much more, and
even more seriously, the question of democracy.'
And of course in so far as the dogma, not necessarily
the practice, of the Soviet is merely a violent form
of democratic belief, the more 'radical' the American or any other Democracy becomes, the more such
a question as the Negro Question becomes strictly
the rule in your system of belief, or you must 'capitulate,' as Mr. Locke invites the White Man to do.

But Mr. Locke also has another no less seemingly
powerful argument: he insists that the White Man
cannot dance every night to negro music, and throng
to *Porgies* and *Emperor Joneses*, and continue to be
haughty where the Negro is concerned.

'Prejudice, moreover, as wholesale generaliza-
tion of social inferiority and cultural incapacity
. . . becomes, as a matter of course, more contrary to fact with every decade—yes, with every
day. . . . Apart from the injustice and reactionary unwisdom, there is tragic irony and imminent
social farce in the acceptance by "White America'

of the Negro's cultural gifts, while at the same
time withholding cultural recognition, the reward
that all genius merits and even requires.'

The 'cultural' present that the Negro has made
to White America, and through America to the
whole White World, can be summed up in the word
'jazz.' It is a very popular present and White
people everywhere have tumbled over each other to
pick it up, and it has almost superseded every other
form of activity. But what it is impossible not to
ask is whether it deserves quite so large a 'reward'
as Mr. Locke claims for it. The White arts that the
Paleface has turned away from in order to cultivate
these Black arts, were certainly as good as the latter:
and all that the 'Afroamerican' has succeeded in
supplying is the aesthetic medium of a sort of
frantic proletarian sub-conscious, which is the very
negation of those far greater arts, for instance, of
other more celebrated 'Coloured' races, such as the
Chinese or the Hindu. The Chinese or the Hindu
would never have been captivated by nor even paid
any attention at all to that sort of *inferior* Black art.
But the White has: and it *is* very unreasonable of
him still to deny social equality to the Negro: about
that there can be no question at all, under the circumstances. (It is only the circumstances that
ought never to be there.)

The other 'cultural' lights mentioned by Mr.
Locke are, for example, Roland Hayes and Paul
Robeson. That black nightingale and that excellent actor are handsome presents to our civilization: and if the Negro community has not had a

band of distinguished philosophers, men of science, and poets to point to, it is, I am sure, merely because the Negro has not had the opportunity of producing them: there is no race that is not able to produce distinguished philosophers, men of science, and remarkable poets, in profusion. Where Mr. Locke is mistaken, in my opinion, is in talking about the 'cultural' gifts of the Negro to the White up-to-date, and as already handed over.

What Mr. Locke might say with great reason is somewhat as follows: 'Although the Blacks have produced nothing but a barbarous, melancholy, epileptic folk-music, worthy only of a patagonian cannibal; and although this sort of art has been fastened upon the White World, as a result of a given set of circumstances, that is no reason at all why the White Man should look down upon *all* Negroes, or should too lightly assume that, given equal opportunities, the Negro would not produce something that would put the foolish jazzing White in the shade.' That would be unanswerable, I think.

Mr. Locke, again, writes: 'Successful peoples are rated, and rate themselves, in terms of their best. Racial and national prestige is, after all, the product of the exceptional few.' In order to have grasped that highly undemocratic truth Mr. Locke must have risen far above the level of the average Paleface. When he says that 'it is not in the interests of democracy itself to allow an illiterate, unprogressive White man the conviction that he is better than the best Negro,' one is not so sure of the soundness of his purely democratic principles.—The general impression that his article made upon me was that he stressed too much the 'cultural,' in rather too resounding a way, which left him open to too profound a retort. And the 'democratic' basis seems to me as things stand an impossible one for argument.

At this point I will return from my consideration of the evidence provided by a series of books, both in Europe and America, to the main current of my argument.

## § 16. *Final Objections to me as 'Champion.'*

THE German philosophers of the beginning and the middle of the last century have perhaps provided us with the best example of 'internationalism' of any people in modern times, that is, such men as Goethe or Schopenhauer. Schopenhauer's father gave him the name of 'Arthur' because Arthur is the same (he argued) in all european tongues—at least it is not exclusively german. (It is interesting to note that the 'Arthur Press' received that name for a reason of a similar order.) And Schopenhauer himself never ceased to criticize his countrymen for their german-ness. Nietzsche after him did the same. Goethe before him was quite as confirmed an 'internationalist,' in the sense that he always advocated a universal language of Volapuc for Europe, and hoped for a confederacy of states and an abolition of frontiers.—Today we are, with Fascism, with Irish, Czech, Catalan, Macedonian, Indian, Russian, Turkish, Polish, etc. etc., nationalism (which invariably takes the form of abolishing every local custom and becoming as like everybody as possible), at the other pole to that attitude of mind

so common a century ago.    This appears to me very
regrettable indeed.    I should like everybody to be
imbued with the spirit of internationalism, and to
keep all their local customs.

I have, in addition to my often expressed desire
for a universal state, another craving, up till now
unexpressed (that is publicly).    I would, if I were
able to, suppress all out-of-date discrepancies of
*tongue*, as well as of skin and pocket.    I desire to
speak Volapuc, to put it shortly.    I cannot help it,
it is if you like a crank, but I should like to speak,
and write, some Volapuc, not english—at all events
some tongue that would enable me to converse with
everybody of whatever shade of skin or opinion
without an interpreter—above all that no shadow
of an excuse should subsist for a great Chemical
Magnate to come hissing in my ear: 'Listen!    That
low fellow' (magnates always speak in such lofty
terms, partly for fun) 'says "ja"—-I heard him!
Here is a phial of deadly gas.    Just throw it at him,
will you?    He won't say "ja" any more, once he's
had a sniff of that!'

But this is not the end of the matter, where my
many disqualifications are concerned.    I am actually conscious of the many difficulties that must
beset any honest Paleface, called to the defence of
his skin.    Although people of a lightish complexion
have overrun the globe, they have, he would be
compelled to confess, taken with them, and stolidly,
irresistibly, propagated a civilization which is exceedingly inferior to many civilizations found by
them in full-swing, possessed by people of dark, or
'Coloured' complexion.

68

So, confining ourselves to 'skins,' if this Paleface is told that he has been foolishly arrogant—his 'superiority' at the best a very temporary material or technical one—he cannot find much to answer. Further, the charge has to be met of having imposed a rotten, materialist civilization upon all sorts of people with great cruelty often, of having wiped out races of very high quality, such as the Indians of North America, in the name of a God who was all compassion: so he is convicted of hypocrisy of the ugliest, of the 'civilized' kind, on top of everything else.

How can the White Man confront these charges? As an Anglo-Saxon he cannot point to America and England today, and claim that spectacle as a justification of his dominion. What is he to do? If a timid man, as the Paleface often is, all those vindictive pointing fingers will put him quite out of countenance.

Now I of course can find him the necessary arguments to dispose of his passionate critics, and I am only too glad to, for his opponents are a stupid crew for the most part—just 'to amuse myself' I would help my Paleface. But all the same I recognize that his case is dangerously open to attack.

Beyond this, as an artist I am convinced that all the very finest plastic and pictorial work has come out of the Orient, and that Europeans have never understood the fundamental problems of art in the way the Indian, Persian, or Chinese have done. These hasty remarks will have served, nothing more, to define the nature of my disqualifications for the rôle of White deliverer.

# CONCLUSION

AS to the definition from the *Institutes*, quoted by Green, and all that deeper argument of a view of life in which the principle of the 'common good' expands so that it includes all that we decide to recognize mystically as possessing a spiritual essence, however remote in time and place, and as to the 'notion that there is something due from every man to every man,' I will hazard the following remarks, which will serve as a Conclusion to this introductory essay.

In Rome what constituted 'abnormality' was the being either a slave, a stranger or a minor (of whatever age) within the potestas of some head of a family. A slave and, originally, a stranger, a 'peregrinus,' was legally a 'thing,' coming under the 'jus quod ad res pertinet.' The absolute legal roman *persona* was only enjoyed, I suppose, by the eldest male of a roman family. But originally the status of a non-Roman was as 'abnormal' as that of a slave. All animals were naturally 'things'—a lion in the forest or a wild bee was a 'res nullius,' but a watch-dog or a slave was not 'wild,' so could not be affected to another person than his owner by capture—though if you felt like it you could acquire a lion, for *it* (as we still say) was a 'thing' not entangled legally with a 'person.' You would then become its unique entanglement, and it would cease to be wild, but would remain a thing.

To be normal was to be free in the roman state, but it is now generally supposed that the 'slave' in

# CONCLUSION TO PART I

Antiquity, although outside the law of persons, was nevertheless not treated as a *thing* by his master to any greater extent than let us say a drapery assistant or a charwoman is treated as a thing. The female slave, of an averagely humane roman citizen, did not call herself a 'lady' but a 'slave'; there probably the difference ended. It is unlikely that there was any contemptuous disability attached to her state to compare with that of the victorian 'skivvy' or 'slavey.' If the choice lay between being a 'slavey' and a 'slave,' in fact, any rational person would prefer to be a 'slave' I should think—without ambiguity, sentimentality or, in a word, offence.

What I am attempting to get at here is that very important factor of 'sentimentality' in the relations of human beings, especially as that applies to the wholesale reform of those relations, at present in progress all over the world. It is the verbal problem, really; and the history of 'sentiment' is one of the survival of words, after the fact they symbolize has long vanished. It is possible under certain conditions to have a person as a slave in the most effective sense—to make him work himself to the bone, live upon crusts of bread, call you 'sir' or even 'lord,' and be in short entirely at your disposal, and yet for you to have no *legal* right whatever over him, indeed for him technically to be 'free and equal'—even for you to be, ostensibly, *his* servant. We are all accustomed to this situation as illustrated in the expression 'servant of the Public,' for instance. 'Dictatorship of the Proletariat' affords another example. In such cases a minority governs a majority, often with an iron hand, either telling the majority that it is its 'servant,' or, in the other case, telling the majority or Proletariat that it, the Proletariat, is sovereign, paramount, and engaged all the time in ruling itself. These (and many similar instances will no doubt readily occur to you) are all matters simply of *words*: and what I am describing is of course the sort of government that we call today a 'democracy'—either with elective representatives or with a small body of people who are kind enough to 'dictate' to it. But in all cases it is government by words.

Everything that the word 'democracy' implies, however, we get from the Romans and the Greeks. And in spite of the fact that all the circumstances of physical life and of our present society have suffered an absolute change, yet in our institutions we still perpetuate these ultimate distortions of a law framed for a political body in every respect different from our own. The roman body was compact and efficient, if nothing else, and is not to be despised. But either we should retrace our steps and acquire that body (which is impossible) or else adjust our laws for those vast, sprawling, dreamy polyp-organisms we call nations, but so that those laws will enable such degraded organisms to issue once more as a formal structure of some kind, somewhat higher than at present.

If, again, we cannot all be 'free' in the roman sense, or be 'persons' as were all Roman Citizens, then should we use their words? It is impossible not to question the propriety of that: for not until we cease to *call* ourselves free shall we be able to recognize how unnecessarily servile we have become. The word 'free' is merely, as it were, a magical counter with which to enslave us, it is full of an electrical property that has been most maleficent where the European or American is concerned.

But beyond that I suggest that very few people can be 'free' under any circumstances, or equally you may say that very few people can be 'persons,' still to employ the roman terminology, but in this case abstractly. It is the 'democratic' conceit that is at fault, is it not?—it seems as though it were the love of fine words that has undone us, as much as anything. That is where the 'sentimentality' comes in and plays its destructive part. (It is that 'lady' in char-lady that has given us a false security and made us blind to the novel facts upon which we must at last concentrate our gaze and recognize that we are beset.) If people managed to resist those verbal blandishments, they would, it is true, be sadder (at first) but also wiser. That is of course the ideal—to be wiser; and no one can accuse me in this of indulging in a verbal blandishment with my word 'wise,' for who on earth, in a general way, ever wanted to be *wise*? 'Free,' yes: but never wise.

But in saying that very few men are able to be 'free,' or very few to be 'persons,' one must I suppose be prepared for every hair upon the body of the true democrat (or doctrinaire of the dictatorship of Demos) to bristle. 'Ah! that is very nice indeed, that is charming!' he says: 'in a nation of fifty million people there are to be a handful of "great" *persons* (according to your aristocratic plan and whatever you may mean by your mystic of the *person*)—that is to say, at any one time, a statesman

73

or two, a poet or two, a man of science or two, and so on, and no more. But what of the rest of the community?—where do they come in? Are they not to have an equal share in the statecraft, art, science and all that constitutes a civilized state?'

In the first place the plan is, of course, not mine at all, but nature's. 'Nature' has repeatedly been interrogated, often angrily, upon this very point—it is a burning question. Why does not nature produce a dense mass of Shakespeares or Newtons or Pitts? That has been the idea; and means have been considered and plans worked out for assisting nature in this respect. But it is conceivable that nature after all may usually produce as many as are needed of these 'persons,' and that this ratio may be according to some organic law that we are too stupid or too conceited to grasp.

It is always possible that nature may not desire a structureless, horizontal jelly of a society, as does the modern democrat, but a more organic affair. A 'moral situation,' it may even be, does not enter into the comprehension of that legislator or creator which we habitually call 'nature.' Just the correct number of Shakespeares, Newtons and the rest may have been regularly supplied to us, and overcrowding at the top (a top and bottom being perhaps part of this hierarchical, non-moral, creative intention) have been guarded against.

But we will return from this region of idle speculation to that of practical politics. It is not disputed by anybody that we have evolved a very mechanical type of life, as a result of the discovery of printing and its child, the Press—the Cinema, Radio and so forth, and the immense advances in the technique of Industry. There is much less differentiation now, that is, between the consciousness of the respective members of a geographical group, and between the various groups or peoples, than before machines made it possible for everyone to mould their mind upon the same cultural model (in the way that they all subject themselves to the emotional teaching of a series of films, for instance, all over the surface of the globe).

The more fundamentally alike nations become, the more fiercely 'nationalist' is their temper: but also the more *impersonal* they grow (in the nature of things, in a more intensely organized routine of life), the more they talk of freedom, and of their 'personality.'

Both these paradoxes of the present age are, I believe, the merest habits. There is very little sign that the majority of people desire to be 'persons' in any very important sense: their conversation about 'developing their personality' is a sentimental habit, merely, it would seem. If they were cured of this habit nothing would ever be heard of their 'personality' again. But government on a democratic pattern entails an insistence upon these mythical 'personalities' on the part of their rulers: so the habits remain and flourish. It is impossible to bring them up-to-date, for they are too chronologically absurd to do that with. And the same system requires that some purely sentimental and unreal notion of 'freedom' should, at all costs, be sustained. (It is like the cry *La Patrie est en danger!* There was *once* a 'country,' that was culturally and

PALEFACE

racially intact, and so susceptible of being put in
'danger'; and in consequence the martial cry still
evokes a situation that is dead, and people flock to
defend that grinning corpse or historical spectre.)


Only a *person* can be susceptible of a *right*—that
is not a roman law but a universal one. What is 'due
from every one to every one' (in the words of Green)
is either (1) a merely sentimental *cliché*—and that is
what it generally amounts to in contemporary democracies; or it is (2) an entirely non-sentimental compulsion—namely that that is due to merit, to personal character or to personal ability. There is
nothing else 'due' from one person to another.

Another and more exact way of stating this would
be to say—There is nothing 'due' at all from one
person to another: but there are persons who attract,
or compel, those services spoken of by Green, described by him as mysterious debts on account of
which all truly moral men are constantly denying
and impoverishing themselves (of the things of the
mind as well as of the body—in order to be 'the poor
in spirit') so that they may adequately render what
'is due from every one to every one.' But this something in fact is 'due' not because the object of it is
'human,' nor because the skin in question is white
or black: it is 'due' because in some way we recognize an entity with superior claims to ours upon
our order, kind or system: as I see the matter, that
is the only ground for an obligation that exists. The
sentimental, or the moral, elements, have no part in it.

76

## CONCLUSION TO PART I

This obligation that all men are under to personal power or to the vital principle that resides in *persons*, is apt to be bitterly resented. What the 'puppet' owes to the 'person' (to make use, as in the *Art of Being Ruled*, of Goethe's terminology) is the cause of many heart-burnings and revolts, and is, where that is possible, withheld. This is the case more than ever where an aggravated 'moral situation' exists, as at present. Indeed a 'moral situation' is essentially a revolutionary situation, in the most frivolous sense, when for a time the unreal and purely sentimental values, in a dissolving society, get the upper hand. The Power to whom the direction is being transferred dare not yet openly announce itself (this is, I suppose, somewhat the case in Russia), there is only one Master-principle visible, above the surface, still ostensibly effective, and that is weak. So the pack flings itself upon it, and all for the moment is confusion.

For what is the essence of a 'moral situation'? It is of course, and always has been (since those days when, to be the curse of the West, 'morals' were first invented), a situation in which a society loses its organic structure and disintegrates into its individual components—into its millions of individual units. This may in itself be desirable; but it naturally isolates or disconnects for the time all that is most powerful and exposes it to attack. As this society becomes, instead of an organic whole, a mass of minute individuals, under the guise of an Ethic there appears the Mystic of the Many, the cult of the cell, or the worship of the particle; and the dogma of 'what is due from everybody to everybody' takes the place of the natural law of what is due to character, to creative genius, or to personal power, or even to their symbols.

I do not need to point out how intense this mysticism of the Monad or 'the Many' has become, nor how it has resulted everywhere in wholesale aggression, aimed at anybody, either in the past or present, possessing those 'great' qualities to which 'something is due' from everybody. (The daily belittlement of or the personal attacks upon, in books or in the Press, the 'great men' of our literary Pantheon is one of the obvious signs of this sansculottist temper.) It is almost as though the duty of the truly moral man was as much to destroy what he regards as 'great' (or possessed of the enjoyment of the powers and delights of the mind) as to deny himself such enjoyment: and a sentimental value for what is little or ineffective, or merely distant, or incomprehensible, must be eagerly professed.

I will now apply myself to the question of how we are to define (1) a person; (2) the term 'human'; and (3) the conception 'the common good,' those terms of critical importance that we have been up till now using without much definition.

The idea 'person' I associate essentially with the idea of 'organization.' What we could say was 'due' to what is highly organized on the part of what is less highly organized—that is the principal character of this obligation. If I were working this out more thoroughly here, I should have to go into the question of how I understood this version of the law of persons and the law of things, insisting that in every case our human laws must be in the nature of a 'law of things.' For it is upon that basis that I should naturally think of it.

All that is 'due' from one creature to another is, as I should describe it, in reality due to God, whose 'things' we are—only the fictions as it were of that Person. It would be best for me to recall here (since the existence of a spiritual power or God, or any reference even to that power, is involved for most people with the sickliness of some debased ethical code) the *unsentimental* nature of this obligation I am supposing to exist. And this character of compulsion, this intellectual character, applies as much to what is 'due' to God, as to what is 'due' elsewhere: and what is exacted from us elsewhere is an expression merely of a more absolute dependence.

So our dependence or our independence is, I should say, an organic phenomenon, a matter of concentrations and dispersions, which we familiarly regard as the 'personal' attributes, when they become highly concentrated. As to political independence, or political 'freedom,' it has very little to do with personality, and so, in a fundamental sense, very little to do with independence. Political independence is the gift of a society, whereas independence of character, or the being a person, is a gift of nature, to put it shortly. That gift is held for our natural life, irrespective of function. A person can only be 'free' in the degree in which he is a 'person': and if the most potentially effective and the wisest members of a given society are obscured or rendered ineffective, then it can only mean that that society is about to perish, as an organism, for it cannot survive in a condition in which what is most vital in it is obscured or not permitted to function.

How it is that we are able to say that only a *person* can be susceptible of a *right* is because no sentimental value is attached here to the word 'right': because, in short, the law we are presupposing is a non-moral law. Every ethical system has those 'rights,' infested with sentiment: but such mere systematizing of expansion-impulses is not worthy of the name of law.

Does being *susceptible of a right* mean anything else than being a creature who has recognized his willingness (or whose willingness is assumed) to abide by a set of rules, said to be for the 'common good' of the community, and who so comes to form part of a certain social system? That is all that 'human' meant for an early Roman or a Greek. A stranger was 'abnormal,' susceptible of no rights, and no more 'human' than a wild bee or a lion in the forest.—To be beneath the same law—that is to be 'normal,' and to be 'human': let that be our definition.

In the modern nation—and this is of course the case particularly with America—the working of this principle is very easy to follow. The 'Frenchman' as the 'American' is a person *beneath the same law* as all other 'Frenchmen' and 'Americans'—though he may by birth and training be a Russian, who emigrated upon the Revolution, a Spaniard or Italian, a Polish Jew or an African ex-slave. 'Human' in the same way is a term describing anybody beneath the same law as ourselves—it is a term of the same order as 'American' or as 'Russian.'

But all the natural leaders today in the White world are strictly speaking *outlaws.* They are in an 'abnormal' position. (Some are intelligent enough to realize this, but others still believe that they are functioning, or that it is still possible to function, traditionally.)

I, for example, am an outlaw. I am conspicuous for my clear appreciation of that fact.

What can I possibly mean by saying that the best individuals of the european race are outlaws? I mean of course that we are now in the position of local tribal chiefs brought within a wider system, which has gathered and closed in around us; and that the *law* or *tradition* of our race, which it is our function to interpret, is being superseded by another and more universal norm, and that a new tradition is being born. (Of this more universal norm there are as yet no accredited interpreters—for the Soviet leaders are too involved in opportunist politics to lay claim to that position. I am perhaps the nearest approach to a priest of the new order.)

The reason we are outlaws then is that there is no law to which we can appeal, upon which we can rely, or that it is worth our while any longer to interpret, even if we could. We, by birth the natural leaders of the White European, are people of no political or public consequence any more, quite naturally. Even, we are repudiated and hated because the law we represent has failed, not being as effective as it should have been or well-thought-out at all, I am afraid; having been foolishly and corruptly administered into the bargain. There is not one of us (except such a venerable and ineffective figure as Shaw, for instance) who is in a position of public eminence; nor will a single one of us, who is worth anything, ever be allowed to attain to such a position. We, the natural leaders in the World we live in, are now *private citizens* in the fullest sense, and that World is, as far as the administration of its traditional law of life is concerned, leaderless. Under these circumstances, its soul in a generation or so will be extinct, as a separate unit it will cease to exist. It will have merged in a wider system.

Speaking, simply in order to make quite clear what I mean, about myself, if I were a politician, like Shaw, a man of platforms and cameras, I should be very disappointed in the face of this situation. But there are many reasons why it suits me quite well to be denied a public life, to be treated as a dangerous outlaw—still to illustrate my argument by means of personal statement: I do not desire personal notoriety (and that is really all that is at stake), I would rather slip a book I had written into the hands of the Public than I would make a thousand speeches: my abilities, and my interests, again, do not lie in the economic or the political field at all, but in that of the arts of expression, the library and

the theatre. But, far more important than anything else is the fact that I do not happen to regret
the norm that is being superseded and rather find
my sympathies on the side of the more universal
norm which is (as I see the situation) to take its
place. I am a man of the 'transition,' we none of
us can help being that—I have no organic function
in this society, naturally, since this society has been
pretty thoroughly dismantled and put out of com-
mission; though, of course, if you ask me that, I
would prefer a society in which I was beneath a
law, which I could illustrate and interpret. But I
have no desire to walk into the Past. I am content
to think a world-law will be better than a law for
Tooting Bec, and politically speaking to leave the
matter there.

But these various circumstances tend to make me
a sort of extremist: for since what we have lost was
not absolutely to be despised, and should be bitterly
regretted if nothing is put in its place as good as it;
and seeing how many chances there always are that
after wholesale destruction no one will have the
genius or the *bonne volonté* even to do anything but
batten upon the ruins and call that the 'New-world,'
I am what is called a 'bitter' critic of all those symptoms of the interregnum that suggest a compromise
or a backsliding or a substitution of opportunist
romantic policies (prepared to follow every sinuosity
of the landscape, rather than build spectacular
escapes) for a policy of creative compulsion.

The reasons, then, that I should give for not regarding as a tragedy the fact of the personal eclipse
of all that is most intelligent in the Western com-

munities, and the falling apart of those communities in the mass (as they grope their way back to an unconsciousness), are as follows. Our political disorganization is our own doing, is it not? it has been at our own hands, as socialists, liberals, radicals, or artists, and not at the hands of another and hostile organism, that we have been overcome: or it has come about through physical necessity, in the person of our revolutionary Science, all terrestrial societies being called upon to coalesce into a vaster unit—namely a world-society. If this can be effected without more violence and confusion than the human organism is able to endure, it should be the reverse of a misfortune, I think I am right in believing.

But there are extremely few people in the world at this moment who regard the situation in this light. That is a very great pity and likely to involve a great deal of violence and confusion. The remnants of our Western Governments, in the grip of a network of financial groups, or War and Trade Trusts, are behaving as though we were called upon to revert to a super-feudalism and the Dark-Ages, and the Communists tend to play up to every gesture of violence and to allow their doctrine to be converted into a proletarian imperialism (this must be taken as nothing more than an impression of one not more informed than the next and merely judging from report).

How these remarks affect the questions to be canvassed in *Paleface* is as follows. The anti-Paleface campaign has all the appearance of attacks upon a disintegrating organism, by some other intact and triumphant organism: it has very much too *human* and personal a flavour. What it seems to imply is that the White World is 'finished,' that it is a culture or political organism that is going to pieces under assaults from without and from within, quite on the traditional, historical, *Decline and Fall* pattern. And the *Revolt of Asia*, the *Dark Princess*, and such books, suggest that it is the 'Coloured Races,' or the non-European, who have done it or are doing it, and are to be the beneficiaries of a reversal of political power. That is why the tactless assaults of the Borzoi big-guns have to be checked and are certain in the end to cause a disturbance and make it worth somebody's while to take up the cause of the 'Paleface.' That championship is a title that is going begging, but for the moment only.

As good little revolutionaries, at all events, we Palefaces have to claim our revolutionary rights—that is my message in *Paleface*. We ask nothing better than to go over into the reformed world-order, am I not right? but we will not be *pushed* over, no, nor barked at as we go by the Big Borzois and other mongrels, or in short, march out to a chorus of Dark laughter. That, if I understand my fellow Palefaces, is the position. We are somewhat touchy about the legend of our despotisms: this is as much *our* Revolution as anybody else's. Indeed, it is we who have made it possible. It is *more* ours, we can claim, than anybody else's. The White component in the world-combination will be of exactly the same importance, as shown by the revolutionary-weighing-in machine, as every other: but we will not be so gratuitously revolutionary as

85

to allow the Paleface interest to weigh *less*, that is the idea. Even a White revolutionary has his rights, that is my meaning in *Paleface*. But I am 'purely and simply amusing myself,' as Paul would say. I have no official position, White, Red or Black, nor do I covet one.

America has been called the 'Melting-Pot'—it is where more than anywhere else the world-state is being prepared, in a big preliminary olla podrida. I have called this book a *Philosophy of the Melting-Pot*: so there is no occasion to explain how it is that America is the scene I have chosen for my main illustrations.

The outlaws like myself who are preparing the new Law and the new Norm have a very heavy responsibility. It is their business to detach themselves entirely from the specific interests of the human component or group from which they have come, whether Paleface, Negro, Indian or Jew. That is why you find me, in *Paleface*, in a position of defence where my poor downtrodden Paleface brother is concerned. And because a certain short-sighted cockiness in the Paleface makes him sometimes scorn my assistance and causes him to be blind to the novel dangers of his situation, I do not for that reason abandon my impartial ministrations.

The new Law will effectively take shape, it is very likely, in the continent of America, for the same reason that the metropolitan position of Rome caused the *jus gentium* to be developed practically there rather than elsewhere, in the ordinary course of the daily routine of the Praetor Peregrinus.—In Rome the magistrate appointed to deal with the cases in which foreigners were involved (and to whom the roman code was not applicable) was the Praetor Peregrinus.  As Rome grew in importance, foreigners from all quarters of the world made their appearance; and the Praetor Peregrinus had forced upon him what was to some extent a constant exercise in comparative jurisprudence.  It would be discovered no doubt after a time that, underlying the respective codes of even the most widely separated states (whose subjects the Praetor Peregrinus had before him) there was a sort of rough system common to all.  It was upon this more universal system (as it sorted itself out in his daily practice) that the Praetor Peregrinus would base his judgments.  In arriving at any decision involving a conflict between one code and another, he would naturally choose that law that experience had shown him to be of the more universal application.

The main principles of the *jus gentium* were finally incorporated in the roman system, which would benefit by acquiring a more universal applicability. The well-known though disputed identification by Sir Henry Maine of the *jus gentium* with the *jus naturale* ('*jus naturale* is *jus gentium* seen in the light of the Stoic Philosophy') may serve to emphasize still more the significance of this juristic evolution, consequent upon the meeting and trafficking of nations.

We are in a world in which we are all in some sense outlaws, at the moment, for our traditions have all been too sharply struck at and broken and no new tradition is yet born. Some such process as occurred in the administration of the Praetor Peregrinus is occurring today in every quarter of the globe—there is no country that is not in that sense metropolitan. Meantime, we are, technically, in an 'inhuman' situation. This is a very delicate position. It is necessary, I think, in consequence, to insist a little upon the essential (though imperfect) *humanity* of any ill-treated and threatened group— such, for instance, as the Palefaces—who so recently were the rulers of the world, and who are, as a result, looked at somewhat askance, in the new dispensation, and perhaps hustled, on occasion.

As to the 'common good,' what can be said briefly on that head, in connection with the things we are discussing, is as follows.

No successful human society could be founded upon a notion of the 'common good' which attempted to weigh out to everybody an equal amount *and* kind of 'good.' The 'pleasures of the mind,' for instance (which Green denied himself), cannot be equally distributed unless you have a community composed of standard minds, turned out according to some super-mechanical method. It is exactly that sort of regularity or quantitative fixity that it is necessary to avoid, for the sake of the mutual satisfaction of the members of any social group.

The 'common good' can only mean organic 'good,' the functional 'good' belonging to some social organism. There cannot be any 'good' common to an unorganized mob of 'things.' It is only when a mob of things is organized, and has become possessed of *persons* (interpreting and administering its laws and its tradition) that it can be said to have a 'common good.' A 'common good' is, in short, an expression of the law of 'normal' beings (in the juristic sense of beings beneath a common law), and it reduces itself, in the end, to the proper working of their particular law—where that law is healthy and effective, operating in a naturally closed system.

A society is formed, in the first instance, it might be said, by the secretion of some spiritual quiddity (which is the germ of the norm or law) by some single powerful family, or group of active families. It is this norm, as it matures and acquires the strength of habit, that holds them together. From the start that norm is incarnated in the chiefs and leaders of the group, and becomes *personal*, as it were. It is to those leaders that everything is 'due' on the part of the other members of the group.

For Green, however, the 'common good' would mean something entirely different from the laws of this organic complex of relationships. For him the 'good' had become a (falsely) personal 'good,' and human society was conceived as a horizontal egalitarian plane of equal and undifferentiated 'persons.' There were no 'things' in this world at all—except 'lower animals,' stones and trees. For him, as a typical nineteenth-century revolutionary moralist, until every man, woman and child (but especially every woman and child), in the entire world, had been accommodated with all the 'pleasures of the

89

mind' of Plato, Green could know no peace. And
(to turn from the pleasures of the mind of Plato to
things about which there is at any time likely to be
more trouble) if one individual had a wireless set, or
a Bentley or a Morris-Oxford, then everybody must
have them—quite irrespective of the fact that it is
evident to any fairly intelligent and observant person today that the possession of these machines is
not spiritually of very great advantage to the average man, and so such possessions can hardly be regarded as eligible for a position among that aggregate
of things we agree to call the 'common good.'

The 'common good' can, then, only be defined,
in a general way, as the law of any social organism.
But perhaps *any* social organism is too sweeping:
for a society can be so low in the vital scale that it is
incapable of realizing anything that can properly be
described as a 'good' at all. Most of our Western
democracies are rapidly reaching that biologic level.
So it must be the law, I think, of a fairly active and
*perpendicular*—a well-proportioned, elastic, orderly
—society.—As for the indefinite expansion of the
idea of the 'good,' or of the 'human' without limit
of time or place—so that any number of units may
be embraced by a law that is unique—there again
the emotional or sentimental expansiveness of the
protestant moralist seems to me to be at fault, and
to provide for us, in place of a well-built society, an
emotional chaos. That type of feeling must to my
mind result in social ideas that are at once meta-
physically impossible and foolish, or, from the standpoint of the engineer or the artist, in structures that
will be disgustingly unsatisfactory or else quite

90

CONCLUSION TO PART I

meaningless—a sort of rainbow-bridge, of crude and stupid tint, stretched from nowhere to nowhere.

I do not wish to seem too severe or even perhaps a trifle roman, but I must pursue my analysis of this type of ethics a step further, for else the word 'human' will be left up in the air, I am afraid, or get mixed up with Green's 'lowest animals.' And yet the 'Je suis Romain—je suis humain' of Maurras is a formula for the provençal countryside—and a very good one—rather than for the american 'Melting-pot,' into which we all must slip (and, in my view, *should* slip, although I say so without any dogmatism).

Outside what would popularly be regarded as the 'human' norm, lie all the other forms of the animal creation. In order to know what we really mean by 'human,' we cannot escape considering that irrational world; any more than in considering what appears on the face of it the 'human' world, can we help discriminating between the rational and the irrational. There is no question but that a dog, for instance, of a charming character, is more worthy, in the abstract, of our interest and sympathy, than are very many men, both Paleface and Coloured. If you isolate that particular 'lower animal,' and that inferior man, then the animal is the more 'human'—gentler, better, and more rational. To that proposition, I am sure, I shall have no difficulty in receiving your assent (although if the *Borzois* are listening, they no doubt will bark, for they will perceive that this might raise difficulties for them).

A deer or a horse is a nobler creature physically, perhaps, than many men; and some individual

91

horses and deer would be superior spiritually to
them.    Yet those animals could not be said to come
within a human canon, or to be themselves 'human':
and therefore there is nothing 'due' from us to them
or *vice versa*—or only a sentimental something,
which is in its purest state that something that
Green, or the primitive Christian, seizes upon, exag-
gerates, transfers to men, and proceeds to convert
into the peculiar property of man, calling it 'love'
and the ethical sense.    But indeed it is most unreasonable when the 'lower animals' are excluded
from such 'human' canons.

Ethics as conceived by the author of the *Prolegomena to Ethics*, whom I have chosen for my illustrations in this essay, should be entirely confined,
perhaps, to questions regarding our relations to
animals, other than men.    The science of Ethics
altogether might find its true rôle in the regulation
of such relationships.    Dogs, horses, cats and cows
are the natural, and the true, clients of the moral
philosopher, I believe.    As such, the exercise of
ethical emotions would give rise to very grave
problems indeed: and they would involve questions
very much more difficult to meet than those raised
by the purely human variety of ethical speculation:
we should immediately be confronted with the problem of the pork-chop and the mutton-cutlet, in
fine, or of the draught-horse.    And I need not point
out to the reader possessed of an acute political eye
what repercussions this newly demarcated ethical
science would have in the world of revolutionary
politics.    In a flash everything would be in an
uproar.

## CONCLUSION TO PART I

I believe the problem of the mutton-cutlet will yet come into its own, and become one of first-class political importance.—But of all neglected problems of that order, the *Paleface* problem is to my mind the first on the list—if only because, in that instance, we ourselves are the mutton-chop. I am sorry to terminate this part of my essay upon this sordid animal note.

# PART II

## PALEFACE

OR

### 'LOVE? WHAT HO! SMELLING STRANGENESS'

*'There is something direct, brutal, and fine in the nature of Uncas. It is not quite an accident that in our games he is always* the Indian, *while I am the despised White, the Paleface.'*
> *A Story-Teller's Story. Sherwood Anderson.*

*' I went often to the movie studios and watched the men and the women at work. Children, playing with dreams—dreams of an heroic kind of desperado cowboy, doing good deeds at the business end of a gun—dreams of an ever-virtuous womanhood walking amid vice — American dreams—Anglo-Saxon dreams.'—(Ibid.)*

*' The Indian way of consciousness is different from and fatal to our way of consciousness. Our way of consciousness is different from and fatal to the Indian.'*
> *Mornings in Mexico. D. H. Lawrence.*

*' The consciousness of one branch of humanity is the annihilation of the consciousness of another branch. That is, the life of the Indian, his stream of conscious being, is just death to the White man.'—(Ibid.)*

# INTRODUCTION

IN the following essay I quote very fully and examine at considerable length passages from Mr. D. H. Lawrence, Mr. Sherwood Anderson, and other writers using popular narrative to present ideas and even religions. That so much careful attention should be given to artists in fiction, or to works written, it is felt, in the first instance, to amuse, may seem strange to some people. It is not usual to honour them in this way. Were it the analysis of the conditions favourable to a virus, of some definite 'social problem' (with the accompanying statistics, references to philosophic and sociological treatises, and so on), it would not appear at all strange to devote a great deal of space to a minute examination of things that were in themselves, perhaps, not very important or interesting.

What I wish to stress, then, is that these essays do not come under the head of 'literary criticism.' They are written purely as investigations into contemporary states of mind, as these are displayed for us by imaginative writers pretending to give us a picture of current life 'as it is lived,' but who in fact give us much more a picture of life as, according to them, it *should be* lived. In the process they slip in, or thrust in, an entire philosophy, which they derive from more theoretic fields, and which is usually not at all the philosophy of the sort of people they portray. The whole of *Paleface*, in fact, deals with and is intended to set in relief the automatic processes by which the artist or the writer (a novelist or a poet) obtains his formularies: to show how the formulas for his progress are issued to him, how he gets them by post, and then applies them.

According to present arrangements, in the presence of nature the artist or writer is almost always apriorist, we suggest.  Further, he tends to lose his powers of observation (which, through reliance upon external nature, in the classical ages gave him freedom) altogether.  Yet *observation* must be the only guarantee of his usefulness, as much as of his independence.  So he takes his nature, in practice, from theoretic fields, and resigns himself to see only what conforms.to his syllabus of patterns.  He deals with the raw life, thinks he sees arabesques in it ;  but in fact the arabesques that he sees more often than not emanate from his theoretic borrowing, he has put them there.  It is a nature-for-technical-purposes of which he is conscious.  Scarcely any longer can he be said to control or be even in touch with the raw at all, that is the same as saying he is not in touch with nature: he rather dredges and excavates things that are not objects of direct perception, with a science he has borrowed ;  or, upon the surface, observes only according to a system of opinion which hides from him any but a highly selective reality.

The mere fact—with the artist or interpreter of nature—that his material is living, exposes him to the temptation of a drowsy enthusiasm for paradox, since 'life' is paradox (sprinkled over a process of digestive sloth), and all men live, actually, upon the amusement of surprise.  'What man is this who arrives?  A beautiful, a wonderful stranger!' they say: and all strangers are wonderful or beautiful.

'What will the day bring forth? There will be some pleasant novelty, at least of that we can be certain! —a novelty with whose appearance we have had nothing to do.' 'Life' is *not*-knowing: it is the surprise packet: so, essentially unselective, if nature can be so arranged as to yield him as it were a system of surprises, the artist will scarcely take the trouble to look behind them, to detect the principle of their occurrence, or to reflect that for 'surprises,' for the direct life of nature, they are a little over-dramatic and particularly pat. So he automatically applies the accepted formula to nature; the corresponding accident manifests itself, like a djinn, always with an imposing clatter (since it is a highly selective 'accident' that understands its part): and the artist is perfectly satisfied that nature has spoken. He does not see at all that 'nature' is no longer there.

You are merely describing, you may say, the famous 'subjective' character of this time, in your own way and a little paradoxically. If I could surprise anybody into examining with a purged and renewed sense what is taken so much for granted, namely our 'subjectivity'—though who or what is the subject or Subject?—I should have justified any method whatever. But I am anxious to capture the attention of the reader in a way to which he is less accustomed, a less paradoxical way.

In Western countries the Eighteenth-century man and the Puritan man are perhaps the most marked types that survive, disguised of course in all sorts of manners, and differently combined. We have learnt to live upon a diet of pure 'fun,' we are sensationalist to the marrow. Ours is a kind of Wembley-

life of raree-shows, of switchbacks and watershoots.
We observe the gleeful eye of Mr. Bertrand Russell
as he appears suspended for a moment above some
formal logical precipice. Or there is Mr. Roger Fry
in the company of his friend, Mr. Bell, sustaining
delightedly shock after shock from the handles of
some electric machine, or in other words from the
unceremonious vigour of some painting which,
charged with a strange zeal, outrages in turn all the
traditional principles of his English training and his
essential respectability. Then there are the round-
abouts for the Peter Pan chorus, swings for exhibi-
tionists, mantic grottoes and the lecture-tents of the
gymnosophists. Oh it is a wild life that we live in
the near West, between one apocalypse and another!
And the far West is much the same, we are told. In
a word, we have lost our sense of reality. So we
return to the central problem of our 'subjectivity,'
which is what we have in the place of our lost sense,
and which is the name by which our condition goes.

Elsewhere I have described this in its great lines
as the transition from a *public* to a *private* way of
thinking and feeling. The great industrial machine
has removed from the individual life all responsibility. For an individual business adventurer to
succeed as he could in the first days of industrial
expansion, will to-morrow be impossible. It is
evidently in these conditions that you must look for
the solid ground of our 'subjective' fashions. The
obvious historic analogy is to be found in the Greek
political decadence. Stoic and other philosophies
set out to provide the individual with a complete
substitute for the great public and civic ideal of the

happiest days of Greek freedom: with their thought we are quite at home. I will take the account of these circumstances to be found in Caird.

'Even in the time of Aristotle a great change was passing over the public life of Greece, by which all its ethical traditions were discredited. . . . By the victories of Philip and Alexander the city states of Greece were reduced to the rank of subordinate municipalities in a great military empire; and, under the dynasties founded by Alexander's generals, they became the plaything and the prize of a conflict between greater powers, which they could not substantially influence . . . we may fairly say that it was at this period that the division between public and private life, which is so familiar to us but was so unfamiliar to the Greeks, was first decisively established as a fact. A private non-political life became now, not the exception, but the rule; not the abnormal choice of a few recalcitrant spirits, like Diogenes or Aristippus, but the inevitable lot of the great mass of mankind. The individual, no longer finding his happiness or misery closely associated with that of a community . . . was thrown back upon his own resources. . . . What Rome did was practically to pulverize the old societies, reducing them to a collection of individuals, and then to hold them together by an external organization, military and legal . . . its effect (that of roman power) was rather to level and disintegrate than to draw men together.'—(*Evol. of Theology.*)

There is not much resemblance, outwardly, be-

tween the pulverization by one central power, such
as that of Rome, and the pulverization of our social
and intellectual life that is being effected by general
industrial conditions all over the world.   But there
is, in the nature of things, the same oppressive re-
moval of all personal outlet (sufficiently significant
to satisfy a full-blooded business or political ambition) in a great public life of individual enterprise:
and, in the West, at the same time, through the
agency of Science, all our standards of existence
have been discredited.   Many people protest against
such an interpretation of what has happened to us
in Europe and America: they do not see that it has
happened, they say that at most 'there may be a
danger of' it: yet every detail of the life of any
individual you choose to take, in almost any career,
testifies to its correctness.

As to what is at the bottom of this immense and
radical translation from a free public life, on the one
hand, to a powerless, unsatisfying, circumscribed
private life on the other, with that we are not here
especially occupied.   But the answer lies entirely,
on the physical side, with the spectacular growth
of Science, and its child, Industry.   The East is
in process of being revolutionized, however, in
the same manner as the West.   Let me quote Mr.
Russell:

'The kind of difference that Newton has made
to the world is more easily appreciated where a
Newtonian civilization is brought into sharp contrast with a pre-scientific culture, as for example,
in modern China.   The ferment in that country
is the inevitable outcome of the arrival of Newton

upon its shores. . . . If Newton had never lived, the civilization of China would have remained undisturbed, and I suggest that we ourselves should be little different from what we were in the middle of the eighteenth century.'—(*Radio Times*, April 8th, 1928.)

If you substitute Science for Newton (for if Newton 'had never lived' somebody else would) that explains our condition. We have been thrown back wholesale from the external, the public world, by the successive waves of the 'Newtonian' innovation, and been driven down into our primitive private mental caves, of the unconscious and the primitive. We are the cave-men of the new mental wilderness. That is the description, and the history of our particular 'subjectivity.'

In the arts of formal expression, a 'dark night of the soul' is settling down. A kind of mental language is in process of invention, flouting and overriding the larynx and the tongue. Yet an art that is 'subjective' and can look to no common factors of knowledge or feeling, and lean on no tradition, is exposed to the necessity, first of all, of instructing itself far more profoundly as to the origins of its impulses and the nature and history of the formulas with which it works; or else it is committed to becoming a zealous parrot of systems and judgments that reach it from the unknown. In the latter case in effect what it does is to bestow authority upon a hypothetic something or someone it has never seen, and would be at a loss to describe (since in the 'subjective' there is no common and visible nature), and progressively to surrender its faculty of observation, and so sever itself from the external field of immediate truth or belief—for the only meaning of 'nature' is a nature possessed in common. And that is what now has happened to many artists: they pretend to be their own authority, but they are not even that.

It would not be easy to exaggerate the naïveté with which the average artist or writer to-day, deprived of all central authority, body of knowledge, tradition, or commonly accepted system of nature, accepts what he receives in place of those things. He is usually as innocent of any saving scepticism, even of the most elementary sort, where his subjectively-possessed machinery is concerned, as the most secluded and dullest peasant abashed with metropolitan novelties; only, unlike the peasant, he has no saving shrewdness even: and this is all the more peculiar (and therefore not generally noticed, or if recognized, not easily credited) because he is physically in the very centre of things, and so, it would be supposed, 'knowing,' and predisposed to doubt.

Listen attentively to any conversation at a café or a tea-table, or any place where students or artists collect and exchange ideas, or listen to one rising— or equally a risen—writer or artist talking to another —from this there are very few people that you will have to except: it is astonishing how, in all the heated dogmatical arguments, you will never find them calling in question the very basis upon which the 'movement' they are advocating rests. They are never so 'radical' as that. Not that the direction they are taking may not be the right one, but they have not the least consciousness, if so, why it is right, or of the many alternatives open to them. The authority of fashion is absolute in such cases: whatever has by some means introduced itself and gained a wide crowd-acceptance for say two years and a half, is, itself, unassailable. Its application, only, presents alternatives. The world of fashion for them is as solid and unquestionable as that large stone against which Johnson hit his foot, to confute the Bishop of Cloyne. For them the time-world has become an absolute, as it has for the philosopher in the background, feeding them with a hollow assurance.

But this suggestionability, directed to other objects, is shown everywhere by the crowd. The confusion would be more intense than it is, even, if every small practitioner of art or letters started examining, in a dissatisfied and critical spirit, everything at all, you might at this point object. And, if that is the case, why attempt to sow distrust of the very ground on which they stand, among a herd of happy and ignorant technicians entranced, not with 'mind,' but with 'subjectivity'? Was not the man-of-science of thirty years ago, in undisturbed possession of all his assumptions as regards the 'reality' he handled so effectively, happier and brighter, and so perhaps more useful than his more sceptical successor today?

This argument would carry more weight, if the opinions to which it referred were not so fanatically held. It is very difficult to generalize like that: sometimes it is a good thing to interfere with a somnambulist and of course sometimes not. You have to use your judgment. The kind of screen that is being built up between the reality and us, the 'dark night of the soul' into which each individual is relapsing, the intellectual shoddiness of so much of the thought responsible for the artist's reality, or 'nature' today, all these things seem to point to the desirability of a new, and if necessary shattering criticism of 'modernity,' as it stands at present. Having got so far, again, we must sustain our revolutionary impulse. It is an unenterprising thought indeed that would accept *all* that the 'Newtonian' civilization of science has thrust upon our unhappy world, simply because it once had been different from something else, and promised 'progress,' though no advantage so far has been seen to ensue from its propagation for any of us, except that the last vestiges of a few superb civilizations are being stamped out, and a million sheep's-heads, in London, can sit and listen to the distant bellowing of Mussolini; or in situations so widely separated as Wigan and Brighton, listen simultaneously to the bellowing of Dame Clara Butt. It is too much to ask us to accept these privileges as substitutes for the art of Sung or the philosophy of Greece.—It is as a result of such considerations as these that a new revolution is already on foot, making its appearance first under the aspect of a violent reaction, at last to bring a steady and growing mass of criticism to bear upon those innovations that Mr. Russell would term 'Newtonian,' and question their right to land upon the shores of China, and do there what they are said to be doing.

# INTRODUCTION TO PART II

In the arts of formal expression this new impulse has already made its appearance. But the deep eclipse of the extreme ignorance in which most technical giants repose, makes the pointing of the new day, in those places, very slow and uncertain.— Really the average of our artists and writers could be regarded under the figure of nymphs, who all are ravished periodically by a pantheon of unknown gods, who appear to them first in one form then in another. These are evidently deities who speak in a scientific canting and abstract dialect, mainly, in the moment of the supreme embrace, to these hot and bothered rapt, intelligences: and all the rather hybrid creations that ensue lisp in the accents of science as well. But is it *one* god, assuming many different forms, or is it a plurality of disconnected celestial adventurers? That is a disputed point: but I incline to the belief that one god only is responsible for these various escapades. That is immaterial, however, for if it is not one, then it is a colony of beings very much resembling one another.

So then, before discussing at all the pros and cons of the 'subjective' fashion, it is necessary to recognize that it is not to the concrete material of art that we must go for our argument: that is riddled with contradictory assumptions. Most dogmatically 'subjective,' telling-from-the-inside, fashionable method —whatever else it may be and whether 'well-found' or not—is ultimately discovered to be bad philosophy—that is to say it takes its orders from second-rate philosophic dogma. Can art that is a reflection of bad philosophy be good art? I should say that you could make good art out of almost anything, whether good or bad from the standpoint of right reason. But under these circumstances there is, it follows, no objection to the source being a rational one: for reason never did any harm to art, even if it never did it any good. And in other respects we are all highly interested in the success of reason.

But if, politically and socially, men are today fated to a 'subjective' rôle, and driven inside their private, mental caves, how can art be anything but 'subjective,' too? Is externality of any sort possible, for us? Are not we of necessity confined to a mental world of the subconscious, in which we naturally sink back to a more primitive level; and hence our 'primitivism,' too? *Our* lives cannot be described in terms of action—externally that is—because we never truly *act*. We have no common world into which we project ourselves and recognize what we see there as symbols of our fullest powers. To those questions we now in due course would be led: but what here I have been trying to show is that first of all much more attention should be given to the intellectual principles that are behind the work of art: that to sustain the pretensions of a considerable innovation a work must be surer than it usually is to-day of its formal parentage: that nothing that is unsatisfactory in the result should be passed over, but should be asked to account for itself in the abstract terms that are behind its phenomenal face. And I have suggested that many subjective fashions, not plastically or formally very satisfactory, would become completely discredited if it were clearly explained upon what flimsy theories they are in fact built: what bad philosophy, in short, has almost everywhere been responsible for the bad art.

My main object in *Paleface* has been to place in the hands of the readers of imaginative literature, and also of that very considerable literature directed to popularizing scientific and philosophic notions, in language as clear and direct as possible, a sort of key ; so that, with its aid, they may be able to read any work of art presented to them, and, resisting the skilful blandishments of the fictionist, reject this plausible 'life' that often is not life, and understand the ideologic or philosophical basis of these confusing entertainments, where so many false ideas change hands or change heads. As it is, the popularizer is generally approached with the eyes firmly shut and the mouth wide open. And the fiction in its very nature takes with it the authority of life—people live it, as it were, as they read: so it is able to pass off as *true* almost anything. The often very elaborate philosophy expressed in this sensational form very often not only misrepresents the empirical reality, but misstates the truth.

I dignify this critical work with the title of *system*, because as literature stands today, it in reality amounts to that. It is a system that will enable any fairly intelligent man, once he opens his mind to it, and seizes its main principles, to read under an entirely new light almost everything that is written at the present time. Works of sociology, fiction, history, philosophy, claiming to be on the one hand conceived 'objectively,' according to the non-human

methods of ideal Science, will be found on close inspection, in most instances, to be All-too-Human,
and to be serving ends anything but scientific; and,
in another class, works of fiction claiming only to be
ingenuous works of *art*, will be found to be saturated
with political doctrine, or with attitudes of mind
imposed upon the Many in the first place not by
pure pleasure experts, anxious only to excite the
palate of their clients, but by political experts, de-
vising means of ruling people by working on their
senses and emotions.

In order of course to employ this system effectively the reader must acquaint himself with many
things of a sort that do not come his way in the
ordinary course of life. He must accustom himself
to regarding the means by which people are ruled
today as very much more shrewd and elaborate
than is generally believed. He must entirely dis-
card all the notions of the essential brute stupidity
of 'power' that formerly sometimes would have
applied in Europe, but certainly does not at present.
If he finds it difficult to believe that he is ruled with
such a 'ruthless' cleverness, let him study for a
moment the highly 'psychological' methods by
which the Soviet rules its subjects. The Soviet do
their ruling in public, indeed: they explain and
explain, as did the german theoreticians of war:
there is no excuse, therefore, for any one to-day not
to be *au courant* with the way that he is likely to be
ruled. For he can be sure that those open professors
of intrigue and herd-hypnotism are not the only
practitioners at work. Those who do *not* publish
daily accounts of how they reach their ends are at

least likely enough to be not less clever than those who do.

In the following pages, then, it is my intention to squeeze out all the essential meaning that there is in the works I select, and to leave only the purely literary or artistic shells. That the Public, at the present moment, should have that essential matter isolated for it, seems to me of very great importance.

Again, Mr. D. H. Lawrence, an english writer, supplies the most important evidence in the review of the contemporary american 'consciousness.' But, first of all, many american and english books are read almost equally on both sides of the Atlantic; Sinclair Lewis is as much at home here in England as he is in America, and Mr. Lawrence is, I believe, more widely read in the United States than in England. His name is invariably associated, in America, with that of Sherwood Anderson. In the 1925 *Americana* of Mr. Mencken a scornful Middle West reviewer refers to 'Sherwood Lawrence,' as though that composite name covered one person. So my choice of Lawrence is explained. A further reason, however, is that his *Mornings in Mexico* reveals the true aim of Sherwood Anderson and others of his school better than they have, to my knowledge, so far revealed themselves. This does not mean that Mr. Lawrence is better qualified to express what they all equally wish to say: it happens, only, that he has provided, in his book, an ideal material for such an analysis as the present one.

There is one more point. No criticism of America as a whole is involved in my choosing, in this instance, american writers. America appears to me

111

much stronger and more admirable than those of her writers who are most prominent in criticizing her, and who for a long time have been busy attempting to convert the essential American to something that would be far less effective or desirable than what at present he still is. Also these writers are committed to a policy of driving him into a position that would be a much less enviable one than that he occupies at present. This situation, with the 'Coming of Age of America,' is changing, but it is unlikely that menckenism will be dropped, and if it is succeeded by a mere jingoism, its effects will remain, not far beneath the surface.

It is my sense of the immense importance of America to the Western World that has impelled me to scrutinize the mind of contemporary America, as displayed in some of her most influential writers. My admiration for that very forcible publicist, Mr. Mencken, is not in contradiction with that. Mencken was absolutely necessary to destroy the self-complacency that well-being must bring. Also he has been of enormous use, no doubt, in cutting off the American from his self-indulgent, comfortable Past, which is no longer actual today. That Past had to be evacuated, the anglo-saxon romanticism had to be knocked out of Americans, or out of the English, by somebody. But it is no doubt true, as most of the writers of the reaction see today, that such a critic as Mencken, become an institution, should be dissuaded from philosophizing, as it were, his function.

# ROMANTICISM AND COMPLEXES

§ 1. *The Paleface receives the Dubious Present of an 'Inferiority Complex.'*

THE once proud, boastful, super-optimistic American of the United States has become just a White 'man-in-the-street' with a pronounced 'inferiority complex.' (I speak of the educated, or book-reading, American.) This fact, or something like it, is patent to anybody who has followed american thought of late and had opportunities of meeting a good many Americans.

'Never glad confident morning again'—for the American of the United States. This, most Europeans would here exclaim, is a change for the better. —What I propose to consider is the first cause or causes of this transformation: and if it is, in reality, a change for the better or not, as it affects America, and as it affects us, in the other parts of the anglosaxon World. I will take the last point first.

The toning-down of the American is coeval, I suppose, to give it a fairly exact convenient date, with the activities of Mr. Mencken. I do not of course mean that this great transformation has been effected by the editor of the *American Mercury*. But the *Americana* of that writer is not calculated to inspire a very acute sense of self-respect in the american bosom: and certainly attacks by Mr. Mencken upon the traditional american conceit must have been a powerful factor in bringing to the surface this gradual sensation of insecurity, the habit of self-criticism, the dissatisfaction, to which I am alluding. At the present moment this has grown, it would seem, into what is actually an 'inferiority complex.' Or that is how the situation presents itself to me.

That the influence of Mr. Mencken, both in his own writings and through his disciple Mr. Sinclair Lewis, is of a popular, rather than an intellectual, order is true. But we are concerned here with the wider general discouragement and disillusion of the large book-reading mass of a prosperous modern democracy: so that does not affect our statement.

## § 2. *White Hopes with a 'Complex.'*

THERE is among the younger writers a powerful movement to americanize. The tendency is to isolate America from Europe, and to produce an art that shall be starkly *american*, for the Americans. This, at the present time, finds expression in numerous attempts in the literary field, at all events, to depict essential phases of american life. The scene usually chosen is that part of the United States that is least affected by the more recent european immigration, and therefore most american, in the old sense.

Mencken, I should say, means very little to the people engaged in these latter activities. As a publicist who ten, or five, years ago shook things up, and who at all times has used his influence to get a good book read and so prepared the way for the present more intelligent standards, they would respect him. But as a political publicist he would not interest them. These are, as it were, the intellectualist White Hopes. But they are White Hopes who have passed through very dark barrages of disillusioned thought; and the character of all they do will bear traces, I think, of the rough handling they have received. They are *White Hopes with a complex*; or White Hopes composed of many complexes. As such the more far-sighted literary fans will, no doubt, think twice before putting their money on them. This is a general statement, without reference to any particular writers.

But more than that, in its search for the savage and the primitive (resulting usually in rather artificial romantic constructions) this movement has a philosophy which is scarcely that of the superb natural physical vigour (innocent of expedients to look strong, or to terrorize with exhibitions of violence, innocent also of an intensive and romantically overheated sex-philosophy) of the early, purely european, American. It has all over it the stigmata of the neo-barbarism of the post-war gilded rabble, of café, studio and counting-house. And the neo-barbarism, so elaborate and sophisticated, is *european*—not anything that can be called 'american,' in origin. It is of the Ritzes and Carltons, of the Côte d'Azur, of the luxurious vulgar philistine bohemianism of the european cities. Greenwich Village today, without drink, is a dirty neglected and empty slum. It is to prosperous bohemian Europe you must look for the necessary *mise en scène* of this philosophy.

The pan-american movement, then, so excellent as a direction, so far, except in a few cases, does not seem to have emancipated itself from the essential european post-war decay. However much it buries its head in the tawny sands, or super-rich and fat Zolaesque red loam, of Arizona, Indiana, or Ohio, its *bottom* (so to speak)—its tell-tale ecstatically wriggling back-side, remains in the Café du Dôme, Montparnasse. And there is no true bridge between the primitive America it is sought to resuscitate and the Café du Dôme. Glance into the Dôme, any one who questions this, and who happens to be in Paris. You would think you were in a League of Nations beset by a zionist delegation, in a movie studio, in Moscow, Broadway, or even Zion itself, *anywhere* but in the mythical watertight America of the present reaction, whatever that *pur sang* America may be worth as an idea, and it seems to me a good one.

These suggestions I allow myself to make very much under correction, however: and that anyway is not the subject of my essay, except indirectly. It had to be alluded to to obtain an accurate perspective for the satire of Mencken—Lewis—Nathan.

§ 3. *The opposite 'Superiority Complex' thrust at the same time upon the Unwilling Black.*

ANYTHING that affects the general mind, however, in the way that the attacks of Mencken have, does also, without their knowing it, usually influence the intellectuals. Such a man as Sherwood Anderson, for instance (who, in his turn, was the originator of the *America-pure* school), has been very much influenced by all those waves of opinion and suggestion militating *against* the American believing in

116

himself quite as firmly as formerly he did, and so against this dream of a watertight America. What I shall have subsequently to say with regard to the books of Sherwood Anderson will, I think, make this aspect of the matter very much clearer. Ambition of that sort should certainly be made of sterner stuff than such as Anderson is able to supply.

It would not be an exaggeration, in consequence, to say that *Americana* is making a present to the White American of a formidable and full-fledged 'inferiority complex,' that is, in so far as he is the widely-advertised, popular focus of all the disillusioned thought of the post-war Western mind in the United States.

Parallel with this, many writers of american nationality are busy providing the Negro, the Mexican Indian, the Asiatic Settler, and indeed anybody and everybdy who is not a *pur sang* White, of the original american-european stock, with a 'superiority complex.' This in some cases is not an easy matter. The American Negro, for instance, is difficult to galvanize into pride of that sort, and is apt to remain obstinately 'inferior.' Similarly, the Kaffir requires a good deal of hard pumping before he swells into an aggressive race-class warrior ready to scorn, bare his teeth and drive out, the White. But still the good work goes on. The almost demented energy and ingenuity on the part of the *pumpers* is one of the most curious features of these unique events. All this is of course the complement of the other little present—that of the 'inferiority complex.' A mechanical reversal is in progress, or promises (if that is how you look at it) to occur.

## § 4. *The Nature of Mr. Mencken's Responsibility.*

AT this point I had better make clear what I suppose is Mr. Mencken's position in this racial turning of the tables, and that of those associated with him in these revolutionary enterprises. Mr. Mencken, let us say, became more and more impressed with the futility of the machinery of Democracy, which he was able to observe in full and indecent operation all round him, in the rich and exaggerated american scene. It showed itself capable of idiocies of unequalled dimensions. The Poor White showed how unable he was to defend himself against his interfering rulers, of whatever shade of race or politics. The Rich White was not a specially high type of magnate, and he manipulated his power with a sickly unction of cordiality and righteousness that gave the intelligent american patriot (such as Mr. Mencken) a violent nausea, and every sort of misgiving for the future of american life. This violent nausea translated itself into violent acts of criticism and persiflage. The more truly patriotic, the more disgusted he would be.

I am not acquainted with Mr. Mencken; but that, as a description of what has brought about his famous critical attacks, would, I suppose, be generally accepted by educated Americans. In any case he has convicted the American Democracy (mainly out of its own mouth, in his *Americana*, which are extracts from newspapers, handbills, advertisements, etc.) of surprising stupidities. Generalizing from this body of evidence, he concludes that such a form of Democracy as has developed in America is fundamentally bad and absurd.

Passing on from the general statement to my private view of the matter, I do not see how any one surveying the evidence Mr. Mencken has collected could deny that a radical change of some sort was to be desired for this great key-nation of the modern world. By key-nation I mean that what the United States are today, the other most 'advanced' countries we know, from experience, will become to-morrow. Karl Marx, in his day, told people to watch Industrial England, on the same principle. So what America really *is* is of as great importance outside its frontiers as within them. But those changes should perhaps be quite different from what Mr. Mencken would bring about, if he were called in to do the changing, as well as the smashing. Radical the changes no doubt should be. But there are so many *radical* things that are the opposite, even, of what is meant, currently, in America by 'radical.' Even the choice of this epithet for *one* direction only of change, or revolution, reveals, surely, a very much narrowed view of life's possibilities.

§ 5. *What is 'Change' or 'Progress,' and are they One or Many?*

On the other hand, once it has been decided to transform anything or anybody, from its or his present state into some other condition, it is important to know (especially if you are the person who is to be transformed—it does not matter so much if you are the transformer or reformer) just which of an infinite number of possibilities is to be that 'new.'

119

# PALEFACE

*It is usually a lack of imagination that makes people so blindly, uncritically, susceptible to the 'new.'* That fact should be self-evident, for in practice you have it borne in upon you continually. It is because they cannot imagine anything new themselves that they are forced to accept the 'new' officially provided for them.

Take, for example, the novelties of fashion. Each fresh novelty is accepted with a sort of fatalism as the *only possible* novelty, as an inevitable creation, as though it had dropped from the sky, instead of, as is the case, been invented by a fat little man somewhere in Paris. (I here use—for different purposes —a device of Mr. Lawrence's: *vide* p. 186.) But whatever happens at all is accepted by the majority as the *only thing* that could possibly have happened. In short, it has *happened*, they feel—the 'new' has happened; not that some other person a little shrewder and more active than themselves has *done it to them.* And all the *other* things that might quite well have 'happened' (if somebody else had been there at the controlling centre) are not so much as dreamed of.

In a thick fog of the *actual* the generality of people dwell, deeply unconscious of all the multitudes of possible things, of possible 'changes' and 'novelties,' that do *not* issue from that fog into the spot-light of *actuality.* The 'up-to-date' is thus the emanation of some person, or some small inner ring of people. But it is superstitiously regarded as a fatal cosmical event.

Bankok, New York City, Venice, the London of the Regency, a medieval flemish town, are all appearances that differ very much from each other. They all grew and have been tried to answer the requirements of some community, or of the leaders of a community. But there are many factors in the choice of form. Venice, in the midst of its lagoons, was a marine fortress and a trading centre. Manhattan was a narrow rock, hence the skyscraper, it is said. The skyscraper, elsewhere in America, is often, we are told, a mere ornament, something a rising town must have before it can become a full-fledged 'city.' The competitive skyscrapers in New York have similarly been the supreme advertisement of Big Business: the rising big business, like the rising big town, had to have a skyscraper. The biggest business, it was assumed, would have the biggest skyscraper.

The forms of cities do not grow according to the requirements of the greatest happiness of the greatest number. They are usually the inventions of minorities. The hill of masonry that goes up behind the Battery at New York is no doubt as much the panache of mercantile conceit as it is a geographic expedient. It is one of the avatars of the principle of beauty, as much as the venetian palaces. And, in the distance, it is beautiful as well as impressive, though differently from Venice. It is the difference between the towered and terraced most recent battleship of the 'Rodney' type and the state-barge of the Doge.

The upshot of these remarks is as follows (though I cannot go into it very carefully here): First, the geographic conditions, and indeed generally the *physical* conditions, are not so important as is usu-

121

ally supposed in deciding the character of 'Change' or of 'Progress' in the outward form of cities. There is a kind of physical and climatic absolute, no doubt. But the reality is, very often not that absolute, but some sort of perversion. Hence it would lie much more in your power than you are accustomed to think to *change* yourself, just as it would be to change your environment, in any of a great variety of ways, provided you had the imagination and the necessary power. *'Change' is much less than is generally believed a single-gauge track.* It is not a single-gauge track at all. It is a multitudinous field of tracks and lines, only *one* of which is used. That single line—the one that is used, the one that 'happens'—we call 'the new.' As we proceed along it we call that 'progress.' It is my argument that there is an *absolute* progress for any given community, but that they are seldom able to investigate it, and seldom attain it.

But all philosophy of history today—and Spengler is a most perfect example of that—assumes an absolute *arrest* somewhere or other. There is, on any analogy, advance or 'progress' between the amœba and Socrates. (The amœba's opinion of Socrates, I am assuming, we should not regard as a contribution to values: else the amœba becomes merely another romantic outcast or superseded 'race,'about which we grow touchy and diffident.) But *now* there is nothing but a rising and falling of peoples and cultures, on a dead level as regards value. Change is always merely—change. It is quite evident that if this had been the philosophy of the earliest men no arts, sciences, or anything but wild animal life would have resulted. Yet what people call 'Progress' today is generally not an advance. Those are the two main facts in this connection: that is the centre of the confusion.

Under these circumstances the men of imagination of this period of 'change' and violent 'progress' are under no obligation to keep their eyes fixed on the *one* track and direction that what is called 'modern' and 'progress' is taking. The fatalism of that fixed stare, of that 'what is, is,' is perhaps natural enough, but, in its turn, can only claim to be *one* attitude. And, as to 'progress' or 'change,' there are millions of extremely different forms available. You should, for that one out of the many, of your personal choice (not yet existing, but quite available), *wish*: and you should steadily oppose what you do not wish. As for the many individuals of imagination and with certain powers, they have to learn once more to wish, or will, quite simply. That is the first step. This all Europeans have for fifty years been taught *not* to do, until today *to will* is very difficult for them: they have had such a thorough grounding in impotence. But certainly what no one in his senses would wish or will is the America of Mr. Mencken's *Americana* or the Europe of Herr Spengler. And it would also show very little imagination —less even than that displayed by those who shut their eyes and open their mouths and swallow the hastily-manufactured 'new'—to will yesterday back. For it is yesterday that conceived in the first place the America of *Americana,* and the Europe of spenglerism.

Imagine such an artist as Leonardo da Vinci alive

at this time and suddenly given *carte blanche* (in some access of official enthusiasm) to change radically London, New York, or Berlin into the most beautiful city he could imagine; or else suppose him entrusted with the creation of Canberra or a new Delhi. *If* you can imagine such an event as that, then you will immediately see the bleakness and unreality of what is generally called 'Progress,' or the false revolutionary fatalism we describe as 'Change.'

## § 6. *From White Settler to Poor City-White.*

I will now return to the 'inferiority complex' of the White Man. That the seeds of that reversal of feeling do not date from the end of the War, but from long before it, is obvious. If we consider for a moment the circumstances in which the White Race has found itself for a long time now, and the temper of many of its literary spokesmen, poets and statesmen, we shall see that clearly.

The colonization of the New World, Australia, and of large areas in Asia and Africa, by the European, opened a new epoch of World-history, of a different character from any preceding it. It was the domestication, or imperialization, of the entire globe, with the White as overlord.

For the most part the White peoples who overran the world, and, with the help of their rapidly developing Science, enslaved the greater part of it, wiping out entire races and cultures, were possessed of a meagre cultural outfit, and only a borrowed religion. It is a commonplace that Cortez and Pizarro were less 'civilized,' on the whole, than the

Aztecs, Mayans or Incas they subdued. The Anglo-Saxons, who were responsible for the major part of this european expansion and colonization (although not the first in the field) possessed less cultural equipment, and a more naïve and crude variety of religion (their well-thumbed Genevan Bible in their breast-pocket), than the other White partners of this World-conquest.

As far as the Anglo-Saxon is concerned, there was never any unnecessary diffidence or lack of self-persuasion about his conquest. Whether he wiped out the 'Redskin' of America to make room for himself, captured and enslaved the Negro and put him on his plantations, or subjugated the highly civilized Hindu, he can seldom have suffered from anything in the shape of an 'inferiority complex.' Quite the reverse, of course. He was quite sure that he was in every way a better man than the people he over-ran. He was more 'civilized,' more 'moral,' he was a 'gentleman,' he was 'White,' he was *cleaner* (that came next to his 'godliness'), he was faultlessly brave: he was, in short, of a different and better clay. Some of his enemies were brave, some 'gentlemen' (like the Turk): but none possessed *all* those qualities that were his. If to succeed is what you want, and not to fail, that is the only spirit in which to effect a conquest.

The great opportunities that offered themselves to the early colonist and trader reinforced this opinion. He was repaid for his colonizing enterprise by the possession of land—even if his family at home had never possessed an acre—and, if not too stupid, could easily grow rich. The hard and

125

active life made a better man of him, too, than many
of his stock that remained in their country of origin.
With his scientific weapons he was like a god amongst
the 'heathen' and the 'poor Indian' (who worshipped
stones, 'heard god in the wind,' and was 'untutored'
in White science). So there were substantial
grounds for a sensation of superiority. A century
ago the White was in full possession of a 'superiority
complex,' in consequence, and until the War (when
all the Whites, in one glorious *auto-da-fé*, for four
years did their best to kill and ruin each other) he
retained it.

From those early days of White conquest down to
the days of the 'Poor White' (the subject of Sherwood Anderson's books), and to the present educated
city-White, with his gradually crystallizing 'inferiority complex'—the subject of this essay—is a road
of disillusionment and decline, to some extent.
White Civilization, especially in America, built itself up with great rapidity into a towering baby-
lonian monument to Science; but the old freedom
and sense of power shared by every White Man in
the early days naturally was crushed, or overpowered, at least, by the great technical achievements of the same instruments that had secured him
his new empire. So, if you compare that empire
with the roman, for instance, it has been in his hands
a remarkably short time. Today the average White
Man experiences great difficulty in realizing how the
engine has been turned against himself, and how his
'conquest' is already a thing of the past.

This slowness to understand, this indolent, in-
stinctive, self-protective *living in the past*, or else

126

just sheer ignorance of the World-situation today, accounts for many things: certainly it would account for an attitude of astonishment or incredulity that such a plain statement as the present one must expect to encounter. For, in a sense, it is what we all know to be the situation: and yet, when stated in so many words, and associated with a few of the things that obviously must ensue from it, it may at first, to many readers, seem fantastic.

Better than a great deal of argument—for the purpose of convincing people that I am not talking quite in the air—will be to quote, at adequate length, passages from a variety of sources which will, I think, plainly show the reality of this deep and powerful current of doubt and confusion that has overtaken the White Man. And I will begin with the most obvious, as far as America is concerned, namely, the destructive work of Mr. Mencken.

§ 7. *'Americana' of Mencken.*

THE *Americana* of Mr. Mencken are so well known that there would be no object in quoting them at any length. It must be admitted, in general criticism of these documents, that another sort of patriot than this earnest, clever, germanic editor could easily throw doubt on their value and significance. Perhaps the most useful way of considering them would be to approach them from the standpoint of this hypothetic patriot, of another persuasion. Their very qualities, even, will be best brought out by this method. I will proceed to do this. But by adopting this procedure I wish to make it clear that

I would not minimize the great debt of America to Mr. Mencken, or to Sinclair Lewis, for holding up their hostile mirrors.

In the first place, then, it could be said that the *Americana* consist mostly of ridicule of religious emotionality. But all religion, looked at with the uninterested eye of the outsider, or from the exclusively secular or scientific standpoint, lends itself to ridicule. For instance, to the Anglo-Saxon of two centuries ago, the religious 'superstitions' of every race whatever, except the Anglo-Saxon, provided much amusement. A 'heathen Chinee' at his devotions, 'Fuzzy-wuzzy' at his, the 'Indian native,' or the Coolie, at his (cf. *Mother India*); the Jew muttering away in his dingy synagogue; even 'the Dago' at his, was a joke at which the Anglo-Saxon laughed heartily. And, of course, his laughter increased his self-esteem.

From this point of view, Mr. Mencken's *Americana* is merely the Anglo-Saxon at *his* devotions being laughed at, in his turn. It is the turn of the Anglo-Saxon, merely. It is a mistake to regard the *Americana* as exclusively referring to the more savage states of America. The evangelism of Dakota is no funnier than the same sort of thing in Wales or Scotland. The London Salvationist, at the corner of any street, would provide Mr. Mencken with perfect *Americana* jokes. *Americana* is an attack upon the Anglo-Saxon Protestant at his devotions, more than anything else, as *Mother India* is an attack upon the religious habits of the Indian. (But Mr. Mencken is a different sort of critic to Miss Mayo.)

Therefore, all that comes under the head of *ridi-*

*cule of religion* could be matched anywhere in the world. Horatio Bottomley, in the days of his most florid publicity, was as grotesque as any 'moron' in a 'backward' southern State. Abandoning the beautiful forms and ancient etiquette of devoutness, the Protestant everywhere inevitably grew vulgar in the *form* his worship took. This was unavoidable. As time went on he grew worse, more vulgar instead of less. In America he has perhaps gone furthest, but not so very much ahead as all that. The richest, and so the most aggressive and cocksure Protestant will be the most ridiculous. And possibly the spirit of american Advertisement, taking a hand in the Alleluiah business, has made a slightly more fantastic-looking thing of it than can be found elsewhere. That is the utmost that can be claimed for the criticism of *Americana*.

That is all there is to that, and it is more than half of the matter of Mr. Mencken's book, and the richest and funniest portion.

Here is an example from the Louisiana cuttings (p. 98, *Americana*, 1925) of 'How Christianity is being spread among the girl-students of Tulana University, etc.':

'What per cent. of your students read the Bible daily? You? How many minutes a day do you pray? Ever pray thirty minutes by watch? Honest!

'In how many rooms on your campus is there a deck of spot cards? A Bible?

'How about smoking, cursing, drinking?

'What per cent. of your students go to Sunday-school? Preaching? Once a day? Twice?

Prayer-meetings at a Church? Contribute to the
Church? Belong to the Church school? Study
the Sunday-school lesson?'

That is a fair specimen of the more normal evidence provided by Mr. Mencken. It is not particularly funny. It is depressing reading: but surely
it could be matched anywhere in the christian world.
The anxious, insistent, 'humorous' note has a uni-
versally familiar ring.

Really these collections called *Americana* throw
a more interesting light upon the people who are
amused and delighted (apparently) by them, than
they do upon the people whom ostensibly they are
supposed to hold up to ridicule. As you read them
you are inclined rather to glance aside and survey
your *fellow-readers*, and to wonder what variety of
snobbery, or superiority complex, has brought together this large 'reading-public.'

The critic of these collections, again, would have
occasion often to object that things quoted as
solemn statements were evidently intended to be
jokes. They are not usually very good jokes. They
look, in fact, as though they had been specially con-
cocted to catch Mencken's eye. Here is one from
Massachusetts (p. 121):

'Effects of Woman Suffrage as disclosed by the
Lynn *Telegram-News*, a great intellectual and
moral organ.'

[These are Mencken's headings, describing the nature
of the cutting.]

'Many of the village belles . . . of Danvers, . . .

have started wearing dog-collars. Dog-collars
are not only being worn by schoolgirls, but are
even worn by teachers. . . . The girls do not always
buy their dog-collars. That fact was brought to
light when many complaints were heard from dog
owners to the effect that dogs have mysteriously
lost their neck pieces.'

This looks like a clumsy joke of the 'sly' order,
written by some tired newspaper-man in the silly
season.

Here is a 'dispatch' from Orono, Maine, appearing
'in recent public prints':

'If Henry James, society novelist and short
story writer of the late Nineteenth Century, were
to reappear today, one-fifth of the University
of Maine freshmen class would expect him to be
arrayed as a two-gun bandit, according to the
results of a questionnaire made known to-day.
Martin Luther was the son of Moses; the author
of Vanity Fair was William Shakespeare; Dis-
raeli was a poet; and Moses was a Roman ruler,
according to some of the other answers submitted
in reply to questions.'

Every civilized country has and has always had
its examination jokes—*What the Eton boy answered
when asked what he knew of the Orinoco or Oregon,* as
an instance of the sort of thing. (Oregon, or for
that matter Orono, he would probably describe as a
cheese, or a game of cards.) In all this type of story
two reflections are apt to remain in the mind of the
person to whom it is told: first, he feels that the

story has probably been made up by somebody to make him laugh; which he doesn't mind if he has got his laugh satisfactorily. Or else, if the story is authentic, he usually has the impression that the dunce who is its hero was not quite such a dunce as he looked; and even may have been a much shrewder fellow than his examiners.

The above cutting from 'public prints' in Maine is no exception to this rule. That Moses was a roman ruler was evidently the freshman's idea of a joke. That Martin Luther was the son of this roman ruler was a subtle extension of the joke—both, to me, have a theological and learned look. Or perhaps the freshman was a reader of *Americana*, and wished to make a parade of his ignorance of the sacred text, seeing that so many 'morons' showed a lamentable familiarity with it. In any case, if the 'freshman' of Orono could be convicted of a benighted ignorance, as a magnificent compensation the newspaper men of all the 'public prints' of Orono shine brightly as a well-informed body of men, conversant with the work of Henry James, thoroughly acquainted with the Scriptures, and with some knowledge of the Reformation. So, as it is America in general we are having held up to us, not any particular class, Orono, Maine, does not come off so badly.

Then a great number of the extracts have reference to the absurdity of Prohibition. Prohibition is, of course, a joke played upon the American People of a very perfect kind. That such a joke *could* be played does not say much for their collective political sagacity, it could be argued. But can any

European today assert that this is not a joke that may equally be played, successfully, upon his people at any moment now?

The War provides some *Americana* fun, as well. But the War is another joke, like Prohibition, that has been played on all of us without exception. So, *people who live in glass houses,* etc.

I will go on, for a moment, with these possible criticisms of Mr. Mencken's excellent satire:

> 'Progress of Methodist *Kultur* in the home of the Creoles, as reported by a press dispatch from New Orleans.'

> 'The old Absinthe House, one of the landmarks in the old French quarter of New Orleans, where, according to repute, Jean Lafitte planned his piratical forays and boasted of what he and Napoleon Bonaparte would do to Messieurs les Anglais, was badly damaged last night. Prohibition agents did it all for one quarter of an ounce of absinthe, according to their official report, filed today. In the old courtyard, a door, priceless relic of the old hotel, was smashed. The book in which artists, statesmen, writers and lesser or greater notables had signed their autographs was cast carelessly upon the wreckage-littered floor. Because a few drops of absinthe was found in the place, charges of possession and sale of intoxicants were placed against the proprietor.'

This shows how the idiotic drink-war resulting from the Volstead Act leads to vandalism: 'priceless relics' and an old and historical building suffer. This is Rheims Cathedral, damaged by german shellfire, over again in a small way—that is the idea. Only here it is not the Germans but their former enemies doing the same thing.

And here we have to note another feature of the *Americana*: namely, that many of them are designed to turn the tables upon the 'Allied' war-propagandist. Mr. Mencken, being of german origin, naturally resented that propaganda, and, in the heat and folly of the moment, its frequent unfairness. But such material for a turning-of-the-tables of this sort could be found in any community. It is merely the tale of general human stupidity. And, of course, the Germans did destroy an irreplaceable work of art, and would have destroyed others had they been able.—This undercurrent of nationalist passion in Mr. Mencken, it could be claimed, weakens his criticism.

When he says that there have been rumours of the suppression of his paper, he refers to the american police as *Polizei*. He refers to the 'goose-stepping' habits of the american masses. So he rubs it in. If he had conveyed that Americans were mesmerized and drilled without this familiar war-time tag of *Polizei*, the effect would have been stronger. But Mr. Mencken is, I should say, a very honest man, and he has strong feelings.

Kentucky should be a good state for Mr. Mencken. If you refer to *Americana*, 1925, you can fairly take that as an example. But it is surprising how little he gets out of it to his purpose. Of course, there is the usual extravagant Salvation Army language quoted. But that vernacular of provincial religion is rather engaging than otherwise, and an example of extreme high-spirits on the part of very simple folk indeed—whose principal offence seems to be that they do not want their kind to intermarry with Negroes, and that they believe in the hebrew sacred books so deeply that they object to people teaching that men are descended from monkeys, instead of having been created along with monkeys and all other things, all in one simultaneous Fiat. (The ultra-sophisticated beliefs of Mr. D. H. Lawrence, which I shall be examining shortly, lie somewhere between the two—between Mencken and the kentuckian 'moron'—as Berman would call him, after Mencken.)

The first of these two arch-offences I regard as a substantial virtue; the bitter contempt directed upon the second by many people I do not share: so all this part of *Menckeniana* I find dull or pointless.

Here is the example from Kentucky of high-spirits, combined with imperfect education:

'Solomon, a Six-Cylinder Sport. Could you handle as many wives and concubines as this "Old Bird"? Rev. B. G. Hodge will preach on this subject Sunday night at Settle Memorial.'

The simple mind, in ruminating on the behaviour of one of the most celebrated personages in its Scriptures, is struck by the vigorous picture of this preternaturally wise old Jew presented to it. What more natural? The Rev. B. G. Hodge announces that he will discourse on that theme to his rough high-spirited flock. What could be more appropriate? I can see nothing worth getting excited about there. And it is only very mildly funny.

135

On the next page, again (p. 90), the amusements
of Dean Paul Anderson are pilloried.    Those amusements appear to be, as a matter of fact, neither more
nor less intellectual than—Lady Dean Paul's, I was
going to say, though I only know what hers are from
reading the accounts in the society-page of the
London papers: I will say, instead, those of any
typical member of the intellectual cream of London
Society.    Mr. Mencken is, I daresay, a shade snob-
bish about his kentuckian 'moron.'    The *ignorance*
of that moron is the burden of his song.    But is that
obvious butt as a fact so very much more ridiculous
(though entirely innocent of cultural pretensions)
than the masses at Saratoga Springs, the Lido, Deau-
ville, and so on?    The Society Columns, to which I
alluded above, are certainly not particularly funny.
Their smooth and nerveless adulation (except where
any real artist, or real person at all, comes to be mentioned) makes dull reading.    The midde-class audience of Mr. Mencken would not get much of a chuckle
out of them; but they would be suitably impressed.
Are 'Society' morons, however, fundamentally less
ridiculous, mean or irritating than devout and
clamorous rustics?    I don't believe that they are:
they seem to me far more so, and terribly smug, into
the bargain.    Apart from my intention here to give
a kind of typical adverse statement where these collections are concerned, I am not an ideal Mencken
reader at all, I confess, in spite of my admiration for
their spirited compiler.

Another Kentucky cutting is about a Missionary
Training School: ' . . . in future no student wearing bobbed hair will be admitted,' etc.    But bobbed

hair suits some women's heads and not others.
Therefore a tyrannical orthodoxy on one side results
in as much injustice to Nature, and the skulls and
hair provided by Nature, though no more, as that of
'goose-stepping' fashion on the other. So this again
is a disappointing cutting.

The more I go into it, and proceed to give effect to
my idea of finding an *answer* to Mencken, the more
I find I should agree with the other sort of american
patriot rather than with Mr. Mencken. But still
there remains Mr. Mencken's great service in stirring
the pot round, and that with honesty, it seems, and
not with malice. Also, in straining every nerve to
find fault—if only in that—he has done good. For
he has demonstrated the *limits* of average imbecility,
as well as its extent: he has done the worst that can
be done, and it actually is not so impressive as all
that. He has even revealed many unsuspected
virtues in the 'moron of the Backward States.'
Other services rendered by his method I will refer
to later in this essay.

## § 8. *'Complexes' as between Whites.*

As regards *other Whites*, many Whites, at one time
and another, have suffered from an 'inferiority complex,' but never as regards people not Whites. The
english farm-labourer or mechanic, in the past, has
suffered from an 'inferiority complex' where a Dun-
dreary Swell was concerned: but Buddha would be
for him a 'nigger.' This was absurd. But it was
the requisite for White world-success.

Americans at the time of Edgar Allan Poe, or

those of the period of *The Virginians*, certainly experienced no 'inferiority complex' where their european cousins were concerned.   They were the cadets and equals of one great family.   But since that time, for various reasons, the educated American has felt 'inferiority'; or, not to use the language of Freud, he has felt provincial, and been rather terrorised by the thought of the 'cultured' backgrounds of polite european life.   This had less to do with the culture question, I believe, than with the great sway, in the european mind, of the aristocratic idea.   As all the great european families, who have not been exterminated by war or revolution, have intermarried with their bankers and brokers, the aristocratic idea has lost its sway entirely: and, that factor eliminated, the other, the cultural one, by itself, could scarcely offer much opposition.   So the American today not only has no reason to be, but in fact is not at all, impressed with the European as such: although, if he had his choice, he might prefer to live in Europe rather than America.   And here is a paradox (the paradox involved in the subject-matter of this essay):  for in most cases he would rather, probably ('America'-movements aside), live in Europe: he probably at no former time would have been so ready as today to say good-bye to America;  and yet he has ceased to believe in Europe or in Europeans, or to have any illusions about them.   There is no spreadeagleism at all discoverable to the European descending on the eastern shore of the United States today, nor in american books does it play any part.   'The American' of the british newspapers is, indeed, a complete myth—an Uncle Sam cartoon of very long ago.   Yet it is not the thought of Europe that instinctively humbles him.   It is the thought of himself.

In spite of all this, the new 'inferiority complex' of the American, which has nothing to do with Europe at all, is partly composed of the material of european criticism of America reaching him indirectly.   And to that subject I now will turn.


## § 9. *The American Baby.*

IT is a widely-held notion in Europe that the American is a kind of baby-man: that the American is not adult, that he remains all his life a child.   And that is of course one of the things that Mr. Mencken's criticism suggests.   Mr. Sherwood Anderson says, 'Most american men never pass the age of seventeen.'   This would equally well describe most men everywhere: but when the typical educated European thinks of the inhabitant of the United States he thinks of something childish, super-young, undeveloped, excitable and helpless.   He thinks of him (and of the American Woman equally) as a creature of 'crazes' and impulses, who when not 'crazy about' this is 'crazy about' that;  a half-cooked, foolishly-eager, snob of every idea that can get itself advertised and describe itself as novel and 'stimulating' (the last invariably-used adjective suggesting some radical impotence in the public): but generally and to sum up all the rest, as substantially prone to an ever-deepening juvenility, ever more of which merely receptive quality is willed for itself by this spoilt-child of fortune—for that is precisely what it wishes to be, an irresponsible child, sheltered from the rough embarrassments, fatigues and battles of the surrounding universe. It would indeed not at all surprise this type of European if the entire American Nation, pressing on back into the rosy lands of self-deceiving childhood and breathless illusion, vanished, one fine day, into the womb out of which it came.

That this cannot, in reality, describe the great mass of the population of America I need not say, nor is that my view, or that of the better-informed European. But it is still a widely-held opinion. So, if european opinion ever reached and touched America, it would not lessen the 'inferiority complex' being manufactured for it on the home-soil. So to the older White countries America cannot look for help in the analysis of its 'complex.' For them America is a baby, the baby of Europe and—after a hundred and fifty years—a peculiarly infantile one, making on all-fours for the womb of its origin.

§ 10. *Was Walt Whitman the Father of the American Baby ?*

ALTHOUGH I know, as I have said, that the whole of America is not a gigantic baby, tied to the apron-strings of some 'cosmic' Mama, nevertheless it really does seem that the american mind is today more infantile than it was in the days of Edgar Allan Poe, for instance. The Virginians and New Englanders of that day it would have entered nobody's head to accuse, even, of this peculiar infantilism. The american mind was at that time, no doubt, much abused by the enemies or rivals of the master-state of the New World, but that state was governed and represented by adult Europeans at a few removes tempered in the sternest roman traditions of english enterprise. So it does seem that America, as it has grown older, has grown younger and younger, in the sense that there is a patch or streak in the mind of the american aggregate that gives some colour to the more recent european myth of the American Baby.

If we take this patch, or this tendency, and if we isolate it, and so form an entire Baby, and proceed to call that 'America' (which is what has happened, I believe, in the case of the european belief I am here discussing), then who was responsible for that particular child? For, as it did not exist a century ago, it must have made its appearance in the interim.

Walt Whitman was, I feel sure, the father of the American Baby, looked at in that light. Walt showed all those enthusiastic expansive habits that we associate with the Baby. He rolled about naked in the Atlantic surf, uttering 'barbaric yawps,' as he called them, in an ecstasy of primitive exhibitionism. He was prone to 'cosmic' raptures. A freudian analyst specializing in inversion or perversion would have said, observing his behaviour over a suitable period, that he was certainly the victim of a psychical 'fixation,' which incessantly referred him back to the periods of earliest childhood. He was a great big heavy old youngster, of a perfect freudian type, with the worst kind of 'enthusiasm' in the greek sense of that word. He was also, it should be remembered, the epic ancestor of the now celebrated american 'fairy.'

141

Walt Whitman, as the father of the American Baby, is a hint, only, to the american analyst of these questions, and I of course may be wrong in stressing that particular figure.   But he does seem to fit so wonderfully the requirements of the case: so I at all events recommend him in that capacity.


§ 11. *The Healthy Attitude of the American to his 'Babylon.'*

WHEN I visited New York I found the pictorial effects exceedingly curious and beautiful.   This was not a view in any way shared by the more intelligent New Yorkers, I was glad and surprised to find. They, who lived in the place, and understood the motives of the builders and their masters, regarded it as so much vulgar and childish display.   The 'Down-town' towers and cathedrals produced nothing but a contemptuous and rather bitter mirth in them.   For me it was purely the satisfactions of the eye that made me like it.   In every other way I was in agreement with them.   For towards everything, and all the people, that are *behind* the creation of these 'swinging gardens of Babylon,' I feel about as they do.

Strange as it was to find this disillusioned and hostile attitude on the part of the intelligent educated men, it was far stranger to find it as well amongst the workmen and average of the community.   Far from boasting of their city, they seemed to take very little interest in it, except occasionally to remark that they did not like New York, and that one of these days—I should see—it 'would all blow up,' since Nature did not approve of such structures as were to be found there, and Nature would have the last word!

These traces of Nature-worship are reminiscent of Whitman, it is true. It was the good side of Whitman—the very ancient gospel that was the matrix of his own, but which he was not able to incarnate, and only succeeded in making exaggerated and ridiculous.

## § 12. *Sherwood Anderson.*

I NOW come to the part of this brief preliminary essay where I propose to show, by means of citations from books, the reality of my argument. And Sherwood Anderson comes first in order of importance as a witness, though actually the first writer I shall use is english, and not american. It may be as well to point out at once that I am in no way attempting here any estimate of the value of the writings I use as evidence. I take the good and bad writer (as I see it) indifferently. Provided, for good or bad reasons, or for very mixed reasons, he exerts, or recently has exerted, influence, that is enough for my purpose.

Of all the children of Walt Whitman, Sherwood Anderson is perhaps the most celebrated: and he has exercised a very great influence upon all the young school of american fiction, and indeed throughout the intelligent life of America. So the feelings and tendencies to which his work testifies are authentic evidence in such an examination as this.

Now, although, as I have said, I am certainly offering no opinion upon the value as writers of the people I have chosen to quote, there are certain judgments or classifications that it is impossible not to make in taking up the evidence. It will be better, in a few words, to make clear at the start what these must be.

## § 13. *The Essential Romanticism of the Return to the 'Savage' and the 'Primitive.'*

IF there is one thing more than another that is quite certain about Sherwood Anderson, and what almost may be called his 'school,' it is that they are extreme *romantics*. At least one member of this 'school,' or person influenced by Anderson and writing on somewhat the same lines (Hemingway), has turned upon his inspirer, and very ably caricatured him, choosing for his satire exactly this quality in Anderson—namely, his incurable romanticism. Hemingway himself appears to me much drier and less sentimental than Anderson, and so his action may be the result of a genuine impatience with the absurdities of *Dark Laughter*. But how far this essential romanticism can be weeded out of the raciness-of-the-soil of american creative writing, I do not know: I am not familiar enough with all the circumstances to be able to offer an opinion about that. Bullfighters and Boxers occupy the centre of the stage in Hemingway's books; if *Action* is your god, if you are a romantic and regard strong romantic tendencies as a highly desirable thing in an artist, then you will be glad to meet these gladiators so constantly at the heart of the business; but if you are not so romantically inclined you will get tired of such a physical infatuation, and the insatiable taste for violence—for sangre y arena, for blood and sand, blood and iron, and all the other accompaniments of the profuse discharge of human blood. It is possible to feel that the blood-stream, perforations through which it pours out, things that make it beat and throb hotly, and so on, are not the only subjects of interest.

You may even go further than that, and feel that our literature today is becoming a sort of mortuary games; more and more a roman brutality is invading our books; so that the communistic fever into which everyone was plunged during the War, especially those who took part in it—the gladiators watched by the politicians and financiers, for whom the War was a sort of immense Circus—is perpetuated in print. This fascist or marinettian (futurist) appetite for violence—and possibly in the case of Hemingway this particular romanticism has been encouraged in him by that perfect 'American Baby' of the Whitman tradition, Ezra Pound—is perhaps the most characteristic note of all to be found in these writers. Theirs are 'American dreams — Anglosaxon dreams,' in the words of one of the principal dreamers.

*Torrents of Spring* (Ernest Hemingway) may be, however, a sign, on the part of the strongest and latest of this school, of a turning of the tide. For if you repudiate one romanticism you are apt to repudiate others, and with luck the whole gaudy pack may come tumbling down.

Corrected in some, especially those following Anderson who have benefited no doubt by contacts

which have militated against too naïve a romantic
afflatus, with Sherwood Anderson the pure romance
of whitmanesque tradition remains. At a first
reading he looks a little like a Strindberg softened
in the prosperous optimistic air of America, and
brought up in the shadow of Whitman.

Two sisters of Strindberg have written a biography
of the great swedish writer (*Strindberg's Systrar
Berätta*, reviewed in the *Observer*, August 21st, 1927,
from which I quote). His sisters, apparently, take
Strindberg at his own persistently stormy, romantic
valuation. '*In his sisters' opinion, he was possessed
by a dark demon.*' How that description seems to
fit what many romantic persons today would like to
be the figure under which the world should know
them! We are in the presence of a school of 'dark
demons,' in short, with Bernard Shaw behind them
demoniacally grinning, but in a lighter and more
mischievous mood; and behind him, all the mephis-
tophelian 'darkness' of Nietzsche. Behind that
comes the debonair 'darkness' of Lord Byron.


§ 14. *Possessed by 'a Dark Demon.'*

BUT we have in England a much more complete
and much more up-to-date Anderson, who is very
widely read in America: that is Mr. D. H. Lawrence.
No one, I suppose, will be found to deny Mr. Lawrence the title of 'romantic'; and I think it is quite
evident that he is possessed by a very 'dark demon'
indeed, that takes him to the darkest and most
mysterious corners of the earth in search of other
'demons' of similar complexion. He succeeds in

146

rooting out quite a fair number of devils still, and their 'mysterious,' mechanical worshippers. Literature is indebted to the activities of this 'demon' of his for many excellent pages; though it is certainly our business to show (on our way to the Melting-pot, in short all the way to the final mix-up), we who are possessed by the White demon, the *daimon* of the White Man, the authentic one, I mean, that that is as compelling as the 'dark' for the purposes of art, without the perils for our race (in its march towards the Melting-pot) of the 'dark' familiars. But that is not in any way what we are talking about here, for the same could be said of Anderson, who does not always write badly, as of Lawrence.

Mr. D. H. Lawrence's book, *Mornings in Mexico*, had just appeared when I was in New York this summer (1927). His 'dark demon' may be observed in it working at high pressure on the material provided by Mexico: and I am taking this book, along with those of Anderson, to reveal what I am driving at in this review of the contemporary mind.

In general outline my argument will be this:— Against this Dark Demon I oppose everywhere (for the sake of argument and 'purely and simply to amuse myself') a White Demon or *daimon*; the spirit of the White Race against the spirit of the Dark Race—the 'mystical' 'dark' race of the romantic-White imagination (not against—naturally —any flesh and blood Black brother, or fellow-slave, of the moment). Against this over-excitable, over-susceptible romantic-White, too, I bring the discipline of my criticism, and offer him as cold a bath as possible, where, for the period of immersion, at least,

he can keep cool.    With its White Demon I believe
the White Race can be saved (instead of perishing
on its way to the Melting-pot), if this demon can
only be properly utilized.    He is a marvellous force,
who has manifested himself on many occasions, and
often given us evidence of his magical power.    If
we do not entirely throw him over, he can yet be our
saviour: *he was the 'daimon' of Socrates*, this White
Demon we have inherited: he has a vivid and
spectacular history that it would be unwise for his
antagonists to allow themselves to forget.    It may
be that very rapidly many people of our race will
stop kowtowing to the 'Dark Demon,' and turn
again to him.    And ultimately he may blanch or
bleach the entire Melting-pot.

But there is no reason at all why we should not be
on excellent if 'distant' terms with the 'Dark One,'
even as in Byron's *Vision of Judgment* we find that,
when they met,

> ' His Darkness and his Brightness
> Exchanged a greeting of extreme politeness.'

There is no reason why we should not be exceedingly polite to all that is 'dark.'

From here onwards I am assembling as evidence
of what I have so far been discussing in the abstract,
quotations from those authors who have suggested
themselves to me as expressing most clearly the
'dark' point of view.    So at this point I am terminating the first division of my survey.

# THE 'INFERIORITY COMPLEX' OF THE ROMANTIC WHITE, AND STUDENT SUICIDES

§ 1. *Romance on its Last (Physical) Legs.*

THE passion for 'the primitive' among the civilized, or (the same thing) the appetite for the 'dark' and exotic among the Whites, made its first appearance in Europe, in its present form, in the earlier part of the last century, at the time of the Romantic Revival. So its romantic genealogy is not in question. Baudelaire in 1850 went about with a mulatto mistress, and wrote some of his most beautiful poems to her crinkly head, her 'tenebrous' flanks, her 'mysterious' eyes—full of night and 'savage' properties. Later, the french boy-genius, Rimbaud, followed much the same lines, disappearing at the age of twenty as a trader into Africa. Still later, at the beginning of this century, Paul Gauguin kicked the dust of Europe off his shoes and departed to live with the South Sea Islanders, whither the romantic Scotsman, Robert Louis Stevenson, had preceded him. Going very much further back, the Templars succumbed to the mystical attractions of the lowest kind of orientalism, and exchanged the europeanized Master of St. Peter for Baphomet: and at their trial it was alleged that the Grand Master of the order had passionately remarked that 'one hair of the head of a Saracen was more valuable than the whole body of a Christian.'

149

Nietzsche writes, in his *Joyful Wisdom*, 'The barbarians have always loved the South; and once they got there, never wanted to come back into the North again,' etc.

This was partly wanderlust, no doubt, partly appreciation of a gentler climate and a nice blue sky. But the European, like every other man, has always had a fancy for the 'mysterious' lands outside his own, inhabited by marvellous and strange peoples. He has always 'smelt strangeness,' and mistaken that for love. History is quite choked with that counterfeit.

Today these mysteries have been exploded. The Age of Newton, as Mr. Russell calls it, has destroyed what was imposing and native in the great eastern civilizations; and Bolshevism, with the full encouragement and assistance of the West, is westernizing (and bolshevizing) the Eastern populations still more, as it 'nationalizes' them in the Western sense; our popular musical-comedy actors and actresses spend week-ends in Hawai or Samoa; there is no 'Darkest Africa,' or it is full of trippers shooting tame tigers; our Earth has narrowed and is everywhere accessible and open to inspection. What difficulties the author of *Arabia Deserta* encountered in his attempt to make-believe to himself that he was in the heart of an inaccessible, fanatical, and perilous land—a sort of 'Darkest Africa'—any reader of his wonderful book will remember. So the position of Romance is not what it was before the turbine engine, wireless, etc. It will still be its old 'romantic' self for ever (for the romantic cannot change its 'dark' ethiopian skin) but henceforth it will be a shabby and diminished one. Romance will never be the same Romance again, at least for a long time. The more imaginative 'romantics' have taken to Time-travel instead, disquieted with the vulgarity of Space.

Under these circumstances the romantic mind is not so easy to justify to-day as it was even at the time of Gauguin: infinitely less so than it was for Baudelaire. There is scarcely any excuse for being a romantic to-day, indeed, of the type of Hardy, Zola, Baudelaire, Livingstone, Lafcadio Hearn, Stevenson or Gauguin. Yet there are still a great number of just the same sort of *physical romantics*, as they might be classified. But usually we find them a little apologetic and uneasy or full of an epileptic movement and borrowing more and more from madness to substantiate their dream.

The *class-romantic*, like Tolstoi—romancing about 'the peasant'—even he still exists, although Bolshevism has almost eliminated him. But with his political enthusiasms few people have any patience today. On the whole that sort of romantic may be said to be extinct.

All these romantics I have been mentioning have enormously assisted the overthrow of european power; and they all have been like those cinema actors and actresses in the movie studios described, in one of the epigraphs to this essay, by Sherwood Anderson in the words:

'Children, playing with dreams— ... American dreams—Anglo-Saxon dreams!'

What was it that caused all these Northern dreamers to dream things so physically, or politically, disastrous to us, their descendants? Was it that instinct of the aristocrat *to throw himself down,* to return into the untaught and dispossessed mass beneath him, dramatized in Strindberg's *Mademoiselle Julie*? Whatever the answer is, these Playboys of the Western World of the last century, from Byron and Shelley, those typical romantic revolutionary aristocrats, down to the present time— down to the people we are now discussing—have ruined us with their *dreams*—American dreams, French dreams, Russian dreams. The generous impulses of some of these aristocratic dreamers, to relieve distress, to give happiness to the poor, have only resulted in debasing the Poor White still further, till he bids fair to become the despised servant of the coolie. The last action of the last of his feudal masters was one that will soon result in a greater abasement than ever before for him. This could be made, by a fanatical proletarian, to look like malice! Already in the East the White who is not Poor (and so despised) is no longer respected. So it is impossible for us today, as average Whites, for whom the Melting-pot is not the reality but only the transition, who at last see clearly this whole chain of uncomfortable events, to thank those dreamers for their expensive idealism. We can do nothing but deplore their political short-sightedness, and all that sentimental 'liberalism' or 'radicalism' that has brought us where we are instead of to a position where we should have been dictators of the Melting-pot, free to jump in or not as we like—not at least liable to be pushed in, like a small boy into his first swimming-bath.

# CONSCIOUSNESS AND ANNIHILATION

## § 2. *The Consciousness of One Branch of Humanity is the Annihilation of Another Branch.*

IN another quotation, used as epigraph to this essay, Mr. Lawrence writes:

'The Indian way of consciousness is different from and fatal to our way of consciousness. Our way of consciousness is different from and fatal to the Indian.'

He then continues:

'The two ways, the two streams are never to be united. They are not even to be reconciled. There is no bridge, no canal of connection. The sooner we realize, and accept, this, the better . . .'
—(*Mornings in Mexico*, p. 104.)

To have been able to reach that conclusion is an achievement for a White Man.

'*The consciousness of one branch of humanity is the annihilation of the consciousness of another branch,*' again he says.

How entirely true! Then why does Mr. Lawrence, it is impossible not to ask, go on smelling round the indian Heaven and coquetting with the indian gods? just as Mr. Anderson, before Mr. Van Vechten, philandered with the *Nigger Heaven*? Why cannot he learn to leave them alone, or at least to keep this as a private luxury, and not try to communicate it to the rest of the world? Why does he attempt to teach this alien (and, for the White, he announces, 'fatal') 'consciousness' to us? As well ask, of course, why a man always wishes to proselytize about his pet vice. The more unusual it is, the more he wishes every one to share it.

But Mr. Lawrence's explanation is that he has 'a little ghost inside' him, which 'sees both ways.' And this arrangement he recommends to us. We should all get such little optical ghosts. I will quote the whole of this passage:

'The consciousness of one branch of humanity is the annihilation of the consciousness of another branch. That is, the life of the Indian, his stream of conscious being, is just death to the White Man. And we can understand the consciousness of the Indian only in terms of the death of our consciousness . . . the same paradox exists between the consciousness of white men and Hindu or Polynesians or Bantu. It is the eternal paradox of human consciousness. To pretend that all is one stream is to cause chaos and nullity. To pretend to express one stream in terms of another, so as to identify the two, is false and sentimental. The only thing you can do is to have a little ghost inside you which sees both ways, or even many ways. But a man cannot *belong* to both ways, or to many ways. One man can belong to one great way of consciousness only. He may even change from one way to another. But he cannot go both ways at once. Can't be done.'—(*Mornings in Mexico*, pp. 105, 106.)

All this appears to me exceedingly sound. But, having regard to the locality in which it is uttered, what has taken its author there, and what he elsewhere undoubtedly is proposing to us, it is certainly puzzling. The little two-way-looking ghost is the solution, of course, or the excuse for this glaring paradox. But that is scarcely satisfying.

There is a great deal of argument today as to whether the idea expressed in the proverb that 'There are seeds in the body of the hare that are fatal to the body of the lion' is a true one or not. One set of disputants will tell you that 'all people are the same' (in the face of much evidence to the contrary); and the other set will tell you that East is East and West is West, and that the *consciousness* of a race is deeply fixed, that it obstinately goes on its way, and when its consciousness is starved, inhibited or destroyed, it, too, the race, ceases to exist. Perhaps the truth is not quite on the side of either of these disputants, but somewhere else and not to be answered by such a simple statement.

But still there are many facts that suggest that a race *has* a soul (or 'consciousness,' or whatever you like to call it): that it is vulnerable and of vital importance to the race. I will quote a passage from my book, *The Art of Being Ruled*, to illustrate this.

§ 3. *When the 'Consciousness' or Soul of a Race is Crushed, the Race Collapses.*

'The Chukchee . . . in spite of their hardiness, are, however, subject to annihilating collapses of vitality, of which the phenomenon of "arctic hysteria" is a celebrated symptom. But another symptom is equally striking. Prolonged slumber, lasting many weeks, is common with them—a suddenly recurring hibernation or estivation. A

155

man will collapse, feeling unwell, and go to bed
and to sleep, and so remain until he either dies or
recovers.  So the rigour of the climate, claiming
of them unnatural hardihood and powers of resistance, overwhelms them in this way once it passes
their guard.  After the subjection of the neighbouring tribes by the Cossacks some fifty years
ago, it is said that the whole population suddenly
collapsed: they lost all interest and zest in life,
neglected their usual occupations, sank into a
listless poverty, and became almost a burden
and menace to their conquerors.'—(*Art of Being
Ruled*, p. 295.)

The neighbours of the Chukchee, deprived of their
freedom and of the natural expansions of their deep-
rooted 'way of consciousness,' or soul, sink back into
their arctic torpor, languish, and die.  In my book,
*The Art of Being Ruled*, I suggested that it was not
only geographically unimportant races, like these
sub-arctic tribes, that were prone to these collapses
if suddenly interfered with, or defeated, to such an
extent that the deepest 'consciousness' or soul is
impaired.  Also great nations or races, I contended,
may similarly suffer, and sink into a discouraged
torpor, just as much as may a small tribe.  And in
that book I suggested that there were many symptoms in post-war Europe of such a collapse.  I cited
the widespread phenomenon of male-inversion as an
example of the form that this collapse was taking.
As the starch went out of them, the males relapsed
into what in Sodom are technically called 'bitches,'
in a process of almost physiological transformation.

156

## SUICIDE EPIDEMIC AMONG THE WHITES

The trying and unnatural conditions of the Machine-Age, the elimination of individual ambition involved in the phenomenon of the Trust or Corporation, the suicidal White War, and the shattering tremors conveyed to us by the recent gigantic revolution in Russia, and all it forebodes—these things are enough to account for anything.

### § 4. *Dr. Berman and the Suicide Epidemic among the Whites of the United States.*

I HAVE stepped aside for a moment from an examination of the ideas of Mr. Lawrence, as presented in *Mornings in Mexico,* to make quite clear what is really the issue in his romantic pronouncements. I shall be returning to his book immediately: but I will interpolate another quotation here, of another order, from a book that appeared during the month of August in New York, namely *The Religion of Behaviourism,* by Dr. Louis Berman. Dr. Berman I have dealt with elsewhere (cf. *Time and Western Man*). But the short book about Behaviourism he has just produced offers another and pleasanter aspect of his talent, or rather phase of his peculiar evolution. What has effected this desirable change in Dr. Berman I do not know. But much that he says here appears quite sensible.

The discouragement, confusion, and decay or collapse of communities (whether very large or very small) is what we are considering. It is our belief that the White race, since the War (which in every sense was a mortal blow to it), is, now (despite the great advantages still remaining with it, and the reasons for self-esteem to be found in its great position in the world, its supremacy up to the present), suffering from many of those symptoms of discouragement, disbelief in itself and its destiny, and material collapse, that have often been noticed in other peoples. When it is a small organism, a small people, it decays and disappears quickly. With such a great and elaborately organized system as the White European World, these signs are far more difficult to detect. And Dr. Berman's chapter on 'Suicide as a symptom,' dealing with the recent epidemic of american student suicides, is what has made me go aside to examine this book before proceeding with Mr. D. H. Lawrence.

Dr. Berman gives an account of the phases of the extreme mechanical doctrine of Behaviour (of which the principal exponent is Professor Watson), which he calls a 'religion.' But he cites Bergson as the author of all that is anti-Behaviour, of all that is *Gestalt*, of all that is admirable, according to him, in the contemporary world. He attacks Science, under its extreme (and its most comic and ridiculous) form, Behaviour. So he still stands not so far from where he formerly did. For the significant opposition in the contemporary world is not between Bergson on the one side, and Behaviour on the other. They are much nearer together than they would each have us believe. For if Behaviour comes out of Evolution, does not also *Creative Evolution* and Bergson come out of Evolution? The real opposition is very different from that.

'Behaviourism or Watsonianity,' says Dr. Berman, then, 'was begotten by Darwinism out of the modern scientific spirit. . . . As a child of Darwinism . . . America may be expected to disgrace itself about it as soon as its implications reach the democratic mind. The uproar . . . concerning the teaching of evolution . . . will turn out to be the foam of a passing ship as compared with the howls which will be emitted . . . when the full significance of the New Faith finally filters down to their level ' (that of the 'backward and moronic' mass of Americans).

The sooner the 'morons' of America 'disgrace themselves' with regard to 'Behaviour,' the better, in my view of the matter. But I hope while these 'morons,' as Dr. Berman calls them, are about it, that they will disgrace themselves about *Creative Evolution* and Bergson as well, and any other sort of Evolution they can lay their moronesque hands on.

But Berman has been *reading*: I feel quite certain that Berman must have been reading some improving book or other—I wonder which it was? For listen to him:

'The Smart Set has become the Smart Crowd, indeed the Smart Mob . . . urbanites and suburbanites, wise because instructed by radio, tabloid and press agent, pride themselves on being intellectually hard-boiled when they are only somewhat parboiled. . . . Behold the spectacle then of our men and women of ideas accepting the charge of being cleverists, careerists, trivialists, as a compliment, but shrinking with the horror of that most horrible of all horrors—the horror of ridicule—from the stigma of being called sentimentalists, emotionalists, feeling-ists.'

Ah, so the 'morons' do not only consist of Mr.

159

Mencken's favourite victims, the inhabitants of 'the backward States of the Union'! They are also to be found among the 'Smart Crowd,' these 'morons': and now 'our men and women of ideas' turn out to be 'morons'! That is a slight advance for Dr. Berman. *I am sure Berman must have been reading some very enlightening book.* But he will never tell us which it was, so let us be grateful that something or other has happened to Dr. Berman that has made him slightly more sensible, and leave it at that.

Well, the conditions described in the above extract are suitable to *discouragement*, and to a view of life that may at last persuade people that such an existence as that is so futile that it is hardly worth living: that is Dr. Berman's argument. (And a very good one, too.)

'Behaviourism then is sympathetic to the age,' he says.

'By extravagantly exalting movement, by placing' what a man is doing 'so implicitly in the foreground . . . '——

[I must interrupt Dr. Berman. If he is seriously going to switch over to this line he *must* immediately drop all that Bergson and *Gestalt*. For surely Bergson, of all people, was *the* mercurial philosopher of incessant *movement*, of flux and fuss. So he *cannot* abuse those who 'exalt movement' in one part of his book, and kowtow to Bergson in another.—I will now continue the quotation.]

'——by regarding seriously the half-truth that language is a series of muscle twitchings, essentially in the same class as walking or running, and

160

by reducing the emotions to "nothing but" visceral reactions. . . . Behaviorism appeals to the worshippers of noise in contemporary art and manners . . . the believers in direct action in politics hail its implications for them. In a time like ours when among proliferating cities, in any branch of human activity, motion and commotion are infinitely preferred to contemplation and insight, the gospel of muscular (and glandular) conduct as the conquering creed of the twentieth century may be expected to be hailed as the very indigenous credo of a democratic people.—The effects have been bad and will become worse.'

Where Berman got all this from I can't guess; but it is quite sensible, or so it naturally seems to the author of the *Art of Being Ruled* and the *Revolutionary Simpleton*.

'The behaviorist, in fact, comes to us with a challenge to all our values, of good and evil, right and wrong. There is no aspect of human life he does not touch with his ubiquitous concepts and attitudes. . . . In the law and in education he is coming, with his defiant technique . . . his language (is) the accepted nomenclature of the experts and his theories the means by which the lives of children are being regulated and mutilated.'

You would think, of course, here that Berman was describing not Behaviourism, but Bolshevism, or at least Psychoanalysis. I do not believe that Behaviourism is the *religious* force that he pretends. It is just the extreme gospel of the Machine Age.

L                    161

Every little average 'goose-stepping, superstitious, sentimental' unit of a present-day industrial mass-democracy is a behaviourist. He would be just as thorough a one without Professor Watson. Why Behaviourism is so intolerable intellectually is not because it *leads*, but because it *follows* the little average 'goose-stepping, superstitious, sentimental' unit of the mass-democracy, and makes a mechanical imitation of this robot in the philosophic field.

Dr. Berman, however, is determined to treat it as a religion. And at all events what he says about the *effects* of it, and of similar doctrines, upon the more sensitive mind is no doubt correct:

'Most to be dreaded of all the injuries that may be inflicted by Behaviorism upon the souls of sensitive personalities (the others do not matter) is the effect upon their sense of freedom, their attitude of initiative, which means their feeling of being intensely and fully alive. The repetitive tom-tom of the Behaviorist drum is insistent that we are wholly and totally the victims of conditions beyond our control, from the moment of birth to the moment of extinction. . . . Without regard to any central theme of individuality, movement begets movement, habit begets habit. . . .

'Consider the value of yourself, of your life, of your strivings and efforts . . . of the feeling of your unique self in the light of the conditioned reaction! . . . How invigorating to weakening morale . . . ! To see himself as the product of muscle-twitchings and gland-oozings is the most degrading spectacle of himself ever presented to Man. . . .

162

# SUICIDE EPIDEMIC AMONG THE WHITES

'In the language of its protagonists: of all the modes ever offered for the use of conscious behavior, Behaviorism has the least survival value.

. . .

'*Information, ideas, theories about ourselves may, must, inevitably help or hinder us to live.* The effect may be to exalt, intensify, inspire, transform consciousness and conduct. Or it may be to depress, infect, sicken, dishearten to the point of death.'

Dr. Berman decides that it is Behaviourism (now, he says, become a religion) that has *disheartened to the point of death* a variety of Americans, especially students, in the course of the year 1927. If the religion of Behaviourism grows it will no doubt (more than any Moloch, he assures us) claim more and more victims.

In a chapter entitled ' Suicide as a Symptom ' he details a long list of student-suicides:

'Recently there occurred an outbreak of suicide among student youths. . . . Within a few months a number of students had taken their lives, leaving behind them letters stating their sense of the futility of keeping alive. The record runs: On January 2nd a University of Illinois student killed himself, writing that he had experienced all that life contained . . . the son of a specialist in mental disorders shot himself in his father's home. He found life "dark and worthless," he wrote his father. On January 23rd a student in the University of Wisconsin shot himself because he was bored with this earth and wished to see how things were over there,' etc.

## § 5. *Races similarly ruined by the White Man.*

AND so Dr. Berman goes through a monotonous list of american students who hang, shoot, poison, or gas themselves because life is *dark* and empty.

He considers this a phenomenon of the same sort as that noted by Dr. Rivers among the Melanesians :

'W. H. R. Rivers . . . once studied the degeneration of the inhabitants of the Melanesian Islands after the advent of the White Man. Particularly was he interested in the fact that in certain of the islands there was almost complete extinction of the native population, *in spite of the presence of plenty of the materials of subsistence and the absence of epidemic or unusual disease.* . . . he came to the conclusion that these peoples were dying out because they were losing their zest in life. And they were losing their zest in life because the coming and cunning of the White Man had undermined their attitude to life so completely as to affect the very Will to Live.'

He then proceeds :

'It seems to me there is an analogy between the state of mind of these students and the native populations.'

In the *Art of Being Ruled* (Chatto and Windus, 1926) I came to similar conclusions : and the quotation I have used at the beginning of this part, relating to the neighbours of the Chukchee, tells the same story, on the authority of a traveller who had lived with those tribes, as is told by Dr. Rivers of the

Melanesians. Remove from a ra-raing Yale student his *ra-ra!*—and put nothing equally stimulating there in its place—remove all his illusions about himself, as a human being (fortunate enough to belong to a particularly cute nation, fortunate enough to be of the class that is sent to Yale, fortunate enough to have large muscles and to be a star in the world of university sport, fortunate enough to have blond curly hair and so to attract the attention of all beautiful girls met, or to be dark and sensitive-looking, and so to receive much attention as a likely prey, etc. etc. etc.)—remove all these, or even an appreciable portion of them, and your student will lose his zest for life, just as the Melanesian or the neighbour of the Chukchee did when deprived of what were for him the equivalent of those satisfactions.

The White Man's superior *cunning* is, however, hardly the word, in describing what he destroyed the Melanesian with. There was not *enough* 'cunning' in the White Man, unfortunately. The descendants of those Whites, students in american universities, *because they are not sufficiently 'cunning,'* because they believe anything that is told them, because they are too 'goose-stepping, superstitious, and sentimental' (though not called 'morons' invariably by Berman and others whenever mentioned—but of course not, seeing that they are the principal clients of Berman and others, the cultured minority), because they have allowed themselves to remain romantic, show a tendency now to destroy themselves. Some mind more 'cunning' than the White has enveloped them and infected them with a 'consciousness' not their own.  And if we look round for the possessor of this more 'cunning' mind than the White mind, able to destroy it with its alien 'consciousness' (as Mr. D. H. Lawrence would call it), then we need not go to a hostile *race*, we can find it in the mind of Science, more 'cunning' certainly than the very simple anglo-saxon administrators, who robbed the poor Indian of his 'zest for life,' or 'Will to Live.'

But if the word 'cunning' is to be the key to this problem of the new 'inferiority complex' of the White, then certainly Behaviourism comes very far down the list, and must be disqualified at once.  For it is very simple and not at all cunning.  Professor Watson, as also Yerkes and most behaviourists and 'testers,' is a very simple, even stupid, man.  Messrs. Freud and Jung—or shall we say Einstein?—have really had much more influence—and Psychoanalysis and Relativity, in all their various popular manifestations, are calculated to produce much more effect, than poor threadbare, mechanical, unglamourous, sexless, *Behaviour*.


§ 6. *Behaviourist 'Summer Conversation.'*

THAT *Behaviourism* has its effect upon popular thought, or at least upon the fictionist, who is the middleman conveying philosophic notions to the minds of people not accessible to ideas in anything but a sensuous and immediate form, of that there is of course plenty of evidence.  I will take a conversation from *The Apple of the Eye*, by Glenway Wescott, a 'first novel,' dealing with life in the

Middle West. It is a conversation between a young man and a boy, the former instructing the latter as to the true character of life. For its possible realism, you have to allow for the very intense puritanic backgrounds provided for it by its american setting.

' Dan lingered beside him. . . .

' "Tell me then,' he asked, "don't you believe in chastity?"

'Mike's eyes brightened at an opportunity to teach. "What a queer question! It has beauty. Before I went to the university I thought it was the only beautiful thing. To live in the spirit instead of the flesh. The flesh nothing but candlewax under the flame. Then you feel that you're like Christ and all the saints. Puritanism appeals to the imagination, but it makes people sick."

' "Sick?" Dan echoed, confused.

' "You see, there isn't anything but flesh." He spoke slowly, in broken phrases, pronouncing the words with obvious pleasure. "We are all flesh; when it's weak, we're weak; when it's sick, we're sick; when it's dead, we're dead. Now we're civilized, we try to pretend that our bodies don't matter. But our minds, our imaginations, are flesh too, and part of the whole. Puritanism is like cutting a muscle in your arm, and trying to move your hand with its own muscles. . . .'

' "Your religion is wrong," Mike went on. . . . "It cuts us in two. It divides the body from the spirit. The body is what we are and the spirit what we think. . . ."

' "And it is only pleasure, your kind of love?" Dan asked wistfully.

167

' "Only? Only pleasure?" Mike shouted, and his laughter turned quickly to an affectionate seriousness. "Listen, boy. It's built on despair. Once we thought life didn't matter, wasn't anything but a preparation for eternity: a vale of tears—with a sunny paradise, very strange and full of songs, all ready for the worthy. That's all over. We've found out we're only cells; they break up when we die. We've found out that we're animals, just animals that remember more and worry more. So life is the only thing that does matter. A few years, thirty or forty or fifty years, hungry years; then we end up here, under the grass; and we're going to have a good time. . . ."

' "And what is a good time?"

' "That . . ." Mike paused—"that is a question." He spoke the words jubilantly. "Joy, delight, pleasure—there isn't any word." Mike stretched himself dreamily. . . ."Fun, without any end. A bunch of flowers, falling, falling, over the eyes, over the mouth, till you're all still and satisfied. . . ." '

That is the central statement of the book (I am not considering it with reference to its merits as a book, but only as evidence for the infiltration of philosophic ideas), and it is behaviouristic more than anything else, I suppose. It is no doubt some such attitude as that, resulting from Behaviourism, of which Dr. Berman was thinking. But Behaviourism alone would not have produced even that, or anything like it. All the influences that, however paradoxically at first sight, fit into Behaviourism, must also be counted into the whole effect. And Bergson and *Gestalt*, and so Berman, is one of them. It will now be possible, I think, for any reader to return to the 'dark' matter of *Mornings in Mexico* with a clear grasp not only of the manner in which I am approaching what Mr. Lawrence has to say, but also with more chances of understanding some of the remoter, and indeed very extended and important, implications of what he *is* saying.

### § 7. *Race or Ideas?*

I WILL quote once more the passage of his with which I began :

'The Indian way of consciousness is different from and fatal to our way of consciousness. Our way of consciousness is different from and fatal to the Indian. The two ways, the two streams are never to be united. . . . The consciousness of one branch of humanity is the annihilation of the consciousness of another branch. That is, the life of the Indian, his stream of conscious being, is just death to the White man."—(*Mornings in Mexico*, p. 105.)

Let us place this side by side with the similar passage from Dr. Berman:

'In the language of its protagonists: of all the modes ever offered for the use of conscious behavior, Behaviorism has the least survival value. . . . Information, ideas, theories about ourselves may, must, inevitably help or hinder us to live.   The effect may be to exalt, intensify, inspire, transform consciousness and conduct.   Or it may be to depress, infect, sicken, dishearten to the point of death.'

So the 'stream of conscious being,' which is the Mexican Indian, 'is just death to the White Man.' That is Mr. Lawrence.   For Dr. Berman 'ideas and theories' are capable of achieving the same result. They can 'depress, infect, sicken, dishearten to the point of death.'

Is it necessary for this different 'consciousness,' between which and ours 'there is no bridge, no canal of connection,' this *soul*, to be incarnated in a Mexican Indian (or a Hindu, a Polynesian or a Bantu, to choose Mr. Lawrence's other examples)?   Or can this be merely a disincarnate idea?   Is the scientific or mathematical man of genius as good for those destructive purposes as the Toltec or Hopi?   Or must it be a *race* ?

The romantic side in Mr. Lawrence, his love of the sensationally concrete, would always dispose him to seek this situation in the psychological clash of races, as others can only see it in classes.   He sees it as a *race* situation and also quite conventionally, as a conventional and wholly melodramatic race situation.   East is East, and West is West, and the unbridgeable *something*—the alien and unassimilable seed in the matrix of the Indian 'consciousness,' will not accommodate itself to the White.   It is a fight to the death.   One or the other dies.

My more abstract interests would naturally make me seek it rather in *ideas* than in *races*.   I admit, however, that the culture of one race, acquiring a political mastery over another, and imposing its ideas upon it, is able and very likely to destroy the soul and so the physical life of another race. There are too many events that testify to it in recent history for that not to be beyond possibility of question. But an *idea* is quite as powerful. Even a race, for that matter, can annihilate another race with a swarm of ideas, or intellectualized notions; ideas proper to itself but with properties of disintegration for another race; or with ideas not necessarily its own, but such as it could manipulate without injury to itself, and which are destructive to its adversary. We have examples of something of that kind. But the *ideas* themselves, swarming over from the fields of scientific research, are just as potent. And though they do no harm to their trained manipulator, they may be harmful enough to those whom they attack. Besides, there is no powerful race with whom we are in contact whose alien 'consciousness' could affect us in this way, unless you count the half-asiatic masters of Russia, whose ideas, it is true, are pouring through our consciousness, and a modified and diluted form of whose gospel has established itself in our midst.

If we *were* in touch with an alien 'consciousness' (there would be no need even to be physically at war with its possessors) in the way that the Melanesians were with the White, or the neighbours of the Chukchee with the Russian, on terms difficult and disadvantageous to ourselves, then we should find that 'consciousness,' no doubt, inimical, confusing and dangerous to our vital impulses, as Mr. Lawrence describes. And in the same way the Whites certainly are finding the attack of alien ideas confusing and dangerous for their Will and Imagination, just as much as though they were clearly, sharply and picturesquely incarnated in some alien people, with whom we came in daily contact, and who had tested us politically. So the racial analogy will serve. But you must fix your eye on something less palpable—on systems of ideas, and a restless mass of theories.

We are almost reminded of the superstitions associated with the tombs of the egyptian dead, and the belief in the *unlucky* nature of the enterprise of the excavator: the late Lord Carnarvon and Tutankamen, for instance. His death seemed to come very suddenly after disturbing Tutankamen.—The White Man has unearthed and brought to light an enormous historical rubbish-heap: there is nothing he has not excavated and brought into his own 'consciousness' for examination. Some of the distant charms and remote systems have released into his 'stream of consciousness' things that are not healthy for it, perhaps?

These general considerations (which presented themselves and demanded to be dealt with at the beginning of this section) disposed of, we can return to the Mexican Indians, Toltec and Hopi.

The Toltec and Hopi, Mr. Lawrence believes, and with that I for one am prepared to agree, might be dangerous for the 'consciousness' of Mr. Lawrence if he did not possess that 'little ghost' looking both ways at once, on account of which he is immune. So they will do no harm to one of the most justly celebrated of english novelists, we can be reassured. And it is very unlikely that the 'consciousness' of the Toltec and Hopi will ever cause any noticeable embarrassment at this time of day to anybody else. At least this would be so *if it were not for Mr. Lawrence* (the only White liable, even, to interference at the hands of these faded daimons).

Through Mr. Lawrence (who makes himself into a sort of Hopi or Toltec for the occasion), they may still add their quota of confusion to the civilized world. For Mr. Lawrence is repeatedly telling his White readers that they are poor specimens compared to his energetic and 'mysterious' Indians, and a certain proportion of his White readers are liable to believe this, and add this 'theory,' or 'information' (whichever you care to call it) to the material of their rapidly developing 'inferiority complex.' (For we are speaking, too, of a 'consciousness,' of which often enough, even, people are not conscious.) It is perhaps by itself a tiny factor, but it fits in with 'The Revolt of Asia against White Civilization,' or what not. So it is worth while to examine it. If we get to understand one or two things of this kind thoroughly, we shall understand the lot.

Section III

# 'LOVE ? WHAT HO! SMELLING STRANGENESS'

§ 1. *'We Whites, creatures of spirit.'*—D. H. LAW-RENCE.

I WILL now turn to Mr. D. H. Lawrence's account of the Mexican Indian, and especially to his chapter 'Indians and Entertainment':

'It is almost impossible for the White people to approach the Indian without either sentimentality or dislike.'

[Mr. Lawrence proves himself in this respect a *good White Man*, I think, in his book about the Indian. There is no sign of dislike, so he is the other sort of conventional White Man.]

'The common healthy vulgar White usually feels a certain native dislike of these drumming aboriginals.'

Mr. Lawrence we can at once agree is not 'a common healthy vulgar White'; he has nothing very 'native' about him, either white or dark.

'The highbrow invariably lapses into sentimentalism like the smell of bad eggs.'

Mr. Lawrence is a 'highbrow,' about that I think there cannot be two opinions. And a 'sentimentalism like the smell of bad eggs,' I am sorry to have to say, rises from all the work of Mr. Lawrence. It

174

## 'WE WHITES, CREATURES OF SPIRIT'

is all slightly 'high' and *faisandé* in a sentimental way.

Anyhow, far from 'disliking' the 'drumming' of these 'aboriginals,' there is no question that he likes it very much; and heavily implied in all his descriptions is the notion that these drumming and other 'native' habits are far superior to ours; the dark ones to the white. If we followed Mr. Lawrence to the ultimate conclusion of his romantic teaching, we should allow our 'consciousness' to be overpowered by the alien 'consciousness' of the Indian. And we know what he thinks that would involve: for he has told us that 'the Indian way of consciousness is different from and fatal to our way of consciousness.'

We will now turn to his account of the specific way in which this 'consciousness' of the Mexican Indian differs from ours.

The 'commonest entertainment among the Indians,' we are told (that is I suppose among the 'common healthy vulgar' Indians, if Mr. Lawrence's romantic soul could bring itself to admit that a Toltec or a Hopi *could* be 'common' or 'vulgar'), 'is singing round the drum, at evening.'

There are fishermen in the Outer Hebrides, he says, who do something of this sort, 'approaching the indian way,' but of course, being mere Whites, they do not reach or equal it. Still, the Outer Hebrideans do succeed in suggesting to Mr. Lawrence a realm inhabited by 'beasts that . . . stare through . . . vivid *mindless* eyes.' They do manage to become *mindless*: though not so *mindless* as the Indian, therefore inferior.

175

'This is *approaching* the Indian song. But
even this is *pictorial, conceptual* far beyond the Indian point. *The Hebridean still sees himself human,*
and *outside* the great naturalistic influences. . . .'

The poor White Hebridean still, alas, remains
*human,* he is not totally *mindless,* though more
nearly so than any other White Mr. Lawrence off-
hand can bring to mind.

The important thing to note in all these accounts
is the insistence upon *mindlessness* as an essential
quality of what is admirable. The Hebridean is not
to be admired so much as the Mexican Indian because he still deals in 'conceptual,' 'pictorial' things;
whereas the Mexican Indian is purely emotional—
'musical,' in a word, in the Spengler sense. (For
the full analysis of this type of thinking I refer you
to *Time and Western Man,* where there is a detailed
account of spenglerism.) And the first impulse to
the anti-conceptualist, anti-intellectual, anti-pictor-
ial point of view in philosophy, and thinking generally, was given by Bergson: just as in Berman's
account of Behaviourism we saw him attributing
the genesis of *Gestalt* to Bergson. So at last we
know just where we are, philosophically, with Mr.
Lawrence. Mr. D. H. Lawrence is a distinguished
artist—member of the great and flourishing society
of 'Emergent Evolution,' 'Creative Evolution,'
'Gestalt,' 'World-as-History,' etc. etc.

§ 2. *Mr. Lawrence a Follower of the Bergson-Spengler*
      *School.*

I will go on quoting to show how completely Mr.
Lawrence is beneath the spell of this evolutionist,

emotional, non-human, 'mindless' philosophy: and how thoroughly he reads it into and applies it to the manifestations of the Indian 'consciousness.'

'The Indian, singing, sings *without words or vision.*'

I am italicizing the expressions that it is particularly necessary to mark in what I am quoting. How the attitude to 'words,' on the one hand, and to 'vision' and the things of vision, 'pictorial' things, on the other, is pure Spengler!

'Face lifted and *sightless*, eyes half closed and *visionless*, mouth open and *speechless*, the *sounds* arise in his chest, from the *consciousness in the abdomen.*'

A 'consciousness in the abdomen' or a visceral consciousness (which otherwise is 'sightless,' 'visionless,' and 'speechless') is what we commonly should call *unconsciousness*. And indeed that is what—if we were to capitalize it under one word—we should take as describing the kernel of this propagandist account. It is as a servant of the great *philosophy of the Unconscious* (which began as 'Will' with Schopenhauer, became 'The Philosophy of the Unconscious' with Von Hartmann, launched all that 'the Unconscious' means in Psychoanalysis, and was 'Intuition' for Bergson, which is 'Time' for Spengler, and 'Space-Time' for Professor Alexander) that Mr. Lawrence is writing.

'*The consciousness in the abdomen*' removes the vital centre into the viscera, and takes the privilege of leadership away from the hated 'mind' or 'intellect,' established up above in the head.

## § 3. *Spengler and the 'Musical' Consciousness.*

THE '*sounds* that arise . . . from the consciousness in the abdomen' should be compared with the 'sounds' or 'sound-symbols' transcending mere words of Spengler. When Spengler is trying to give us an idea of what he means by 'Time,' for instance, he writes:

' "Time"—that which we actually feel at the *sound* of the word, which is clearer in music than in language . . . has this *organic* essence, which Space has not.'

As I have pointed out elsewhere, Spengler's is in the same sense an 'organic philosophy' as Whitehead's. (The 'philosophy of organic-mechanism' is how Professor Whitehead describes his philosophy.)—These names and bare indications will suggest to you the theories that lie behind the romantic interpretations of Mr. Lawrence. I cannot here go into his philosophic derivations any more than to indicate very generally what they are.—So, with him, we see the impulses of the evolutionist, *organic* philosophy reaching the glorification of the 'consciousness in the abdomen'—a sort of visceral, abdominal, mind, involved with the gonadal affective apparatus, and establishing in these 'centric parts' a new revolutionary capital, the rival and enemy of the head, with its hated *intellect*, the aristocratic prerogative of the human being, that is such an offence to communism.

'Every higher language,' says Spengler, 'possesses a number of words . . . about which there

178

is a veil.   No hypothesis, no science, can ever get into touch with that which we feel when we let ourselves sink into the meaning and sound of these words.   They are symbols, not notions. . . . The Destiny-idea demands . . . *depth,* not intellect.' —(*Decline of the West,* p. 117 of english translation.)

In Spengler's language (which, as you see, is 'sound' or 'music,' as he calls it, not anything so definite as *words*) 'Time' is about the same thing as 'Destiny.'   To say that it was *the same* would be to suggest an exactitude which is foreign to Spengler. And upon the *feminine* nature of 'Time' or 'Destiny' Spengler insists a great deal.

'Endless Becoming is comprehended in the idea of *Motherhood.*   Woman as Mother *is* Time and *is* Destiny.'

A glorification of the Feminine principle, naturally, is also a great feature of the writing of Mr. D. H. Lawrence.   The joining up of all these threads is no doubt a tax upon the reader's attention, and I wish it were not necessary so often to set out the evidence of what I am writing.   But if I confined myself to assertion, or to a reference, merely, to where these parallels could be found, and omitted to give the text of some of the things at least to which I refer, my argument would not be so substantially founded as it is, and above all, for practical purposes, would want the convincing appeal derived from 'chapter and verse.'

§ 4. *Communism, Feminism, and the Unconscious
found in the Mexican Indian by Mr. Lawrence.*

ONE of the rhythmical patterns of 'sound' produced by the Indian the latter describes as a 'bear
hunt,' Mr. Lawrence tells us.

'But,' says Mr. Lawrence, 'the man coming
home from the bear hunt is any man, all men, the
bear is any bear, every bear, all bear. *There is no
individual, isolated experience.* It is the hunting
. . . demon of manhood which has won against
the . . . demon of all bears. The experience is
generic, non-individual.'

So we reach Mr. Lawrence's *communism*, cast into
the anthropologic moulds first prepared by Sir
Henry Maine. For Mr. Lawrence is, in full hysterical flower, perhaps our most accomplished english
communist. He is *the natural communist*, as it were,
as distinguished from the indoctrinated, or theoretic, one.

(1) The Unconscious; (2) The Feminine; (3) The
Communist; those are the main principles of action
of the mind of Mr. Lawrence, linked in a hot and
piping trinity of rough-stuff primitivism, and freudian hot-sex-stuff. With *Sons and Lovers*, his first
book, he was at once hot-foot upon the fashionable
trail of incest; the book is an eloquent wallowing
mass of Mother-love and Sex-idolatry. His *Women
in Love* is again the same thick, sentimental, luscious
stew. The 'Homo'-motive, how could that be
absent from such a compendium, as is the nature of
Mr. Lawrence, of all that has long passed for 'revolu-

tionary,' reposing mainly for its popular effectiveness upon the meaty, succulent levers of sex and supersex, to bait those politically-innocent, romantic, anglo-saxon simpletons dreaming their 'anglo-saxon dreams,' whether in America or the native country of Mr. Lawrence? The motif of the 'child-cult,' which is usually found prominently in any 'revolutionary' mixture, is echoed, and indeed screamed, wept and bellowed, throughout *Sons and Lovers*.

At first sight, I am afraid, many of the *rapprochements* that I make here may sound strained, since, I am sorry to say, if things do not lie obviously together and publish their conjunction explicitly and prominently, it is not considered quite respectable to suggest that they have any vital connection. The suggestion of anything 'illicit' shocks, even where ideas are concerned. That one idea should have a hidden liaison or be in communication with another idea, without ever approaching it in public, or any one even *mentioning them together*—that is the sort of thing that is never admitted in polite society.

So the majority of people are deeply unconscious of the affiliations of the various phenomena of our time, which on the surface look so very autonomous, and even hostile; yet, existing under quite a different label, in a quite different region of time and space, they are often closely and organically related to one another. If you test this you will be surprised to find how many things do belong together, in fact, in our highly contentious and separatist time.

Yet it is our business—especially, it appears, mine —to establish these essential liaisons, and to lay bare the widely-flung system of cables connecting up this maze-like and destructive system in the midst of which we live—destructive, that is of course, to something essential that we should clutch and be careful not to lose, on our way to the Melting-pot.

What, you might say, for instance, has Mr. Lawrence's remark about the 'mindlessness' of the Mexican songs got to do with communism ? Or, again, 'mindlessness' or 'communism' to do with 'the Feminine Principle' (as opposed to the Masculine)? I can show you at once what 'mindlessness' has to do with 'communism.' I will quote the latest european advocate of Bolshevism, René Fülöp-Miller, from his book *The Mind and Face of Bolshevism*. It should really be called *The Face of Bolshevism*, since we learn that 'Mind' is of all things what Bolshevism is concerned to deny and prohibit. He is relating how the 'higher type of humanity' is to be produced, the super-humanity of which Bolshevism is the religion.

'It is only by such external functions as the millions have in common, their uniform and simultaneous movements, that the many can be united in a higher unity: marching, keeping in step, shouting "hurrah" in unison, festal singing in chorus, united attacks on the enemy, these are the manifestations of life which are to give birth to the new and superior type of humanity. *Everything that divides the many from each other, that fosters the illusion of the individual importance of man, especially the "soul," hinders this higher evolution and must consequently be destroyed* . . . organization is to be substituted for the soul . . . the vague mystery of the "soul," with that evil handed down from an accursed individualistic past. . . .'

Let us now continue with our quotations from Mr. Lawrence.

*'There is no individual, isolated experience. . . . It is an experience of the blood-stream, not of the mind or spirit.* Hence the subtle incessant insistent rhythm of the drum, which is pulsated like a heart, and *soulless* and inescapable. Hence the strange blind unanimity of the . . . men's voices.'

As you see, it might equally be Mr. Fülöp-Miller on the beauties of Bolshevism. The Mexican Indian of Mr. Lawrence is the perfect Bolshevik. The 'blind unanimity of the men's voices' (the 'keeping in step . . . festal singing in chorus' of Fülöp-Miller) assures 'soullessness.' The 'soul . . . must be destroyed' says the apostle of Bolshevism. '—— the Indian song is non-individual. . . . Strange clapping, crowing, gurgling sounds, in an unseizable subtle rhythm, the rhythm of the heart in her throes: . . . from an abdomen where the great blood-stream surges in the dark, and surges in its own generic experiences.'

To witness all this is, to Mr. Lawrence, heaven. '—— perhaps it is the most stirring sight in the world in the dark, near the fire, with the drums going,' etc. etc.

'It is the dark blood falling back from the mind, from sight and speech and knowing, back to the great central source where is rest and unspeakable renewal.'

On the same principle as 'Back to the Land,' the

cry of Mr. Lawrence (good little Freudian that he has always been) is 'Back to the Womb!' For although a natural communist and born feminist, it required the directive brain of Freud and others to reveal him to himself.

'We Whites, creatures of spirit!' he cries. Ah, the 'strange' things we 'never realize'! (such as the 'strange falling back of the blood . . . the *downward* rhythm, the rhythm of pure forgetting and pure renewal').

## § 5. *The Indian a 'Dithyrambic Spectator.'*

As to the pantheism of Mr. Lawrence's Mexican Indian, the following passages inform us about that:

'There is strictly no god. The Indian does not consider himself as created, and therefore external to God, or the creature of God. . . . Creation is a great flood, for ever flowing. . . .'

*Everything Flows!*—for the Indian, as for Bergson, Mr. Lawrence, etc. In art the Mexican Indian approximates closely to the ideal of the contemporary bolshevik theatre (the principles of which I have discussed in an essay, *The Dithyrambic Spectator*).

'There is no division between actor and audience. It is all one.'

'There is no Onlooker. There is no Mind. There is no dominant idea. . . . The Indian is completely embedded in . . . his own drama. It is a drama that has no beginning and no end. . . . It can't be judged, because there is nothing outside it, to judge it.'

# THE INDIAN A 'DITHYRAMBIC SPECTATOR'

*It is evidently just like life.* It is a form of naturalism, the mystical form. And above all there is no bunk about *mind.* Mind is kept in its place, in the indian idea of drama!

'*The mind is there merely as a servant.* . . . The mind bows down before the creative mystery.'

As to the good and the bad, that again consists in being possessed of a personal will or individuality (which is *wicked*), or not being possessed of any individuality (which is *virtuous*).

'Wickedness lies in . . . seeking to prostitute the creative wonder to the individual mind and will. . . .'

The magician, the Prospero, is the supremely *wicked* person in the indian scheme of things, in the eyes of these 'soulless,' 'drumming,' viscerally-churned-up Calibans. Magic, 'witchcraft,' Mr. Lawrence tells us, is the archetype of all wickedness.

What is *virtue* in woman? Mr. Lawrence becomes very Western at once, under the shadow of a kind of suffragist-chivalry, at the mere thought of 'Woman.'

'In woman [virtue] is the putting forth of all herself in a delicate, marvellous, sensitiveness, which draws forth the wonder to herself, etc.' (To 'draw the wonder to herself' is to be a witch, surely? So virtue and wickedness would get a little mixed up.)

What would the Indian think if he heard his squaw being written about in that strain?—'delicate, marvellous sensitiveness.' He would probably say 'Chuck it, Archie!' in Hopi. At least he would be considerably surprised, and probably squint very hard, under his 'dark' brows, at Mr. Lawrence.

## § 6. *The Under-Parrot and the Over-Dog.*

WHEN we are busy contrasting the White 'consciousness' with the Dark, we are always compelled to remember that there are other 'consciousnesses' as well, perhaps even more hostile.  Mr. Lawrence's first chapter, 'Corasmin and the Parrots,' is devoted to extending the idea of race-'consciousness' (in the sense of different species of men) to the whole animal world.

In the patio of his house Mr. Lawrence sits on a sunny morning in Mexico: and he 'makes an instant friend of the reader' (the publisher assures you on the back of the dust-cover) by telling you that he is only 'one little individual looking at a bit of sky and trees, then looking down at the page of an exercise book.' (*Exercise book!*  Quite like a little child.) He is nothing if not democratic, Mr. Lawrence: just a 'little individual,' like yourself, dear reader, but bringing you a sunlit Morning all the way from Mexico.

In the patio is a dog, called Corasmin.  He is an even *smaller* individual than Mr. Lawrence.  'Corasmin is a little fat, curly white dog. . . . His little white nose is sharp, and under his eyes are dark marks, as under the eyes of one who has known much trouble.  All day he does nothing but walk resignedly out of the sun, when the sun gets too hot, and out of the shade when the shade gets too cool.'

Meantime the parrots in the trees look down into the court, and observe the dog with hatred. All day long they mock him and his two-legged masters; for all the world as the negroes mock the Whites in Sherwood Anderson's *Dark Laughter*.—Chapter One of Mr. Lawrence's book is an account of the 'Dark Laughter' of the parrots, in short.

' "Perro! Oh, Perr-rro! Perr-rr-rro!!" shriek the parrots, with that strange penetrating, antediluvian malevolence that seems to make even the trees prick their ears. It is a sound that penetrates one straight at the diaphragm, belonging to the ages before brains were invented.'

There we are back at the dear old 'mysterious' abdomen, once more! The 'dark laughter' of the mocking parrots goes in at the stomach, straight to the visceral 'consciousness,' disdaining the mere ear and brain. At this point we grow very primitive indeed. We are in the antediluvian world with these parrots, who continue to pour 'vitriolic' mockery over the present masters of this earth, namely men and dogs.

§ 7. *Evolution, à la Mexicaine: (genre cataclysmique, à la Marx).*

HERE is Mr. Lawrence's picture of Evolution *à la mexicaine*.

'Myself, I don't believe in evolution, like a long string hooked on to a First Cause. . . . I prefer to believe in what the Aztecs called Suns: that is, Worlds successively created and destroyed. The

187

sun itself convulses, and the worlds go out like so many candles. . . . Then subtly, mysteriously, the sun convulses again, and a new set of worlds begin to flicker alight.

'I like to think of the world going pop! When the lizards had grown too unwieldy, and it was time they were taken down a peg or two.'

You see it is evolution just the same, with giant lizards and so forth. But a jealous god 'mysteriously' takes things down a peg or two periodically. It is cataclysmic evolution, à la Marx, rather than *evolutionary evolution.*

'Then the little humming-birds beginning to spark in the darkness and a whole succession of birds shaking themselves clean of the dark matrix . . . parrots shrieking about at midday, *almost* able to talk, then peacocks unfolding at evening. . . . And apart from these little, pure birds, a lot of unwieldy skinny-necked monsters bigger than crocodiles, barging through the mosses; till it was time to put a stop to them. Then some one mysteriously touched the button, and the sun went bang, with smithereens of birds bursting in all directions. Only a few parrots' eggs and peacocks' eggs and eggs of flamingoes smuggling in some safe nook, to hatch on the next Day, when the animals arose.

'Up reared the elephant, and shook the mud off his back. The birds watched him in sheer stupefaction. "What? *What* in heaven's name is this wingless, beakless old perambulator?"

'No good, oh birds! Curly little white Coras-

188

min ran yapping out of the undergrowth, the new undergrowth, till parrots, going white at the gills, flew off into the ancientest recesses. Then the terrific neighing of the wild horse was heard in the twilight for the first time, and the bellowing of lions through the night.

'And the birds were sad. "What is this?" they said. "A whole vast gamut of new voices. A universe of new voices."

'Then the birds under the leaves hung their heads and were dumb. "No good our making a sound," they said. "We are superseded."

'. . . Only the real little feathery individuals hatched out again and remained. This was a consolation. The larks and warblers cheered up, and began to say their little say, out of the old "Sun," to the new sun. But the peacock, and the turkey, and the raven, and the parrot above all, they could not get over it. Because, in the old days of the Sun of Birds, they had been the big guns. The parrot had been the old boss of the flock. He was so clever.

'Now he was, so to speak, up a tree. Nor dare he come down, because of the toddling little curly white Corasmin, and such-like, down below. He felt absolutely bitter. That wingless, beakless, featherless, curly, misshapen bird's nest of a Corasmin had usurped the face of the earth, waddling about, whereas his Grace, the heavy-nosed old Duke of a parrot, was forced to sit out of reach up a tree, dispossessed.

'So, like the riff-raff up in the gallery at the theatre, aloft in the Paradise of the vanished Sun, he began to whistle and jeer. *Yap-Yap!* said his new little lordship of a Corasmin. "Ye Gods!" cried the parrot. "Hear him forsooth! *Yap-Yap!* he says! Could anything be more imbecile? Yap-Yap! Oh, Sun of the Birds, hark at that! *Yap-Yap-Yap!* Perro! *Perro! Perr-rro!* Oh, *Perr-rr-rro!*"

. . .

'The third Sun burst in water. . . . Out of the floods rose our own Sun, and little naked man. "Hello!" said the old elephant. "What's that noise?"'

'"*Come on! Perro! Perro!*" called the naked two-legged one. And Corasmin, fascinated, said to himself: "Can't hold out against that name. Shall have to go!" so off he trotted, at the heels of the naked one.

. . .

'And in the branches the parrot said to himself: "*Hello! What's this new sort of half-bird? Why, he's got Corasmin trotting at his heels!* Must be a new sort of boss! Let's listen to him, and see if I can't take him off.

'"Perr-rro! Perr-rr-rro-oo! Oh, Perro!"
'The parrot had hit it.'

I need not point out to the reader, probably, the virtues of this passage as a tour de force of literary art. It is reminiscent of the best manner of Anatole France, only possessing greater freshness—and indeed the whole book is one of the best of Mr. Lawrence's that I have read. Unfortunately I have had

EVOLUTION *À LA MEXICAINE*

to compress this lengthy passage, for all we are concerned with here is the notions underneath it, and
not the literary expression.

What this very vivid mock-account of a series of
cataclysms and aztec 'Suns' reveals is the same
thread of feeling as is to be found everywhere else in
the book, and in those other numerous books whose
underlying ideas, or philosophy, I am scrutinizing
here.   On the earth beneath, strutting about, is the
ridiculous little white dog; up in the trees is the
dignified aristocratic parrot.   But the parrot is
forced to remain 'up a tree' because this ridiculous
little dog is the overlord of the moment, or the servant of the present overlord, Man.   But the 'little
white naked man' is not much less ridiculous than
the little yapping white ball of a dog.   Compared
with the beautiful or at least aristocratical birds
they have superseded, this pair cut a poor figure.
*But they have the power:* they walk the earth.   The
'consciousness' of the little white dog and the little
white man has been too much for the 'consciousness'
of the bird-world.

But the sympathy of the reader, in this play of
fantasia, it is clearly intended, should be found entirely on the side of the birds.   They are the finer
beasts.   And when in later chapters we arrive at the
Indians, and pluck out the 'dark' heart of *their* antediluvian mystery, again we have a defeated race, but
a far finer and profounder one than that that has
superseded it.   Chapter One, with the evolutionary
apologue, is a psychological introduction to a study
of the Indian, especially as contrasted with the
White mind.

191

## § 8. *Race or Class Separation by means of 'Dimension.'*

THE situation in this bird-and-man play is the same situation as *the White and Negro* situation, *the Civilized man and the Savage* situation, or *the White Overlord and subject asiatic races* situation. The play is introduced, at the start of the book, to stress and illustrate the situation to be considered and depicted later on, when the 'consciousness' of the Indian is to be pitted against the 'consciousness' of the White Man.

The monkey at a certain point comes on the scene. He is a survival from another 'dimension.' Mr. Lawrence having introduced the mexican machinery of his 'Suns,' thinks of the word 'Dimension' as being especially vague and picturesque, so he uses that.

'If you come to think of it,' he says, 'when you look at the monkey you are looking straight into the other dimension . . . he's in the same universe of Space and Time as you are. But there's another dimension.'

This other dimension is the thought or 'consciousness' of the monkey, of course.

'He's different. There's no rope of evolution linking him to you, like a navel string. No! Between you and him there's a cataclysm and another dimension. It's no good. You can't link him up. Never will. It's the other dimension.

'He mocks at you and gibes at you and imitates you. Sometimes he is even more *like* you than you are yourself. He's funny, and you laugh just a bit on the wrong side of your face. It's the other dimension.'

As between Dark and White, Indian and European, so between Man and Monkey, there is this *absolute* gulf for Mr. Lawrence, like the cleavage between mathematical dimensions. 'The Indian way of consciousness is different from and fatal to our way of consciousness. . . . There is no bridge, no canal of connection.' For 'Indian' substitute 'Parrots' (why not with a capital P though—is that because we are on the ground and the 'parrot' up aloft?) or Monkeys (why not a capital M, like Indian?) and you have the same situation.

'The Simian way of consciousness is different from and fatal to our way,' etc., or 'The Parrot's way of consciousness,' etc. That is the idea.—It is all arranged to heighten, or deepen, the separation between the Indian and the White—or the Bantu or Hindu or the American Negro and the White.

§ 9. *An Invitation to Suicide addressed to the White Man.*

THE emotion throughout the book from which I have quoted is the dogmatism of 'revolution,' of political revolution, to be precise. In contrast to the White Overlord of this world in which we live, Mr. Lawrence shows us a more primitive type of 'consciousness,' which has been physically defeated by the White 'consciousness,' and assures us that that defeated 'consciousness' is the better of the two. But, since the 'consciousness' of the Indian is death to the 'consciousness' of the White, and eventually, if it prevailed, to the White, physically, as well, it is (however indirectly, and in the form of an entertainment, a book of 'fiction') an invitation to suicide addressed to the White Man. 'Give up, lay down, your White "consciousness," ' it says. 'Capitulate to the mystical communistic Pan of the Primitive Man!  Be Savage!'

Not only the opposition as between beasts and men, or Black and White, is stressed (with, always, the rebellious hypnotic accompaniment of the re-volutionary drum, the primitive tom-tom, and al-ways, that is the important thing, all the sympathy of the reader engaged on the side of the oppressed and superseded, the under-dog—or, in the above in-stance, of the under-parrot); also we are taken into the dark-backward, to more exaggerated opposi-tions.  Once we have got to the earliest birds, and, most ancient of all the dispossessed, the serpent (whom Mr. Lawrence sees biting his tail with an im-memorial rage, and remarking, as he glances malev-olently up at Man, 'I will bruise his heel!'), beyond this we reach *things*—beyond the earliest amœba. Mr. Lawrence does not take us as far as that.  But the philosophers who mainly influence him do.

This will be without meaning perhaps for some readers.  Elsewhere I have shown how *that* most fundamental of all revolutionary impulses works, too.  Mr. Bertrand Russell, for instance, obedient to his liberalist traditions, which he imports into his physics, attempts to stir up the tables and chairs against us and lead them in revolt against the over-weening overlord, Man, who sits upon them, and uses them to write books at, without even asking himself if they may not resent his behaviour, and have their private thoughts about *him*—as he flings himself down upon them, or rests his elbows upon them and scratches his head.

The reason why I direct an adverse analysis against this type of 'revolutionary' emotionality, is not, once more, because I believe that the White Man as he stands to-day is the last word in animal life, or in spiritual perfection, or that he is not often quite as ridiculous as Mr. Lawrence's parrots would have him, and in any case he is engaged in the road to the Melting - pot. I will not here enumerate my reasons for hostility where this revolutionary picture is concerned: I will say, only, that most Aztecs are probably fairly bored with being Aztecs: that the average Hopi, like the average cat, is rather negatively admirable and exceedingly mechanical: that admiration for savages and cats is really an expression of the worst side of the Machine Age—that Machine-Age Man is effusive about them *because they are machines* like himself; and Mr. Lawrence, at least, makes no pretence of admiring his savages because they are *free*—they are no longer for the contemporary 'revolutionary' doctrinaire 'the noble savage' in the rousseauesque or Fenimore Cooper sense, at least not for the best informed doctrinaire: and, lastly, what such gospels as those of Mr. Lawrence or of Sherwood Anderson really amount to is an emotional, and not quite disinterested, exaltation (indirectly) of the *average man*, l'homme moyen sensuel—though in this case *the average Hopi*.

I find the average White European (such as
Chekov depicted) often exceedingly ridiculous, no
doubt, but much more interesting than the average
Hopi, or the average Negro. I would rather have
the least man that *thinks,* than the average man that
squats and drums and drums, with 'sightless,' 'soulless' eyes: I would rather have an ounce of human
'consciousness' than a universe full of 'abdominal'
afflatus and hot, unconscious, 'soulless,' mystical
throbbing.—These few remarks must suffice to indicate the orientation of my attitude in this part of
the debate.

I am now going over into the books of Sherwood
Anderson: and I assure you that, if you have followed my analysis of the passages in *Mornings in
Mexico,* you will be in a much better position to
understand exactly what Mr. Anderson wants to say
to you, at the same time that he spins you an excellent yarn.

I will begin with *Dark Laughter* (it pairs very well
with *Mornings in Mexico,* though, as a book, in
every way inferior, and not even a 'good yarn'); and
I will take my leave of Mexico with a quotation describing the parrots in the patio mocking Rosalino
the indian servant, with *their* 'dark laughter.' In
this way the two types of 'dark laughter' will be
brought into the nearest possible contact, so that
any reader will be able to see how very near they are
together in spirit, as well.

The two parrots 'a quite commonplace pair of
green birds' sit or hang there, with their 'flat disillusioned eyes,' their 'heavy overhanging noses,'
their 'sad old long-jowled faces,' and *watch* the

ridiculous human beings underneath hour after hour, bursting into mockery when tired of watching and noting.

'The parrots whistle exactly like Rosalino, only a little more so . . . Rosalino, sweeping the patio with his twig broom . . . covers himself more and more with the cloud of his own obscurity. . . . Up goes the wild, sliding Indian whistle into the morning. . . .'

§ 10. *'Spring was coming on fast in Southern Indiana.'*

MR. SHERWOOD ANDERSON's book, *Dark Laughter*, ends as follows:

'Why couldn't Fred laugh? He kept trying but failed. In the road before the house one of the negro women now laughed. There was a shuffling sound. The older negro woman tried to quiet the younger, blacker woman, but she kept laughing the high shrill laughter of the negress. "I knowed it, I knowed it, all the time I knowed it," she cried, and the high shrill laughter ran through the garden and into the room where Fred sat upright and rigid in bed.
'The End.'

The negresses in *Dark Laughter* (they are the black servants, and their mocking laughter usually rises from the scullery or kitchen) perpetually release their 'high shrill laughter of the negress,' as they observe with astonishment and derision the feebleness and absurdity of their White Overlords up in the parlour and out on the lawn. 'Up goes the wild, sliding Indian whistle in the morning' from the parrots (mocking the human beings in the court beneath, from which, owing to the overlordship of the human species, they are excluded, and forced to pass their time hanging upon the trees) in Mr. Lawrence's *Mornings in Mexico*: and up goes the 'high shrill laughter' of the negroes in Mr. Sherwood Anderson's *Dark Laughter*. The *negresses* in Mr. Anderson's book are in the rôle of the *parrots* in Mr. Lawrence's book: and the White Overlords in Mr. Anderson's book are in the rôle of Homo Sapiens in Mr. Lawrence's book. But in Mr. Lawrence's book, as in Mr. Anderson's, the *White Overlord*, rather than the more abstract and fundamental Human Being, is the true objective. And the Mexican Indian in *Mornings in Mexico* plays the part of the Negro in *Dark Laughter*. I think this parallel can be missed by no one. So there is a good deal of truth, it seems, in the 'moron' critic's gibe, 'Sherwood Lawrence,' in Mr. Mencken's *Americana*.

*Dark Laughter* is the story of a journalist who, having escaped from his wife in Chicago, gets employment in a small town in the South. He finds his employer's wife ('Fred' is the employer) attractive. She returns his love. She advertises for a gardener. He takes on the job. After what seems a very long time to the negro woman watching from the kitchen and other menial vantage points, Fred's wife and the hired man go up to the bedroom of the wife of Fred, the employer, during Fred's absence, and the 'deed of darkness' is at last consummated.

'A high-pitched negro laugh rang through the house.'—End of Book Ten.

That is the story.  It proceeds to the mocking accompaniment of the laughter of the negro servants who find their masters a great joke.  Fred's wife finds their laughter disquieting, but she dismisses it as follows:

'Soon it would be evening, the negro women come home. . . . About the negro women it did not matter.  They would think as their natures led them to think, feel as their natures led them to feel.  You can't ever tell what a negro woman thinks or feels.  They are like children looking at you. . . . White eyes, white teeth in a brown face—laughter.'

But we, the readers of *Dark Laughter*, know what the negresses think more or less, for we have the following enlightenment, which resolves itself into a sort of 'Attaboy' chorus—the manly straightforward advice of the divinely-inspired black child of nature: 'Get down to it!  Get to business!  Hurry up!  Have her quick!  Don't hang and moon about!'

'Negroes singing:—

" And the Lord said . . .
Hurry, Hurry."

'Negroes singing had sometimes a way of getting at the ultimate truth of things.  Two negro women sang in the kitchen of the house. . . . The two negro women in the house sang, did their work, looked and listened.'

That is the situation.  'Spring was coming on fast in Southern Indiana.'  But the specimen of the White race depicted for us, called upon to be the 'man in the case' or third side to the triangle, and to accommodate Fred's wife, is slow, slow—as slow, in fact, as *the spring in southern Indiana* is fast. And—

'The two negro women in the house watched and waited. Often they looked at each other and giggled. The air on the hill top was filled with laughter—*dark laughter*. 'Oh, Lord! Oh, Lord! Oh, Lord!' one of them cried to the other. She laughed—a high-pitched negro laugh.'

## § 11. '*Torrents of Spring*.'

It is the 'Spring' motif of *Dark Laughter* that Mr. Ernest Hemingway has so ably caricatured in his *Torrents of Spring*. Just as in Mr. Lawrence's *Mornings in Mexico* it is the Indian who takes the place of the Negro, so in Mr. Hemingway's book Indian stands for Negro, and does the 'dark laughing.' It opens with the 'Spring' motif of 'Spring was coming on fast in Southern Indiana,' as follows:

'Yogi Johnson stood looking out of the window of a big pump-factory in Michigan. Spring would soon be here. . . . Near Yogi at the next window but one stood Scripps O'Neil. . . . Scripps O'Neil had two wives. As he looked out of the window . . . he thought of both of them. One lived in Mancelona and the other lived in Petoskey. He had not seen the one that lived in Mancelona since last spring. He looked out at the snow-covered pump-yard and thought what spring would mean.

. · · · · ·

'Yogi Johnson opened the window carefully, just a crack. Just a crack, that was enough. Outside in the yard the snow had begun to melt. A warm breeze was blowing. A chinook wind the pump fellows called it. The warm chinook wind came in through the window into the pump-factory. All the workmen laid down their tools. Many of them were Indians.

.            .            .

The foreman put his finger in his mouth to moisten it and held it up in the air. He felt the warm breeze on his finger. He shook his head ruefully and smiled at the men, a little grimly perhaps.

' "Well, it's a regular chinook, boys," he said. Silently for the most part, the workmen hung up their tools.

.            .            .

'Outside through the window came the sound of an Indian war-whoop.'

That, compressed, is the first chapter of Mr. Hemingway's skit. Chapter Eleven shows Yogi Johnson mortified by the 'chinook' and the sense of maleness disgracefully dormant.

'Yogi Johnson walked out of the workmen's entrance of the pump-factory and down the street. Spring was in the air. . . .

'It's a real chinook wind, Yogi thought. The foreman did right to let the men go. It wouldn't be safe keeping them in a day like this. Anything might happen. . . .

'Yogi was worried. There was something on his mind. It was spring, there was no doubt of that now, and he did not want a woman. He had

201

PALEFACE

worried about it a lot lately.   There was no question about it.   He did not want a woman.   He
couldn't explain it to himself.   He had gone to
the Public Library and asked for a book the night
before.   He looked at the librarian.   He did not
want her.   Somehow she meant nothing to him.
At the restaurant where he had a meal ticket he
looked hard at the waitress who brought him his
meals.   He did not want her, either.   He passed
a group of girls on their way home from High
School.   He looked carefully at all of them.   He
did not want a single one. . . .'

This painful situation is relieved at last by an
opportune stimulus turning up.   This skit amus-
ingly pursues Mr. Sherwood Anderson through all
the phases of his stupidity, especially stressing the
'he-man' foolishness, the 'bursting Spring' side of it.
    Mr. Hemingway's book, it is to be hoped, will put
a stop to *Dark Laughter* for the time, at least, on the
part of Mr. Anderson.   But some form or other of it
(and it becomes, with people more sophisticated than
Mr. Anderson, though otherwise much the same,
White laughter or imitation-'dark') is sure to abound
and to multiply, since it has struck root in the anglo-
saxon mind: and one swallow, that is one Hemingway, does not either make or mar an andersonian
spring—that teutonic zolaesque, meaty, maudlin,
sexish spring, heralding a communist summer—in
which, delirious with the 'chinook,' creatures are
rhetorically invited to *merge* in the 'dark' juicy
matrix of Mother Nature in colossal, 'direct,' 'soulless' abandons.

§ 12. *The Dread of Sexual Impotence.*

THE dread of sexual impotence, thoughts about impotence, taunts about impotence, anxious appeals to the 'chinook'—of such cheerful and 'manly' material as this are many of the pages of Mr. Lawrence and Mr. Sherwood Anderson composed. But there is a strain of frank and free modesty in Mr. Anderson, whenever he casts a glance in the direction of his own 'maleness.' It leaves much to be desired, in his eyes. Throughout his books Mr. Anderson indeed is comparing himself unfavourably, on the score of his 'manhood,' with other men (his brother, for instance, in the account of his childhood). In his *Story-Teller's Story*, and indeed everywhere when he appears in a more or less veiled form, these dark doubts beset him. The adulterous Bruce in *Dark Laughter* feels that a *real man* would behave quite differently from what he does in most things. He would make less fuss, *think* about things less, *act*. He is a bit of a poet, really, that is what it is, not a man of action he says to himself. Perhaps Mr. Anderson is over-modest. He is probably as 'manly' as most men: but, however that may be, he is very much puzzled and befuddled: he is a poor henpecked, beFreuded, bewildered White, with a brand-new 'inferiority complex.'

Mr. Lawrence is quite a different story. He is in full and exultant enjoyment of a full battery of 'complexes' of every possible shade and shape of sexiness. He possesses them *en connoisseur*, and any new one that is suggested to him he receives with an experienced delight. He is l'homme moyen sensuel gloating over the savouriness and variety of the contemporary fare. Beside him Anderson strikes one as a rather muddle-headed, clumsy, in some ways very stupid sensationalist, doing his best for a group of 'dark' influences which he very imperfectly understands, and often misinterprets.

§ 13. *The Manner of Mr. Anderson.*

THIS is in no sense a piece of literary criticism, I have remarked at the outset. But just as it was necessary to say, when dealing with it from another standpoint, that *Mornings in Mexico* was a work of art, that it was worth reading on that score (provided you know how to laugh *whitely* at the 'dark' ideas, and dismiss them as the sticky, over-excited, shallow stuff that they are), so it is perhaps as well to say that Mr. Sherwood Anderson in *Dark Laughter* writes in a manner that is really distracting. What the manner is I don't know: it may be a supremely undeft imitation of Mr. Joyce. I will give you a specimen of it.

'He could hear himself saying it to Harcourt and others—smiling while he said it.

'A brave man. What one does is to smile.

'When one gets out of anything there is a sense of relief. In war, in a battle, when one is wounded —a sense of relief. Now Fred would not have to play a part any more, be a man to some woman's woman. That would be up to Bruce.

'In war, when you are wounded, a strange feeling of relief. "That's done. Now get well."

' "She has gone to Chicago." That Bruce!

204

Shoes twenty to thirty dollars a pair. A work-man, a gardener. Ho, ho!" Or:
' "Go softly. Don't hurry. What's all the shooting about? A little more white, a little more white, graying white, muddy white, thick lips—staying sometimes. Over we go!
'Something lost too. The dance of bodies, a slow dance.

.   .   .

'Sleep again, white man. No hurry. Then along a street for coffee and a roll of bread, five cents. Sailors off ships, bleary-eyed. Old nigger women and white women going to market. They know each other, nigger women, white women. Go soft. Don't hurry!'

It is, in its least dextrous form, the chopped Mr. Jingle style employed by the author of *Ulysses*, to represent a person thinking: for instance (from *Ulysses*, p. 231):
'Damn good gin that was.—Fine dashing young nobleman. Good stock, of course. That ruffian, that sham squire, with his violet gloves, gave him away. Course they were on the wrong side. They rose in dark and evil days. Fine poem that is: Ingram. They were gentlemen. Ben Dollard does sing that ballad touchingly. Masterly rendi-tion.

" At the siege of Ross did my father fall."

'A cavalcade in easy trot along Pembroke quay passed, outriders leaping, leaping in their, in their saddles. Frockcoats. Cream sunshades.

'Mr. Kernan hurried forward, blowing furiously. His Excellency! Too bad! Just missed that by a hair. Damn it! What a pity!'

Here is Anderson again:

'Once he had read a book of Zola, *La Terre*, and later, but a short time before he left Chicago, Tom Wills had shewn him a new book by the Irishman Joyce, *Ulysses*. There were certain pages. A man named Bloom standing on a beach near some women. A woman, Bloom's wife, in her bedroom at home. The thoughts of the woman—her right of animalism—all set down—minutely. Realism in writing lifted up sharp something burning and new like a raw sore. Others coming to look at the sores.'

In *The Enemy* (No. 1) I said all that it is necessary to say about this jerky sententious way of writing, in dealing with Wush & Co. 'Ulysses. There were certain pages. A man named Bloom.'—'Others coming to look at the sores.' Pick up any monthly magazine devoted to the most popular sort of fiction, and you will read 'He flung out bitterly, in short jagged sentences, as though it was painful for him to speak: "No good. All is over between us.—Things might have been different. If—Ah well. It's too late. Good-bye."' This is intended to represent a person labouring under an emotion too deep for words. In the above passage of Mr. Anderson's the effect aimed at is a sort of bitter brevity—stuff flung out carelessly by a man who in the opinion both of the author and of himself is rather a fine fellow.

The other passage I have quoted, beginning: 'Go softly. Don't hurry!' etc., represents a maddening trick of many not very good writers to-day, who are too nervous and stupid to be simple, and who consider that they have in some way *modernized* what they have to tell, or that they have made its essential banality more difficult to detect, by breaking it up into jerky statements, and stark elliptical noisy clauses. Also it *poeticizes* it. It is a very similar sort of stupidity, or else deceit (according to who employs it), to average free verse. If they are really live wires they say most of their sentences two or three times over, like Miss Stein, occasionally, to vary it a little, breaking off in the middle, or punning and fumbling incessantly with some word.

§ 14. *'Brutal Realism'* cum *the Sophistication of Freud.*

Now, above, in the third passage by Mr. Anderson that I have quoted, Zola is mentioned first, and Joyce afterwards. Zola, standing for 'brutal realism,' or for 'animalism,' like Joyce (in Mr. Anderson's eyes) must have been always at the back of his mind, I suspect. *La Terre* is surely a recognizable forebear of *Dark Laughter*. All that is *suety*, and *stupid*—all the thick, fat *dummheit*—in this book, is the authentic zolaesque romance—Nature, sensuality, hot lowering sulphurous Summers—bursting, sappy Springs; cows mooing for bulls, bulls bellowing for cows, etc. etc. It all is there. But Freud has come in, too. So when the hero is thinking about his childhood, no one will be surprised to find that he first of all describes himself as a small boy, sitting beside his mother on a river-steamer, and 'sensing' that his mother was 'lusting' for a young man who stood near them with a dark moustache; and that then he half withdraws the young man with the dark moustache, and half-exonerates his mother from these fresh sensations, and takes the blame himself. It was *he*, the little boy, who in reality (the author's dutiful eye on Dr. Freud) was 'lusting' for his mother.

'That young man Bruce had once seen on an Ohio river-boat when he was a boy taking a trip up river, with his father and mother. . . . It would be an odd turn of the mind if the young man had never existed—if a boy's mind had invented him. Suppose he had just invented him later—as something—to explain his mother to himself, as a means for getting close to the woman, his mother.'

So much for the usual incest. Next I will take the mystical communism. (Not that Freud's teaching is not an integral part of communism, too, for it is the psychology appropriate to a highly communized patriarchal society in which *the family* and its close relationship is an intense obsession, and the obscene familiarities of a closely packed communal sex-life a family-joke, as it were. It is a psychology foreign to the average European and his individualistic life. The incest-theme is inappropriate to the european communities, on whom no severe religious restrictions of race or of caste have been imposed.) So by 'communism' here I mean what currently we mean when we say communism. Mr. Anderson is describing happenings on the Mississippi before the coming of industrialism, and especially he is glorifying the negroes.

'——black mysticism—never expressed except in song or in the movements of bodies. The bodies of the black workers belonged to each other as the sky belonged to the river. . . .

'Brown bodies trotting, black bodies trotting. *The bodies of all the men running up and down the landing-stage were one body. One could not be distinguished from another. They were lost in each other.—Could the bodies of people be so lost, in each other,*' etc.

He apostrophizes american painters, and calls them 'silly American painters!' He says that silly painters 'chase a Gauguin shadow to the South Seas.' Why don't they stay at home and paint the american Negro? he asks. If they want to find romance—mystical romance, or 'black mysticism,' here it is at their doors.

'The skin colors brown, golden yellow, reddish brown, purple brown. Where the sweat runs down high brown backs the colors come out and dance before the eyes. . . . Flash that up, you silly painters . . . song-tones in words, music in words—in colors too.'

§ 15. *The Black Communism of Anderson.*

I will now quote successively those passages in *Dark Laughter* that contain the gist of Anderson's whitmanesque message of Black and White brother-

hood, or rather of Black-worship, and religious submission to the Black-idea, as being a more *primitive*
one than the White.

The hero is going down the Mississippi. The following passages represent the cogitations of this
figure (expressing, presumably, many of the ideas
peculiar to Mr. Anderson), upon those american
problems connected with race.

'People talked with a slow drawling speech,
niggers were hoeing cotton, other niggers fished
for catfish in the river.

'The niggers were something for Bruce to look
at, think about. So many black men slowly
growing brown. Then would come the light
brown, the velvet browns, Caucasian features.
The brown woman tending up to the job—getting
the race lighter and lighter. Soft southern nights,
warm dusky nights. Shadows flitting . . . in dusky
roads . . . soft voices laughing, laughing. . . .'

This quotation has its ironical significance: for it
shows the 'noble savage' (as represented by the
american Negro) trying to get a white skin as quickly
as possible, at the same time as the White is beginning to hide his head in shame at the thought that
his is not a black, yellow or brown one.

'Was there such a thing as an American? Perhaps Bruce was the thing himself. He was reck-
less, afraid, bold, shy. . . .

'Could you ever really know . . . a nigger?

'Consciousness of brown men, brown women,
coming more and more into american life—by
that token coming into him, too.

'More willing to come, more avid to come, than any Jew, etc. . . . Standing laughing—coming by the back door—with shuffling feet, a laugh—a dance in the body.

'Facts established would have to be recognized sometime. . . .'

'Thinking of niggers! What sort of business is that? How come? Northern men so often get ugly when they think of niggers, or they get sentimental.[1] Give pity where none is needed. The men and women of the South understand better, maybe. 'Oh, hell, don't get fussy! Let things flow! Let us alone! We'll float!' Brown blood flowing. White blood flowing, deep river flowing.

'A slow dance, music, ship's cotton, corn, coffee. Slow lazy laughter of niggers. Bruce remembered a line he had once seen written by a negro. "Would white poet ever know why my people walk so softly and laugh at sunrise?"'

So : 'silly american painters' chasing 'a Gauguin shadow to the South Seas!' No! 'Across the street . . . a nigger woman of twenty arises at five and stretches her arms. . . . Nigger girl with slender, flexible body.'—That's the stuff! Why go to the South Seas? 'Flash that up, you silly painters. . . . Song-tones . . . in colours.' 'Hot days. Sweet Mama!'

§ 16. *'What ho! Smelling Strangeness.'*

OR let's return to 'that Gauguin'—he is, after all, the goods—though he did go to the South Seas,

[1] Cf. quotation from D. H. Lawrence, p. 174.

whereas for half the money he could have stopped right here in New Orleans, and 'flashed up' just as good a brand of Darkie (if that was all he wanted).— 'Do you remember the night when that Gauguin came home to his little hut and there, in the bed, was the slender brown girl waiting for him? Better read that book. "Noa-Noa," they call it. *Brown mysticism in the walls of a room, in the hair*—of a Frenchman, in the eyes of a brown girl. Noa-Noa. *Do you remember the sense of strangeness?* French painter kneeling on the floor in the darkness, smelling the strangeness. The brown girl smelling the strangeness. Love? What ho! Smelling strangeness.'

Love, What ho! it is indeed: for it *smells strangeness*, which is the essence of romantic love, as of every other form of romance. We here get the full flavour of the clumsy and rather drab exoticism of Mr. Anderson. The 'brown mysticism' of Gauguin's dusky mistresses he wishes to transport into the Mississippi, and create a *Noa-Noa* upon its flood. And Niggerland shall henceforth be their Pacific, for those inland populations that have never seen the sea, and each man be a Gauguin in his own back-yard.

§ 17. *The 'Poetic' Indian.*

THERE is an important feature of the teaching of Mr. Sherwood Anderson with which I am much in sympathy. This he inherits too from Walt Whitman. But it is flatly contradicted by the communism of the rest of his work. I refer to his eloquent opposition to the influences of industrial life—to the killing of life and natural beauty that that entails.

## THE 'POETIC' INDIAN

Part of *Dark Laughter* is devoted to a eulogy of life on the great river, Mississippi, and generally of the lands through which it flows.

'A warm rich land of growth—trees growing rank—weeds and corn growing rank. The whole Middle American Empire—swept by frequent and delicious rains, great forests, prairies on which early spring flowers grow like a carpet—land of many rivers running down to the brown slow strong mother of rivers, land to live in, make love in, dance in. Once the Indians danced there, made feasts there. They threw poems about like seeds on a wind. Names of rivers, names of towns. Ohio! Illinois! Keokuk! Chicago! Illinois! Michigan!'

'New York' and 'Boston,' it is true, might appear intensely romantic to a Blackfoot or a Mohican: and they may have remarked to each other, among their wigwams, sharpening their tomahawks, 'These Whites throw poems about like seeds in the wind! *Boston! Brownsville!* How beautiful!' Still I suppose there is some abstract superiority in the indian names set beside the anglo-saxon ones. I am reminded of Matthew Arnold's contrasting of the place-names for which the 'creeping Saxon' was responsible, and those names originating with the Celts.

'As the saxon names of places, with the pleasant, wholesome smack of the soil in them—Weatherfield, Thaxted, Shalford—are to the celtic names of places, with their penetrating lofty beauty—Velindra, Tyntagel, Carnarvon—so is

the homely realism of german and norse nature to
the fairy-like loveliness of celtic nature.'

So, if Mr. Anderson happens to be of 'celtic'
origin, he can match Carnarvon with Keokuk, Tyntagel with Chicago, and Velindra with Michigan, and
hold his head up once more!

§ 18. *The Mississippi and the Manufacturers.*

BRUCE, the hero of *Dark Laughter*, having torn
himself free from domestic life in Chicago,

'spent nearly two months . . . in getting down
river to New Orleans. . . . Nearly every man
who lived long in the Mississippi Valley had that
notion tucked way in him somewhere. The great
river, lonely and empty now, was, in some queer
way, like a lost river. It had come to represent
the lost youth of Middle America perhaps. Song,
laughter, profanity, the smell of goods, dancing
niggers—life everywhere! Great gaudy boats on
a river, lumber rafts floating down, voices across
the silent nights, song, an empire unloading its
wealth on the face of the waters of a river! . . .
In its youth the Middle West had breathed with
the breathing of a river.

'The factory men were pretty smart, weren't
they? First thing they did when they got the
chance was to choke off the river, take the romance out of commerce. They may not have intended anything of the sort, romance and commerce were just natural enemies. They made the
river as dead as a door-nail with their railroads
and it has been that way ever since.

214

# THE MISSISSIPPI AND THE MANUFACTURERS

'Big river, silent now. Creeping slowly down past mud banks, miserable little towns, the river as powerful as ever, strange as ever, but silent now, forgotten, neglected. A few tugs with strings of barges. No more gaudy boats, profanity, song, gamblers, excitement, life.

'When he was working his way down river, Bruce Dudley had thought that Mark Twain, when he went back to visit the river after the railroads had choked to death the river life, that Mark might have written an epic then. He might have written of song killed, of laughter killed, of men herded into a new age of speed, of factories, of swift, fast-running trains.'

When we in Europe discuss America, we picture it only as this 'soulless' (to use Lawrence's word in another connection) desolation of the Machine Age. It typifies to the European the Robot, Machine-life, in excelsis. We forget, or we have no means of knowing, that the more intelligent American sees this, 'sees through it,' as well as we do; and happens to hate it with far more intensity, sometimes, than is found with us.

Earlier in this essay I have remarked that I was agreeably surprised to find those people I talked to in New York about that very remarkable city (which I was seeing for the first time) expressed nothing but a veiled or open dislike for its famous colossalness. They looked pained or bored if I drew their attention to a particularly beautiful skyscraper. It was like talking to a farmer about the beauty of the scenery. And in american books you meet everywhere the same impatience and contempt for all this commercial display of power, scale and speed. Nowhere in the Old World have I ever met such a thorough aversion for all the things that we regard as typically american, and which the American of the popular imagination is always supposed to be boasting about.

§ 19. *Passages from 'Poor White.'*

THAT Mr. Anderson realizes that in this attitude towards the staggering material achievements of his country, he, and the many Americans of his way of thinking, are rebels against an entire scheme of things—the whole of our 'americanized' civilization, in fact—is clear from what happens in his book, *Poor White.* That is the story of a child of Poor Whites on the Mississippi, who discovers a genius for engineering. His inventions are highly profitable to himself and those with whom he is associated, and the town where he is settled rapidly turns from a village into a big factory town. We have a picture of the struggle between the old order and the new—between the craftsman and handiworker, and the new industrialism.

But eventually Hugh the inventor begins turning against his own mechanical-toys, and even loses his power of inventing these. But by this reaction, Mr. Anderson says, he is still in advance of his fellows. He has become *conscious*; before he had been *unconscious* (that is certainly a step in advance: but does it tally with Mr. Anderson's teaching elsewhere?).

# PASSAGES FROM *POOR WHITE*

'He had been *an unconscious worker, a doer,* and was now becoming something else. The time of the comparatively simple struggle with definite things, with iron and steel, had passed. He fought . . . to understand himself, to relate himself with the life about him. The poor white, son of the defeated dreamer of the river, who had forced himself in advance of his fellows along the road of mechanical development, was still in advance of his fellows of the growing Ohio towns.

'*The struggle he was making was the struggle his fellows of another generation would one and all have to make.* . . .

'There was unconscious defiance of a whole civilization in Hugh's attitude. . . .'

The heroine of the story, Clara, hates her husband's and father's machinery even more than Hugh (as far as we are allowed to follow him) comes to do. There is a sensational scene in which a harness-maker has cut a man's throat for importing machine-made harness into the town, and forcing him to sell it.

'In her mind' (in Clara's) 'the harness-maker had come to stand for all the men and women in the world who were in secret revolt against the absorption of the age in machines and the products of machines. He had stood as a protesting figure against what her father had become.' A little earlier Clara's father, Tom, has turned up, in a state of great excitement, with the first motor car to be seen in that part of the country. He takes his daughter and son-in-law for a drive, Clara sitting behind, and

Hugh beside Tom.   Here are two passages, recounting this event.

'As the daughter sat in the motor listening to the shrill voice of the father, who now talked only of the making of machines and money, that other man talking softly in the moonlight as the horse jogged slowly along the dark road seemed very far away.   All such men seemed very far away. "Everything worth while is very far away," she thought bitterly.   "The machines men are so intent on making have carried them very far from the old sweet things."

'The motor flew along the roads and Tom thought of his old longing to own and drive fast racing horses.   "I used to be half crazy to own fast horses," he shouted to his son-in-law.   "I didn't do it, because owning fast horses meant a waste of money, but it was in my mind all the time.   I wanted to go fast: faster than any one else."   In a kind of ecstasy he gave the motor more gas and shot the speed up to fifty miles an hour.   The hot, summer air, fanned into a violent wind, whistled past his head.   "Where would the damned race horses be now," he called, "where would your Maud S. or your J.I.C. be, trying to catch up with me in this car?"

'Yellow wheat fields and fields of young corn, tall now and in the light breeze that was blowing whispering in the moonlight, flashed past. . . .'

  .    .    .

' "You don't know anything about it, and I don't want you should talk, but there are new things coming to Bidwell," he added.   "When I was in Chicago last month I met a man who has been making rubber buggy and bicycle tires. I'm going in with him and we're going to start a plant for making automobile-tires right in Bidwell. The tire business is bound to be one of the greatest on earth and they ain't no reason why Bidwell shouldn't be the biggest tire center ever known in the world." Although the car now ran quietly, Tom's voice again became shrill. "There'll be hundreds of thousands of cars like this tearing over every road in America," he declared. "Yes, sir, they will; and if I calculate right Bidwell'll be the great tire town of the world." '

§ 20. *The Contradiction between the Communist Emotionality of Mr. Anderson and his impulses to counter the Machine Age.*

IT is plain from the quotations I have given that Mr. Anderson is (whatever the origin of those impulses may be with him) insurgent or reactionary where the great mailed fist of Big Business is concerned—rebellious to all that giant orthodoxy of mercantile collectivism which is pulverizing the life of the contemporary world, in herding people in enormous mechanized masses. Any independent intelligence, standing aside from the two great hostile sects of Capitalism and Communism, must deplore in the latter, side by side with its doctrine of deliverance, the fact that its Promised Land looks too, in the distance, so like the film *Metropolis*.

Mr. Anderson no doubt would be incapable of seizing the fundamental liaison of many of his

favourite ideas with the materialist aspect of the
communist doctrine. Where he bestows upon Clara,
in *Poor White,* a lesbian chum, and makes her re-
spond to her life experience *à la garçonne*; or, again,
where he advertises in *Dark Laughter* a passion, as
a child of six, for his mother (so conforming to the
incest motif of Freud), he is far from realizing, I
should say, where these ideologic borrowings would
lead him, had he the curiosity to track them back
to their true sources. All this is hidden from Mr.
Anderson: but that is not for a moment to say that,
had he the energy or intelligence to track the principal and most picturesque notions by which he has
been influenced back where they most truly belong,
he would not be even better pleased with himself
than now he is. Nor do I say that, swiftly navigat-
ing the broad stream of influences (to which he, in
common with everybody else to-day, has been sub-
jected) up to its fountain head, and finding himself
at last in the company of early Generals of the
Society of Jesus, or Grand Inquisitors, closeted with
the chiefs of the Templars or passing into the shadow
of the Star Chamber, or finding himself at length
face to face with the learned priestly rulers of Eastern theocracies, such for instance as the priests of
Sais, who told Solon that the Greeks were only
ignorant children, he would not be in better intellectual company than ever he has been in the Middle
West. What of course I really mean is that he, himself, would certainly be worse off with those master
minds. But his interests are ours, up to a point,
and it is perhaps as well not to allow Palefaces like
Mr. Anderson to make too many mistakes and to

MR. ANDERSON AND THE MACHINE AGE

arrive at the Melting-pot practically Black. Muddle
and blindness is bad, encountered in the spokesmen
of our race: for if such men as Shaw, Russell, Lawrence and so on here in England and Anderson
amongst the best-known dozen in America are not
our spiritual spokesmen, then who are? Not Sen-
ator Borah or Mr. Churchill, I suppose: nor Dean
Inge nor Rabbi Wise. Once the deep cloud of ignorance and misunderstanding were dispelled, it would
be found that many people with even more enthusiasm would stick to their present beliefs. Others,
however, would abandon them. We should all
know where we were, then, the issues would be stark
and plain, and the argument would move more
rapidly to its conclusion—smoothly, more satisfactorily, to the best of all possible Melting-pots.

So I think that the emotional insurgence of Mr.
Anderson against the conditions of Big Business is
flatly contradicted by his communism. I will repeat
the quotation where he is exclaiming about the
peculiar solidarity of the negro workers.

'The bodies of all the men running up and down
the landing-stage were one body. One could not
be distinguished from another. They were lost
in each other. Could the bodies of people be so
lost in each other?'

The answer of course to that last question (the
exclamations of Mr. Anderson have usually the form
of questions) is 'Yes, they can. It is quite easy for
White Men, as well as Negroes, to become *Mass men*,
"not to be distinguished from one another." Intensive Industrialism is able to achieve that for you

221

whoever the bosses.' But Intensive Industrialism is what Mr. Anderson never ceases to fulminate against. And his reasons for hating it appear to be precisely that it *does* merge people in the way that he exultantly describes the Negro workers as being merged, in one featureless anonymous black organism, like a gigantic centipede. So in the same breath he is gloomy and joyful over the same phenomenon! The black skin appears to have the power of disguising the reality from him. A subsidiary confusion is caused, in this instance, by the fact that the mechanical Negroes are given as a characteristic feature of the free natural life of the Mississippi before the arrival of Industrialism, which put an end to the mechanical trotting Negroes— 'running up and down the landing-stage . . . lost in each other.'

## § 21. *White 'Sentimentality.'*

At the beginning of Section III, I have quoted Mr. D. H. Lawrence, where he says, 'It is almost impossible for the white people to approach the Indian without either sentimentality or dislike.'

And I remarked that Mr. Lawrence showed himself to be a *good White Man* in that respect: for there is a great deal of 'sentimentality' about the Hopi in the books of Mr. Lawrence.

Where the american Negro is concerned it is the same thing with Mr. Sherwood Anderson, although it is a different sort of 'sentimentality.' In any book of his you pick up you will find, wherever Negroes occur, that they are used to score off the

White; or are compared, with considerable 'senti-ment,' very favourably with the White 'Over-lord.'

This invariable attitude on the part of Mr. Ander-son is partly the effect of fashionable *primitivist* doctrine: and it is partly the revolutionary, 'radical,' impulse at work. The Negro is 'kept in his place,' is 'looked down on,' is used as a hireling, and laughed at, by the arrogant Lord of Creation, the White Man. Mr. Anderson has learnt his little 'radical' lesson. So, wherever the Negro occurs, and he occurs fairly often in his books, he is made to take the White down a peg or two. What blissful ignorance of really *dark* realities is displayed by these old-fashioned habits—old-fashioned because they came into existence amongst and were proper to conditions that have passed! There are many duskier things than the big black honest open face of the poor Negro.

§ 22. '*I wish I was a Nigger.*'

I will give a few further illustrations of roman-cing about Negroes. Take, for example, the first story, 'I Want to Know Why,' in *The Triumph of the Egg.* It is a story of the passion for horse-racing—it is, as it happens, a very, very emotional, even, in-deed, a *blubbering* story. It is, in fine, the triumph of the Egg—in the overtaxed soul of Mr. Anderson. Negroes are 'flashed up' here and there.

'Often when I think about it . . . I wish I was a nigger. It's a foolish thing to say . . . I can't help it.'

223

Three other boys and himself run away from home and go to the races.

'We got into Saratoga as I said at night and went to the track. Bildad (a Negro) fed us up. He showed us a place to sleep in hay over a shed and promised to keep still. Niggers are all right about things like that. They won't squeal on you. Often a white man you might meet, when you had run away from home like that, might appear to be all right and give you a quarter or half dollar or something, and then go right and give you away. White men will do that, but not a nigger. You can trust them. They are square with kids. I don't know why.'

I have said in my introduction that I am proposing to you an entirely new system of feeling and thought, a new way of looking at the world in which, since the War, we have been called upon to live. 'I Want to Know Why' is a good thing to exercise your teeth on if you are giving this system a trial.

But let us put under the microscope the two passages just quoted, to start with: afterwards the rest of the story can be associated with our results, derived from the scrutiny of that particular portion.

Mr. Anderson of course is writing to start with in the breathless, unpunctuated jargon of childhood: for he is a little simple child once more, running away from home. (Often in *The Triumph of the Egg* he takes many leaves out of the book of 'Trudy' Stein, it is worth noting, for it is, as I have said, the Triumph of the Egg right enough.) So when he says 'I wish I was a nigger,' we should not be justified in paying much attention to that, if it were not that elsewhere, when no longer the irresponsible truant child, he displays just the same proclivities where Negroes are concerned. He is *always*, in one form or another, 'wishing he was a nigger.' So it *is* 'a foolish thing to say.' It is a foolish thing, all right, and Mr. Anderson, in one way or another, is always saying it.

## § 23. *'The Kid.'*

IN the second passage I have quoted, Bildad, the kind dusky Uncle Tom, with the Dickens tear in the corner of his pathetic rolling benevolent black eye, gives the little runaways lots to eat; and then he bustles off and finds the dear little chaps (in the true Dickens manner) a cosy little hiding place.

'Ah, the good kind Nigger! Would that those hard unsympathetic White Men were as good to "kids" as that! Give me a Nigger every time—if you're a little innocent kid (as I am for the moment, in misty-eyed memory) breaking the hard, cruel, White law, which forbids you to run away from home, and which imposes its disgusting White *discipline* upon you. Ah, if the White Mommer and Pop only could understand! As the Nigger understands! The Child is a thing that requires understanding! He is a wild, rousseauesque thing, a fragment of wild Nature. He hates discipline! He wants to run wild! The Nigger is nearer to Nature: he understands the Child. *Up, the Nigger! Down, the White Mamma!* And especially, *Down the White Papa!*'

That is the andersonian idea. The Nigger and the

Children are kindred souls—both are giggling, emotional—laughing and crying—Children of Nature. '——you know how a nigger can giggle and laugh and say things that make you laugh. A white man can't do it. . . .' (*Triumph of the Egg*, p. 10). Only the adult White is no sport, is *against Nature*! It is he that has invented discipline! It is the White that spoils everything! So, down with discipline! Down with the White! Let Children and Niggers, moist-eyed and hand in hand, run wild and free!

That is the andersonian message: and when we have wiped our eyes and put our handkerchiefs away (still sniffling a little, and still red around the eyes) —if we *ever* do that at all, of course!—let us open our little peepers and see what has been happening to us all. We've been having such a hell of a good time, such a lovely luscious cry, and so much luxurious sob-stuff has been our bath for so long (not only as readers of Anderson, but as readers of so many books), that to be a little inflexible, and on the cold side, will be a change, at least. Suppose we begin to do what—in such a radiant, free and highly emotional world—we should never never do at all: I mean, fall into that beastly condition, so abhorrent to all emancipated, freedom-loving Children of Nature, to all Behaviourists, to all Bergsonians, Gestaltites and Emergent Evolutionists—that condition we call (as it were in mockery of our 'reflexes') 'reflection.' How would that new state of mind affect our view of the above passages in 'I Want to Know Why,' indeed of the whole of that piece?

First, we should undoubtedly say to ourselves that it was a little late in the day to indulge in *Uncle*

*Tom's Cabin* emotions. Things have changed too
much throughout the world for the 'conquering'
White Man to allow himself, without appearing
ridiculous, those sentimental superiorities. It is
even an offence to our Black brothers. On the other
hand, the White Overlord (not being an 'overlord'
at all of course) can no longer strictly speaking afford
the luxury of remaining a 'kid.' That is no good:
the World is no longer his nursery, or happy hunting
ground, so his days of charming Childhood, it should
be recognized by him, are at an end. There are
many people, of course, who are only too anxious to
encourage him to remain a child. On all sides he is
encouraged to remain very, very 'young' and harm-
lessly 'boyish,' not to trouble his little head with
thinking, not to allow any anxiety to come into
his eternally young and divinely irresponsible life.
'Just have a good time: just be a "kid"—we'll do
the rest, we'll look after the world!' his mentors
practically say to him. 'You are so young: much
too young to do anything but enjoy yourself—*at our
expense!* Don't stint yourself! The mortgage will
never have to be paid!' Soothed and flattered,
Little Master Paleface simpers and archly contorts
himself, and turns to the toys provided for him—
more insidious, certainly, than bread and circuses—
by his indulgent guides, philosophers and friends.
Some of his toys are getting very noisy and dangerous. 'Why not have another little War with the
next nursery?' his mentor suggests. 'Just one!'
Little Master Paleface frowns, pouts, and blows
out his chest.

If we were acquainted with these backgrounds—

and I am imagining us in order to represent us as *reflecting*, possessed of such knowledge—the sentimental blandishments of Mr. Anderson, and his Uncle Tom up-to-date, would enable us very quickly to dispose of all traces of our emotion. We should not develop a great power of sympathy for the gleeful alliance of 'the Kid' with 'the Nigger.' The age-war, or more properly the war between the master and pupil, or between father and son, so ably fomented in Paleface society as a part of the revolutionary programme, would not thrill us so very much. We should know, for instance, that if the Nigger helped the insurrectionary 'Kid' against his family, it might conceivably be because the Nigger, although not a bad sort, perhaps, might all the same be rather glad to cause a little anxiety and discomfort to the adult White, who lorded it over him rather brutally. All Bildads, bearing in mind what the circumstances are, must be potential insurgents, and must have some sympathy with revolt in any form. We should know (if we were acquainted with the backgrounds specified above) that the order of the White World was far from perfect, but that it was nevertheless a form of order that should not utterly be allowed to decay before we reached the Melting-pot; that discipline is the enemy of the 'good time,' certainly, whether it is discipline in a family, army, school, or state: but that no good time, even, ever was secured for very long by a studied neglect of disgusting disciplines. All these elementary, universal, homely truths, from which there is no escape for successful life, and which are the first conditions of organization or 'mind,' as opposed to chaos or 'sensation,' we are supposing that we possess as a matter of course. Then, certainly, after a good dickensian cry over the kind loyal Black Man, shielding and caring for the runaway 'kid,' Mr. Anderson's eloquent appeals to our hearts and senses would begin to give place to something disagreeable and mathematical, almost like the meter of a taxi.

There is, of course, some exaggeration in this analysis: but it is only by over-stressing the significance of such material that the true meaning of all such writing can be laid bare for the inattentive reader. The reader must be induced somehow to contract the habit of reading between the lines. That is really the way to read such stuff, if you must read it (and masses of people do), the way I have just been reading it for you. Even if sometimes you are mistaken in your enthusiastic detective activity, that is better than always accepting blindly, as purposeless 'entertainment,' what so often *is* saturated with some political philosophy or other—even unknown to its author and even (if a good philosophy) interpreted, it may be, upside down.

What Mr. Anderson *wants to know why* about is, however, not anything to do with White and Black questions, nor is it part of the 'Fathers-and-sons,' the Kid *versus* Dad, revolutionary situation. It is the 'sex-war,' that other fundamental sub-'war,' that provides the material for the main theme of the story. And the homo-sexual sensibility is, I think, brought in to reinforce this part of the business.

When the runaway 'kid' gets home, 'Mother jawed and cried, but Pop didn't say much.' Pop was perhaps a rather cowed type of Poor White, or perhaps he had no desire to add the burdens of the *Kid—Pop* war to those of the sex-war of *Man—Wife.* 'I told everything we done except one thing. I did and saw that alone. That's what I'm writing about.'—It is about that he 'wants to know why.'

What happened apparently was that 'the Kid' (who was sixteen) fell in love with a trainer called Jerry Tilford. But prior to his infatuation for Mr. Tilford, he evidently fell head over ears in love with the horse trained by Tilford—'Sunstreak.'

> 'There isn't anything as sweet as that horse. . . . I was standing looking at that horse and aching. In some way, I can't tell how, I knew just how Sunstreak felt inside . . . he was just a raging torrent inside. . . . I could just in a way see right inside him. He was going to do some awful running and I knew it . . . I knew it and Jerry Tilford his trainer knew.'

So we arrive at his yearning emotions as regards the trainer. Anything that interests him 'the Kid' seems to translate immediately into the hot, 'aching' terms of sexual love. He has a permanent lump in his throat, 'the Kid.' 'If my throat hurts and it's hard for me to swallow,' he tells us, why then the horse he has these sensations about is a good horse. It is the same more or less about trainers. A good trainer, or I suppose a kind Nigger, affects him in the same way. It would require the tearful art of a Charlie Chaplin to give us a proper version of this 'Kid'; only Charlie would have to throw in a 'Nancy' touch to get the emotional impact required.

'I knew it and Jerry Tilford, his trainer, knew.
I looked up and then that man and I looked into
each other's eyes.  Something happened to me.
I guess I loved the man as much as I did the horse
because he knew that I knew. . . . I cried and
Jerry Tilford had a shine in his eyes.'

The orgasm continues: but the point of 'the
Kid's' story lies in the fact that the orgasm is transferred from the horse to the trainer.  'I watched the
race calm. . . .' You expect the crisis of the orgasm
to occur, of course, when Sunstreak passes the win-
ning post.  But nothing of the sort happens.  All
is suddenly 'calm.'  That is the author's little surprise.

'A funny thing had happened to me.  I was
thinking about Jerry Tilford, the trainer . . . all
through the race.  I liked him that afternoon
even more than I ever liked my own father.  I
almost forgot the horses thinking that way about
him. . . . It was the first time I ever felt for a
man like that.'

So Jerry Tilford is his first love.—The race-meet-
ing ends.—But 'the Kid's' passion for Jerry Tilford
does not die down.

'After the race that night I cut out from Tom
and Hanley and Henry.  I wanted to be by myself and I wanted to be near Jerry Tilford if I could
work it. . . . I wanted to be as near Jerry as I
could.  I felt close to him. . . . I was just lone-
some to see Jerry, like wanting to see your own
father at night when you are a young kid.'

PALEFACE

'The Kid' wanders about, tracks Jerry to a farm-house. He drives up with some other men. The Kid watches him enter, 'aching,' of course. But then come the 'fantods.'


§ 24. *The Fantods.*

'I crept up along a fence and looked through a window and saw. It's what gives me the fantods. I can't make it out.'

This is where the great *Why?* comes in. For the farmhouse was a brothel, it seems. And Jerry, his idol, proceeds to defile himself with *women*, who arouse in 'the Kid' the intensest and most correct aversion.

'The women in the house were all ugly, mean-looking women, not nice to look at or be near. . . . I saw everything plain. . . . The women had on loose dresses and sat around in chairs. The men came in and sat on the women's laps.'

And then, of course, Jerry behaves in a way that makes 'the Kid' hate him. 'His eyes began to shine,' and 'then he went and kissed that woman and I crept away.'

While watching all this through the window his emotions are of a Negro demonstrativeness. 'I began to hate that man. I wanted to scream and rush in the room and kill him. I never had such a feeling before. I was so mad clean through that I cried.'

Everything ends in tears, sooner or later. Everything 'ends in a whimper.' He creeps away and he is so upset that he never goes to a racecourse again.

The paroxysms of the over-feminine 'Kid' do, no doubt, represent an important element in the White American nature: the sort of thing that has made it easy to fling it into jazz, that caused the gigantic farce of the lying in state of Valentino, and the rest of the things that give the European his idea of the american hysteria. If there were nothing but that, the noble Red Man, with his legendary calm aloofness, his faultless self-discipline and self-reliance, so that a solitary Brave was as much to be feared as a troop, would indeed be as superior to the White as he is to the jigging, laughing and crying, yapping and baaing, average Negro.


§ 25. *'Uncas' and the Noble Redskin.*

I WILL conclude this scrutiny of the material in which the political message of Mr. Sherwood Anderson is imbedded with some quotations from *A Story-Teller's Story.*

'Uncas—"Le Cerf Agile" . . . has an idea. Drawing a line in the snow, he stands some fifty feet from the largest of the trees in the grove and hurls the hatchet through the air. What a determined fellow! I am of the paleface race myself and shall always depend for my execution upon *la longue carabine*, but Uncas is of another breed.'

These passages are from the account of the childhood of the Story-teller, and this first chapter of his autobiography is full of the dramatization of the early pioneering life that lay just behind his brothers and himself. This sensitive incubation period is full of Indian-worship, and a long preoccupation with the primitive ideal. 'Uncas' is his brother.

'There is something direct, brutal and fine in the nature of Uncas. It is not quite an accident that in our games he is always the Indian while I am the despised White, the Paleface. It is permitted me to heal my misfortune a little by being not a storekeeper or a fur-trader, but that man nearest the Indian's nature of all the Palefaces who ever lived on our continent, "La Longue Carabine"; but I cannot be an Indian and least of all an Indian of the tribe of the Delawares. I am not persistent, patient and determined enough. As for Uncas, one may coax and wheedle him along any road, and I am always clinging to that slight sense of leadership that my additional fifteen months of living gives me, by coaxing and wheedling, but one may not drive Uncas. To attempt driving him is but to arouse a stubbornness and obstinacy that is limitless. Having told a lie to mother or father, he will stick to the lie to the death, while I—well, perhaps there is in me something of the dog-like, the squaw-man, the Paleface. . . .' (*A Story-teller's Story*, p. 19).

Here you get the contrast that is much older and more fundamental than the Negro question—for the American has always had more contempt than anything else for the 'Nigger'—or than the sort of problems raised by Mr. D. H. Lawrence in his *Mornings in Mexico*. *It is the memory of the values that were suddenly confronted when the first White christian colonists found themselves face to face with the pagan Redskin.* The White defeated the Redskin, and even rapidly exterminated him. But it was with a bad conscience. He knew that he had been able to do it only because he possessed his 'longue carabine.' The noble vigour, unbreakable resolution, high code of honour, of these physically splendid races, picked off, thinned out and finally destroyed by his silly little pop-gun, and in the last stages by his fire-water, left an ineffaceable impression upon the mind of the White settler, which can be best defined, perhaps, as a sense of having stolen a march upon Nature, or having sinned against Nature, as the puritan conscience would probably think of it.

§ 26. *Machines* versus *Men*.

THESE red 'savages,' the Whites always have felt, were *noble* 'savages' (and so they have always celebrated them), and not an ignoble, slothful, shambling, jazzing, laughing-and-crying, sort of big black baby, with silly, rolling eyes, and big characterless lips, as the average 'Nigger' is apt too much to be. To mention the 'Nigger' in the same breath as the Redskin would be absurd. They were of different clay. And the proud and splendid races possessing these difficultly-acquired qualities, who inhabited the northern american continent when they arrived, and who contemptuously called them 'Palefaces,' 'squaw-men,' and so forth—these races had been wiped out not by *them*, but by civilization—by european science and its deadly weapons. These *machines* had killed those *men*. Was it right that these *machines* should kill those *people*—and such splendid people, too?

This was the first lesson of the White in the great issue that later on was to occupy such a central position in his life—namely, of Man *versus* the Machine. The Redskin provided the first illustration. In that first picture the White was on the side of the Machine. With his machinery he drove back and then destroyed the Redskin. Later, all human enemies apparently disposed of, the struggle began between the all-conquering Machine and himself. It looked as though his fate might be the same as that of the Redskin. To-day that is the problem more than ever. But it is never stated very clearly, because all the organization of publicity is in the hands of the owners of the Machines. Here and there such writers as Anderson however give expression to it.

## § 27. *Henry Ford and the 'Poor White.'*

I HAVE given above a fair account, I believe, of what must be at the bottom of the anglo-saxon mind of America, though of course that would not at all apply to the mind of a recent german or russian immigrant. It is strange that Henry Ford, who is, I daresay, the greatest living American, should stand for all that is most *mechanical* in the world and at the same time should have almost identically the point of view of Mr. Sherwood Anderson as regards the modern city-life of the Machine Age, and attempt to revive, side by side with, and away from, his vast commercial plants, the atmosphere of the early colonist days in America.

# HENRY FORD AND THE 'POOR WHITE'

Where Ford is discussing, in one of his pronouncements, the criticisms brought against him for 'mechanizing human beings' in his factories, he says, with admirable candour, that he himself could not lead the life of one of his herd of workmen. But he points out that the humanitarian is wasting his sympathy who wrings his hands over the condition of these men; for *that*—Ford says—is the sort of life that brings the greatest happiness to the greatest number. Most men *wish* to be machines. They want to feed and sleep—and mechanical work is a sort of sleep—and be told what to do, nothing more. Food, just enough exercise for health, rest and sleep, a constant supply of new toys, and, above all, no responsibility—that is the idea.

But Ford is truly humane and public-spirited, in the traditional european sense, and if others would agree to follow suit, he would empty his factories to-morrow, I expect, break up his plant, and return to the 'simple life' with great satisfaction. That is where he differs from most of his fellow-magnates. He is a superman of the Machine Age, but he is still, paradoxically, a 'creature of spirit.' He is not himself a machine.

# CONCLUSION

## § 1. *The White Machine and its Complexes.*

IT was originally my intention, as an excursus to this preliminary essay, to provide a carefully sifted list of the great group of 'complexes' carried about by the average White Man to-day. (I use the word 'complexes' as that will convey to the general reader what is meant, and it also particularly recommends itself, since it is precisely Freud and his assistants, who, along with the idiotic word, have supplied the idiotic thing—have helped in short to build up the full Idiot, as he is emerging today.)

It would be necessary, of course, to overhaul this list every six months, as new material arrives by every post. But the main lines could now be definitely established.

I should have grouped these complexes under their specific headings. There would be, for instance, the 'husband' complex (virility-motif); age complex (A. young, B. old, variety); sex complex (shamanistic variety, sentimental frothing capitulation, etc.—the bastard-american negritic hysteria of 'I Want to Know Why'); infantilism (the desire to remain in sheltered tutelage, refusal of responsibility), and so on. With each I should have provided a complete definition, and a set of concrete illustrations, of the fool-proof sort. But as this would have greatly extended the length of my essay, it was necessary to abandon that part of the evidence.

## THE WHITE MACHINE AND ITS COMPLEXES

As the White spirit shrinks, oppressed under its burden of war, business insecurity, blood-tax, domestic interference, domestic disunion, constant threat of revolutionary cataclysm, anti-cataclysm, and so forth, its very position of world-mastery, racial advantage and prestige, is inclined to become a mockery and burden to it. Everywhere to-day the White European (both as a European and also among the great White colonies and nations) is profoundly uneasy, and looks apprehensively behind him at all moments, conscious of a watchful presence at his back, or somewhere concealed in his neighbourhood, which he does not understand. *Dark Laughter* of the hidden watching negro servants is a typical concrete expression of this uneasiness: evidently, when masters become obsessed with their servants, they are then only masters in name. But this threatening something to whose presence I refer is, of course, in a different category of terror and menace from the fairly harmless concrete Negro. Meanwhile inside himself (there he never looks, though it is, of course, there that he should direct the most objective glance that he can muster), the ferment of the intellectualist disease goes on, and 'complex' after 'complex' is introduced, attacks some mortal centre of life and vitality, and a further portion of the White civilized soul is disintegrated: a further stagger, hop or shamble is given to the White machine.

### § 2. '*Inferiority*,' *and withdrawal* '*Back to Nature.*'

So, in the books that we have been considering, where the White Man is confronted by the Black,

239

the Red or the Brown, he now feels inside himself a novel sensation of *inferiority*. He has, in short, an 'inferiority complex' where every non-White, or simply alien personality or consciousness, is concerned. Especially is it in his capacity of *civilized* (as opposed to *primitive*, 'savage,' 'animal') that he has been taught to feel *inferior*.

The trick of this inferiority could all be laid bare by any inquiring person who took the trouble to examine, not the purely curative doctrine of Dr. Freud, but his philosophical, literary, sociological teaching, and its psychological ramifications throughout our society. There are many factors beside Freud: but Psychoanalysis is in itself quite adequate.

The trick of the *inferiority complex* that we have been approaching, via creative fiction, is to be sought in a certain belief that has been imposed gradually upon the White Consciousness, during forty or fifty years, namely, a belief (it reduces itself to that) that man *cannot* 'progress' beyond the savage or the animal: that when he tries to (as the White European has done, as the Hellene did), he becomes in the mass ineffective and ridiculous: therefore, that the sooner he turns about, and retraces his steps until he is once more like the Huns of Attila, or any community whose main business in life is to 'smite hip and thigh' some other rival community—or like the plain unvarnished man-eating tiger, or the wild boar, the better.

This direction of thought, and with the greatest definition this purpose is visible, has moulded all those schools of fiction, or fancy, specimens of which (from the pages of Mr. Lawrence and Mr. Anderson)

I have given in evidence. The particular he-man-ism of Pound is cut from the same stuff (cf. *The Goodly Fere* of Pound, with the sentimental-militant interpretation of Christ).

All through the range of his complexes the con-temporary White Man can be observed at the same occupation, consisting everywhere in a *reversal* and a *return*. For instance, as *an adult* he looks back at *the child,* and he is taught to say in his heart that the child is a 'better man,' so to speak, than he is. Therefore he seeks to become as infantile as possible, and to approximate, as far as may be, to the infan-tile condition. By the Bergson school of thought he has been taught to regard *intuition* (the 'intuition of the Woman,' for example, contrasted with 'the mere logic of the Man') as superior to Intellect. So he looks *back* towards that feminine chaos, from which the masculine principles have differentiated themselves, as more perfect. As the Child is more perfect than, and the conditions of its life more desirable than those of the Man, so the mind of the Woman is more perfect than, and the lot of the Woman—in league with or immersed in Nature—more to be desired than the lot of the Man. So the contemporary man has grown to desire to be a woman, and has taken obvious steps to effect this transformation (cf. pages on shamanistic cult, *Art of Being Ruled*). Then Power or Wealth has been re-presented as not only evil in itself, but not at all to be desired (cf. the 'higher type' of collective man of communism, according to René Fülöp-Miller). And so on through all the series of *backward*-cults, from primitivism or naturalism, to fairyhood.

## § 3. *The Revolutionary Rock-drill and the Laws of Time.*

As people stand and watch the rock-drill at work in the street, so they watch the engine of political destruction at work, asking themselves stupidly what it is all about. Why is all this going forward in our midst in this very strange and open manner? There is something here I don't understand! It is as though the authorities had sent the 'revolutionary' drill, under an armed escort, to break up the public thoroughfare. It's very odd!—I suppose my brain is not able to grasp these new ideas! whispers poor fuddled Mr. Everyman to himself, apprehensively. He perhaps looks round guiltily, to see if his astonishment has been observed.

If one of these puzzled, staring members of the great Public consulted Spengler, that celebrated philosopher would reply, 'Well, according to the time-table of the best chronological philosophy (a time-table as absolute as that of solar eclipses—I have reduced it all to a very orderly and predictable scheme indeed), according to that time-table White Civilization is now virtually at an end. The various White Governments, realizing this, have directed various groups of "social workers" (as you see) to come and break up the White World with that up-to-date psychological equipment you perceive them handling with so much adroitness. Why they use that rather violent and noisy "cataclysmic" rock-drill is because, if they didn't do that, it would take a very long time to break up the firmly cemented White World (lots of money and energy was spent on cementing it, you see, and in making it solid and resistent), *and then we should all be behind the Time-table!* The various governments, as it is, are exceedingly concerned at the length of time it takes to break up any specific bit of civilization. They had not realized how tough their civilization was.'

'But why do the Western governments want to smash up their own property, papa?' you can hear the puzzled Plain Man (making his little eyes and mouth three round O's) inquire of the portentous Professor.

'Because, my little man,' Herr Spengler would reply severely, 'because they *know* they're behind-hand. They would never do anything that might result in my Time-table being contradicted or disproved. They will not risk—never fear!—offending *Time!* Not *Time!* You understand? When you little Plain Men say 'Time is money,' that is sacrilege. *Everything*—not only money—is Time.'

The Man in the Street would be no wiser than he was before, but he would be considerably impressed and frightened. A vast shadow across the sky, labelled *Zeitgeist*, would dimly emerge for him, the god of the rock-drill, a sort of scientific god. When next he saw the engines of upheaval and chaos at work, he would take good care to ask no questions! He would hurry on, trying to look as much as possible like Brer Rabbit; or else like a little innocent Child, 'mindless' and irresponsible, slightly moron-esque—as small and a hundred times as harmless as a fly.

## § 4. *The 'Jump' from Noa-Noa to Class-War.*

WHAT has 'primitivism' in art (taking Gauguin as a model of primitivist thought) got to do with the orthodox revolutionary doctrine of the Mass man, you may ask. That 'jump' is not a very long or difficult one, but it may be that some readers are not sufficiently trained, or have not sufficient political experience, to make it. So I will state very briefly how these things are connected.

All war is compelled to be anti-progressist in the first place; it has to deny not only the notion of 'progress,' but also of humanity itself, as a privileged classification or principle of action. Every Western government has now accepted all that the new conditions of gas and aerial warfare entail. No future belligerent will be able to make use of a propaganda campaign about 'atrocities,' as was the case in the last war : in advance every form of 'atrocity' is taken for granted. That is an entirely new situation in the civilized european world. It imposes a formidable change of attitude upon any civilized government taking up arms today. The first thing on the declaration of war that all the air-squadrons of those governments engaged would have to do would be to go and bomb and murder the sleeping citizens of the nation on whom war had been declared. The method of murder and poison, only upon a vast scale, which formerly was recognized as the peculiar province of Renaissance Italy and actually the monopoly of the Borgias, is imposed upon us by the development of our machinery of destruction.

But the marxian doctrine of 'class-war' is after all

war : and it is impossible for revolutionary method not to keep pace with its militarist opponent. So you get most communists committed to the same anti-humane train of thought as the militarist. And further it is essential for people engaged in preparing for such events to instil into the Public a philosophy which must be 'ruthless,' materialist and mechanical. And so a philosophy must ensue that is a contradiction of commonsense, and it will be quite unlike any other popular philosophy that has ever existed. For here with our rapidly-evolving machines of destruction at our sides we are in a different position to any former men.

The philosophy required will run generally as follows: The tiger is 'ruthless'; the Borneo headhunter used to hunt a man's head as we go out with a butterfly net: *those* are the true models for you, Mr. Citizen! To the 'Tiger burning bright' the political propagandist points enthusiastically: about that apocalyptic beast there is no nonsense, he is 'frankly an animal,' without any sentimental squeamishness, he frankly enjoys the salts he finds in the human blood he taps; as he leaps upon his human prey, and squashes the entrails out of it, he 'thinks' of nothing, he is a machine that *acts*. That is what poor little Mr. Citizen must do when the time comes. And the time is not far off, he is warned: and so with the class-war and the little communist.

No room at all is left for either (1) the chivalry of earlier nationalist war, nor for (2) the sort of humanitarian socialism of Fourier or Saint-Simon, or for that matter for the fabianism in which the very genial and benevolent **Mr. George Bernard Shaw** was nourished.

But people do not believe in the alleged motives for wars any more today, and they are uncertain as to the benefits of revolutions. Henceforth then all those forms of organized violence must be gone into to some extent against human reason; they are henceforth motiveless, and hence mad. That is why the fever and delirium is essential, in those masses who are to participate in them. Organized mechanized violence must be made to assume the inscrutable face of a *necessity*—a necessity of *Nature*, not of man—man, indeed, must be carefully kept out of the picture.

But these same machines, which impose this type of war upon us, and hence also the philosophy that is required by it, in order to make it possible, also take us farther and farther away, in our everyday life, from 'savagery,' or primitive conditions. The petrol engine and rapidly evolving transport facilities of all sorts, along with wireless and the cinema, make nationalism more unreal and unplausible every day. This is another desperate feature of the matter (from the point of view of the promoter of violence) that requires a desperate (philosophic) remedy. The ordered systematic, sensible atmosphere of our everyday life again renders men recalcitrant to programmes of primitive violence. That is why violence today has to introduce itself *à la Borgia*. A propagandist religion of violence and 'action,' that everywhere takes the form of a *return to Nature* cult, in one form or another, is born of these necessities.

§ 5. *How all Backward Steps have to be represented
as Forward Steps.*

ALL this involves a *backward* step, then. From
any standpoint at all that you care to adopt, except
that of a mystical surrender of life altogether, such
violence as is now involved in war must appear to
the eye of reason as retrograde.

And here is the key to the form of a great deal of
contemporary work in every field of activity. *The
backward step has to be represented as a forward step.*
'Progress,' it is true, as a notion, must be violently
attacked and discredited: but at the same time it
would be impossible to persuade people to do anything without some sort of idea of 'progress' or
betterment. So, with an ill grace, 'progressist'
imagery and inducements have got to be used. As
a sister paradox to this, an extreme primitivism has
to be preached, yet all the reality of what is truly
*primitive*, chronologically, has to be removed from
the pictures employed as baits and advertisements.

There is a very hasty sketch of *political primitivism*, as it could be called. It is not difficult to see
how beautifully it agrees with the artistic primitivism of Mr. D. H. Lawrence—with aztec blood-sacrifices, mystical and savage abandonments of the self,
abstract sex-rage, etc., or Mr. Sherwood Anderson's
more muddled and less up-to-date primitivist bag of
tricks. And, in a general way, how useful *art* is, in
a philosophy that *must*, as its first condition, be
*motiveless*.

As to the reason for my interest in these tolstoyan
problems of War and Peace, it is not, of course,

247

humanitarian. You need go no further than the very practical and unsentimental fact, or facts, of the most vital interests of an artist being ruined by orgies of violence and 'action,' to understand my attitude, if you look for personal motive in it. It takes a long time without interruption to do anything worth doing in an art or science, and that (apart from the fact that it is a philosophy for brutes and the most complete 'morons,' as they are called, only) the accursed philosophy we are discussing denies us. You could not describe such opinions as 'selfish,' seeing that the interests represented are identical with everybody else's in this respect, except those of such as make money or acquire power by means of wars of all sorts.

## § 6. *A Working Definition of the 'Sentimental.'*

In my analysis of the primitivism of Messrs. Lawrence and Anderson, especially with regard to their attitude to the Negro or Indian, I point out how in both cases they were careful to accuse all other people who had ever approached Blacks or Indians of being 'sentimental towards,' or else full of hatred for *those coloured aliens*. It seems plain to me that this was a step, merely, to protect themselves against an accusation that they realize they have deserved.

It will be useful, however, to get some meaning into the tag 'sentimental' before we leave it.

*Any idea should be regarded as 'sentimental' that is not taken to its ultimate conclusion.* I propose that as a working definition of 'sentimentality.'

DEFINITION OF THE 'SENTIMENTAL'

What is the 'ultimate conclusion' of anything? you could object.   But that evocation of the distant metaphysical limit has nothing to do with a working definition: we wish for a definition that will take us, not out of sight, but to the limits of our horizon only.

Why I regard the spirit of the works of Mr. Anderson and of Mr. Lawrence as sentimental, is because it indulges in a series of emotions that, if persevered in by the Public they are intended to influence, would cancel themselves.   I regard Mr. Anderson as more sentimental than Mr. Lawrence, because I do not think he suspects what the real issues are at all; whereas I daresay Mr. Lawrence knows to some extent, though just as he was in the first instance a little vague as to where the ideas he used came from, he probably is not over clear as to whither they are bound, or what their affiliations are.   Alternatively, if both Mr. Anderson and Mr. Lawrence see these conclusions with extreme clearness, then they are deliberately employing, at least, the machinery of sentimentality.   But I think they both use it too naturally for it not to be native to them.


§ 7.  *Every Age has been 'a Machine Age.'*

THE further investigation of those questions that have specifically to do with the machine, with an adumbration of what our attitude should be with regard to the machine, must be left to a later stage of this essay.   In order to give some completeness to this first published part I will, however, make a few remarks before leaving the subject.

The hideous condition of our world is often attributed to 'dark' agencies, willing its overthrow. But there have always been such devils incarnate—it goes without saying that there are such evil agencies —'dark' influences of every sort are certain at all moments to be at work. That alone would not account for the unique position of universal danger and disorganization in which we find ourselves all round the globe. It is obviously to its mechanical instrument, not to the human will itself, that we must look. Without White Science and the terrible power of its engines, such evil people as always abound would be relatively harmless.

How we might dispense with the Machine, or, rather, use it differently, can perhaps be suggested by a brief consideration of the mechanical, or geometric, as it appears in art.

Many attempts have been made to associate art with the triumph of the Machine Age. The question, 'Are machines beautiful in themselves?' has been asked for many years now. What people usually neglect to notice is that all the most splendid plastic and pictorial art is in a very strict sense geometric. *Every age has been a Machine Age.* At least you can say that as far as art is concerned, and as far as the machine is the application of geometric principles.

An alaskan totem-pole, a Solomon Island canoe, a siamese or indian temple, is *a machine*, inasmuch as it is, in its concatenated parts, composed of very mechanically definite units, and is built up according to a rigid geometric plan. The bunch of cylinders of a petrol engine has very much the same structural appeal as a totem-pole or the column of a mayan divinity. Engravings of such machinery have something even of the æsthetic appeal of the latter.

So, in the field of art, there is nothing novel in machinery. All primitive people have proved themselves a sort of æsthetic engineers. So, in a sense, a great suspension bridge, or a modern factory building—or a turbine engine—is only reintroducing into our life an element which the most ancient art supremely possessed, but which has been absent in european art, and which existed nowhere in european life to any great extent, until the industrial age.

Life itself, in all its forms, has always possessed this, however. The insect and plant worlds, much more than the animal world, have always carried their structure outside, as it were, and thrust it upon the eye. The insect world could be truly said to be a Machine World, much more than our age, as yet, is a Machine Age.

The idea that plastic and graphic art is a soft, indefinite, fluffy or vague sort of thing, is more than a victorian prejudice. It is almost a european prejudice. Plastic or graphic art is, in fact, nothing of the sort: it is essentially a geometric thing, a thing of structure. But with european art *the structure*, the geometric basis of beauty, has always tended to be covered up, hidden away (and so lost very often), more than is the case with the great æsthetic systems of the East. The hellenic naturalism, the result of the greek scientific bias, has, as I see it, resulted in Europe in an art which, except in the case of a few individuals of very great genius, has been so inferior to the art of China, for instance, that it could almost be said that the European had never understood the secrets of the pure eye at all. It is for that reason that I have said elsewhere that I consider this century has to its credit more art of the best kind than all the other centuries of european art put together, except the age of the Renaissance. This is, no doubt, partly due to the jewish influence, partly to the fact that specimens of the art of the East and of the antiquity of the so-called Ancient East, have become available to the European. (The gothic naturalism, in its severer moments, produced a very great art: but the general effect of the gothic buildings, according to the standard I am advancing, is one of a cloudy, not truly plastic, naturalism, that makes it not a thing of the eye, but of the 'musical' soul—in Spengler's sense.)

§ 8. *What is 'the West' ?*

THERE is a belief, or prejudice, that you cannot be a good plastic artist and at the same time 'a good European.' It would be an important step in the reform and rejuvenation of our beliefs if we could overcome such prejudices. The appreciation of the formal beauties of mexican pottery, for instance, does not in any way involve enthusiasm for mexican gods, though I daresay the Aztecs themselves would scarcely recognize Mr. Lawrence's account of their beliefs. You could 'flash up' for Mr. Sherwood Anderson the perspiring black back of a Negro without wishing necessarily to share Bildad's lodging, marry his sister or daughter, or embrace his beliefs or habits. You could use the colours and forms of a half-dozen magnificent beetles without becoming an insect; you could use the shape of a grasshopper in an arabesque without taking to hopping, just as you could admire the shawl of a Hopi without wishing to be a Hopi; you could make use of the white expanse of an icepack for your picture without yearning to live the life of an Esquimau. These few illustrations will, I hope, be of assistance in bringing out this part of my argument, which is a matter of some importance for what we have been mainly discussing.

§ 9. *The Intellect 'Solidifies.'* (*The Arguments advanced here in their relation to the Thomist Position.*)

THERE is a similar confusion to the above which, since it has a good deal of bearing on what I everywhere have to say, I will attempt to dispel in passing, as well as using it to confirm the present phase of my argument.

Extreme concreteness and extreme definition is for me a necessity. Hence I find myself naturally aligned today, to some extent, with the philosophers of the catholic revival. Against the mysticism of the mathematician I find myself with Bishop Berkeley (though, of course, he is claimed by the enemies of the concrete, strangely enough): I am on the side of commonsense, as against abstraction, as was Berkeley, and as are today the thomist thinkers (though the militant neo-thomist would repudiate any association of their doctrine with that of the great irish idealist): and my position, inasmuch as it causes me to oppose on all issues 'the romantic,' comes under the heading 'classical.'

To show you how this must come about I will quote a passage from a book which I have just obtained, *L'Intellectualisme de Saint Thomas*, by Père Pierre Rousselot, S.J. He is enumerating the charges usually brought against the thomist 'intellectualism.'

'On reproche à l'intellectualisme scolastique d'exténuer et d'abstraire; on lui reproche aussi de "solidifier." Ce nouveau grief, qui pourrait sembler, au premier abord, s'accorder mal avec le premier, n'en est, au contraire, qu'une expression plus adéquate. Abstraire, c'est mépriser le fluent et postuler la permanence; c'est donc cristalliser ce qui se répand, concentrer le diffus, glacer ce qui coule; c'est *solidifier*.'

Neglecting here the particular significance given to the term 'abstraction' by Father Rousselot, it will be evident that what is laid to the charge of scholasticism, in this account, could also be levelled at what I say: or rather I, precisely, would claim the possession of all these characteristics that are here catalogued as crimes. To *solidify, to make concrete, to give definition to*—that is my profession: to 'despise the fluid' (mépriser le fluent) and 'to postulate permanence' (postuler la permanence); to crystallize that which (otherwise) flows away, to concentrate the diffuse, to turn to ice that which is liquid and mercurial—that certainly describes my occupation, and the tendency of all that I think.

That is why I range myself, in some sense, with the modern scholastic teachers.

This does not, however, at all mean that I share their historical prejudices, any more than it means that I share their dogmas. I do neither, in fact. 'Classical' is for me *anything* which is nobly defined and exact, as opposed to that which is fluid—of the Flux—without outline, romantically 'dark,' vague, 'mysterious,' stormy, uncertain. The hellenic age has no monopoly of those qualities generally catalogued as 'classical'; so, according to me, the term 'classical' is used in much too restricted, historical, a sense; in a word, too historically.

§ 10. *The Necessity for a New Conception of 'the West,' and of 'the Classical.'*

THE opposition, as it is understood here, is not between the Roman Cult and Aristotle on the one hand, and the 'modernist' disorder of Nineteenth Century 'romantic,' 'revolutionary,' european thought, on the other. Rather it is a universal opposition; and the seeds of the naturalist mistakes are certainly to be found precisely in Greece: and I believe we should use the *Classical* Orient (using this distinction in the sense of Guénon) to rescue us at length from that far-reaching tradition.

These are statements of principle only, and I am not able here to make them more than that. Bare as they are for the present, I hope they will have served to foreshadow the conclusions to which the whole foregoing analyses of my essay have been intended to lead. 'European' does not mean for me a fixed historical thing, for it is so little that, in any case. If you tried to make of gaelic chivalry and italian science, german music and norse practical enterprise, *one* thing, that would be a strange monster. Which is demonstrated by Mr. Massis in his *Défense de l'Occident*, where his 'West' is confined to the latin soil. This is an evasion only of the problem. It is just against that separatism as between the different segments of the West that we have most to contend. We should have—should we not?—our local Melting-pot.

It is *a new West*, as it were, that we have to envisage: one that, we may hope, has learnt something from its recent gigantic reverses. For it is only by a fresh effort that the Western World can save itself: it can only become 'the West' at all, in fact, in that way, by an act of further creation.

There are a great many common traditions and memories and a considerable consanguinity: that is the 'material,' at least, for one 'West.' As it is, not only such people as Spengler, but also (but with better motives, and perhaps inevitably) the catholic thinkers and the best of the 'patriots,' insist on regarding the problem historically, in terms of a rigid arrest. 'The West' is for almost all of those a *finished* thing, either over whose decay they gloat, or whose corpse they frantically 'defend.' It never seems to occur to them that the exceedingly novel conditions of life today demand an entirely new conception: in that respect they are firmly on the side of those people who would thrust us back into the medieval chaos and barbarity; at whose hypnotic 'historical' suggestion we would fight all the old european wars over again, like a gigantic cast of Movie supers, and so fill the pockets of these political impresarios.

§ 11. *How the Black and the White might live and let live.*

SINCE I have been discouraging, to the best of my ability, those tendencies (found on all hands) of White capitulation and self-criticism, in the presence of the 'rising tide of Colour,' and especially tendencies to invite the White Man to learn and to adopt the primitive communism (real or imaginary), nihilistic mysticism, and so on, of the primitive Indian or the Black, it is necessary to return to what I have said in the '*Moral Situation*,' and to insist once more upon the fact that it is not the Melting-pot I object to, but the depreciation and damage done to one of the ingredients. I should not welcome a race-war, or a holy war, either of an *ecclesia militans* or any other type, as a substitute for all the other obviously less real or fundamental class-wars that have been arranged for us. That is not my idea. Nothing will certainly ever convince me that a White Man is not more deeply separated from a Negro (race-separation) than a Poor White is separated from a Rich White, or a White Fish-porter from a White Miner (class-separation). But I have used a quotation from the *Vision of Judgment*, by Lord Byron, earlier in this essay to illustrate my attitude:

'His Darkness and his Brightness
Exchanged a greeting of extreme politeness.'

I believe that we cannot, in fact, be polite enough to

all those other kinds of men with whom we are called
upon to pass our time upon the face of this globe.
We should grow more and more polite: but, if possible, see less and less of such other kinds of men
between whom and ourselves there is no practical'
reason for physical merging, nor for spiritual merging, or even very many reasons against both—for
there are such people, too. But why war? If the
White World had kept more to itself and interfered
less with other people, it would have remained politically intact, and no one would have molested it: the
Negro would still be squatting outside a mud-hut on
the banks of the Niger: the Delaware would still be
chasing the buffalo. We could have been another
China. Such aloofness today, as things have turned
out, is an ideal merely, though to me it is not an
ideal. I merely put the matter in that light because
for the average unenlightened Paleface that would
seem much better—he would like to be a powerful
boss rather than a cosmopolitan wage-slave in the
Melting-pot, and his ideas do not soar above some
regional dream. It is always from an exaggeration,
however, on one side or the other, that the actual
comes into existence. Everything real that has
ever happened has come out of a dream, or a Utopia.
We are the Utopia of the amœba. Many of our
lives would seem heaven to the apes.

Are the assumptions at the basis of this discussion
as conducted by me entirely false or merely alarm-
ist? Very many other people, better qualified, in
important ways, than I am, to judge, share my
views. Let me quote one or two.

# LIVE AND LET LIVE

'Several years ago I wrote an essay on "The White Man and his Rivals," in which I pointed out the menace to the domination of the European races from the awakening ambitions of Asia. Till about the beginning of the present century it was taken for granted by almost everybody that the permanent supremacy of the Whites was assured. . . . We had forgotten . . . how entirely that preponderance has been due to superiority in weapons and industrial inventions . . . how formidable the Brown and Yellow races are by their intelligence, their vast numbers, and their untiring industry.

'Much has happened since then to confirm my forecast, and now we have an important and very disquieting book by Mr. Upton Close, an American (*The Revolt of Asia*). . . .

'He has formed the conviction that the suicidal war of 1914-1918 ushered in "the end of the White Man's world." . . . Russia as an asiatic nation entirely alters the balance of power between the two continents. . . . Russia has not ceased to be "imperialist" and aggressive under Communism.'

This is from an article by Dean Inge (*Evening Standard*, May 11th, 1927). In the *Criterion* (August, 1927) Mr. T. S. Eliot, referring approvingly to a 'meditation on the decay of European civilization by Paul Valéry,' writes: 'the Russian Revolution has made men conscious of the position of Western Europe as (in Valéry's words) a small and isolated cape on the western side of the Asiatic Continent.'

While I was writing the rough draft of this essay on

259

the Atlantic the following news item appeared in the
*Daily Mail, Atlantic Edition*, August 15th, 1927 :—

### 'SERIOUS BOLIVIAN REVOLT

#### 'Thousands of Rebels Amok

'La Paz, Bolivia, *Sunday.*

'Five thousand Indians, under Communist in-
fluence, have destroyed the railway at Potosi and
Sucre, and invaded the surrounding districts.
They are murdering any who offer resistance.

'The Bolivian Federal Army are fighting the
savages, and heavy casualties are reported on both
sides.

'The revolt has assumed serious proportions
and the Federal Army cavalry captured several
chiefs and executed them, together with 100 of
their followers.—*Central News.*'

#### 'Whites being Killed

'(*From Our Own Correspondent*)

'Buenos Aires, *Sunday.*

'Reports from La Paz, the Bolivian capital, declare that the Indian rising, under native and
foreign Communist leaders, is most serious. Two
hundred thousand well-armed insurgents are now
holding the railway line.

'Whites are being killed and houses burned.
They appeal to the Government, which admits
the situation is grave.'

The sequel to this was reported (September 8th)
in the *New York Herald.*

# LIVE AND LET LIVE

'BOLIVIAN CHARGES

'RED INTERVENTION

'*(Special to the "Herald")*

'LA PAZ, BOLIVIA, *Wednesday.*

'An alleged proof of Communistic activities in South America, directed and financed by the Third International of Moscow, was presented in Parliament today by the Bolivian Foreign Minister, who read letters signed by Bukharin and Zalkind, prominent Russian leaders of international Communism. The exposure was followed by a vote of confidence in the Government.

'The documents included instructions to "Comrade Martinez, member of the Latin-American section of the Communist International," to proceed to Paris to obtain funds. After this he was to return to Bolivia, open a business house to conceal revolutionary work, and foment Communist revolt among the workers.

'One letter was addressed to "Comrade Dastion, Paris." It introduced Martinez and instructed Dastion to give 1,000,000 francs to the Bolivian agitator out of the propaganda fund.'

I have quoted this to show how the regrettable imperialist and also humanitarian zeal of the Soviet probably is responsible for trouble, often, where Whites and the Coloured peoples are found together, as in South America or South Africa.

The 'open conspiracy,' as Mr. H. G. Wells describes it in *Clissold*, rumbles and drags itself for-

261

ward, spitting fire and brimstone, only very imperfectly subterranean: it is a pity that we should have to admit that the Communist is responsible for these Coloured aggressions, and that it should after all be a Paleface (a russian agitator) who requires our White attention. In any case we know that the Indian, like the Negro, is politically apathetic and would do little himself. But no *wars* are necessary to deal with this: only a strong movement of instructed opinion. The Indian, like the Chinese, is friendly and pacific. Even his *black laughter* is imported. The White teaches him that too. Really our White moral zeal is regrettable! for its *immediate* result can only be, when exercised so clumsily, to provide our bosses with labour cheaper than ours, rather like the feminist revolution. It seems to be playing into the White bosses' hands.

§ 12. *The part Race has always played in Class.*

I WILL quote here, without further comment, a passage from the *Art of Being Ruled*. It will, I think, be of assistance where those questions of race that we have been discussing are concerned. Especially it will throw into relief the great part that race must play in class.

'It may be as well to go for a moment into the relation between class and race in the formation of the former. The *classes* that have been parasitic on other classes have always in the past been *races*. The class-privilege has been a race-privilege. Every white man has until recently been in full possession of a race-privilege where other races of other colours were concerned, which constituted the white man as a *class*. The privilege was never developed to the extent that the achaian race-privilege of the athenian citizen, for example, was. But in a general way it formed part of the consciousness of the white man. Cleanliness was next to godliness, and whiteness was the indispensable condition of cleanliness. So to be a chosen people was to be a white people.

'This class element in *race* expressed itself in the application of the term "lady," for instance, to the most modest citizens of the anglo-saxon race. The *lady* in *char-lady* is a race courtesy-title. It is a class-title that it was possible for her to exact on the score of *race*. This rudimentary fact very few poor whites have understood. They have been inclined to take these small but precious advantages for granted, as indicative of a *real* superiority, not one resulting, as in fact it did, from the success of the organized society to which they belonged. They have confused class with race—somewhat to their undoing as far as the immediate present is concerned.

'Today race and colour are as distinctive features as ever: and it is unlikely in the future that *race* will cease to play its part in the formation of class.'

Since writing this I have visited America and have somewhat modified my views in consequence.

## § 13. *Black Laughter in Russia.*

In these last two sub-sections of my Conclusion I will return to the subject that occupied such a considerable space in my criticism of Anderson and Lawrence. The clumsy adulteries of the dull Whites haunted by the *black laughter* of their Negro servants was the contribution of Anderson. Much more thorough and fundamental, Mr. D. H. Lawrence showed us all creatures whatever, in a position of servitude or defeat, 'taking it out' of their oppressors, successors, or masters, by malevolent laughter and mockery of some sort. Thus the parrots 'take it out of' the little dog, Corasmin, or out of his masters (Rosalino or Mr. Lawrence), with their perpetual imitations. The 'high-pitched negro laughter,' and the shrill voices of the parrots, come out of the same situation.

All these are examples of revenge, in the form of mirth, directed against creatures who are evidently 'bourgeois' and recognized as Top-dogs. But Mr. Fülöp-Miller has his story of Black Laughter of another sort. The Black Laugher no sooner has overthrown the overlord or master and stepped into his shoes, than up goes the Black Laughter against him. He is now the 'boss.' That is, at all events, the story. Here it is.

'For the new ruler of Russia, the Mass man, who came to bring freedom to the earth, in a very short time learned how to use the resources and tricks of tyranny better than the cruellest tsars. . . . No one ventured on any protest, any resistance, however slight; there was not a single open word of censure. . . .

'But all at once it became evident that the subtly constricted apparatus of "mechanized obedience" was not entirely reliable. . . . Some-

264

thing disconcerting happened, due to natural forces without any intervention on the part of the subjects: that unpleasant thing the "soul" which in spite of all mechanization had never been completely eradicated, and was sleeping a sleep that looked like death, suddenly woke up in a smile that lurked on the lips of someone somewhere. With this first smile at the failure of the loudly trumpeted experiments of Bolshevism began the real, the dangerous, counter-revolution, for it worked in secret and gradually attained a sinister power. At first one person smiled, then others in increasing numbers. Soon the smilers united in a mystical organization and then mirth at last expanded into uncontrollable elemental laughter. This first revolt against Bolshevik oppression was the rebellion of the despairing; ever more frequently the hidden wrath became irony, ever louder swelled an uncanny mirth, which threatened to shake the very foundations of the whole structure of State authority. . . .

'. . . in the provinces, among the peasants, laughter went in a triumphal march through the village streets, captured the market-places, and began to press steadily forward towards the official headquarters. . . .

'. . . the dreaded masters of the Red Kremlin themselves trembled at this rising of laughers and jokers. In order to prevent an elemental outburst of all-dissolving universal mirth and to deprive this grave danger of all significance, the authorities hit on the clever idea of having recourse to an old institution, which has always been in-

separably bound up with despotism, the office of
the court fool. By this means the powers effectively took the initiative in this mockery of unpopular institutions and guided it into the right
path. . . .

'. . . the old court fool was transformed into
a circus clown and from the ring amused the
people with his malicious jokes.

'. . . "Bim" and "Bom" were the names of
the two "merry councillors" of the new tsar, the
Mass man; they alone among the hundred millions of Russians were granted the right to express
their opinions freely; they might mock, criticize,
and deride the rulers at a time when the most
rigorous persecution and terrorism prevailed
throughout the whole country. Bim and Bom
had received a special permit from the Soviets to
express openly everything which was current
among the people in a secret and threatening way,
and thus to provide an outlet for latent rancour.
Every evening, the thousand-headed Mass man,
fawned upon by the whole court, sat in the circus
and listened eagerly to the slanderous speeches of
the two clowns Bim and Bom. In the midst of
grotesque acrobatics and buffooneries, amid jokes
and play, these two were allowed to utter bitter
truths to which otherwise the ear of the ruler was
angrily shut.

'The circus in which Bim and Bom performed
was crowded night after night to the farthest
limits: people came from far and wide to hear
Bim and Bom, who soon became star clowns.
Their jokes were the daily talk of Moscow. One

person told them to another, until finally the whole town knew the latest insults which these two fools had permitted themselves to make.

'In the dark period of militant communism, people were particularly under the spell of the two clowns; at that time, the loose jokes to which Bim and Bom treated them with untiring energy were the one respite from the continuous pressure of force and tyranny, the only possibility of hearing open criticism and mockery of the ruler, the Mass man. People abandoned themselves voluptuously to these precious moments of intellectual freedom.

'In spite of their impudent criticisms, Bim and Bom were nevertheless one of the chief supports of the Bolshevik régime: the universal discontent would have burst all bounds if it had not been dissolved in harmless mirth by the two clowns. But, however biting might be the satire of Bim and Bom, the Government could rely on their never overstepping the limits of the permissible, for Bim and Bom were completely trustworthy members of the Communist Party, and at the bottom of their hearts loyal servants of their masters. They understood how to draw the fangs of the seemingly most malicious jest before they let it loose in the ring. Their attacks were never directed against the whole, but only against details, and thus they contrived to divert attention from essentials. Besides, every one of their jokes contained a hidden warning to the laughter lovers: "Take care: Look out, we know you! We are aware of what you are thinking and feeling!"'

# PALEFACE

I do not suggest that there is any resemblance between the Black Laughter of Mr. Anderson's negro servants and the official laughter of the Soviet clowns. The poor little provincial Whites of the american story have not the power of life and death over their negro servants. They do not go down into the kitchen beforehand and arrange what the Black clown shall laugh at and what he shall spare. The poor little White is at the mercy of his dark 'inferior,' his traditional sense of 'superiority' dwindling every day: but of course, since he is not in reality superior, he should not have a Black servant, then he wouldn't be laughed at.

The Soviet clowns were apparently rather like members of Mr. Henry Ford's propaganda department, which is supposed to have invented all the terms, such as 'Tin Lizzy,' 'Flying Bedstead,' and so on, that are thrown at the Ford car. Such an official, carefully regulated safety-valve is the greatest advertisement for the thing 'attacked.' It is like the jokes about the Scotchman's meanness, which (I am glad to say) endear the Scot to all Britons.

The kind of *black laughter* I have been considering all along is of quite a different character from that. It, too, of course, describes itself as innocuous. The White is flatteringly assured that he is such a very secure Big White Chief that he can afford to become the laughing-stock of the rest of the world. But in practice that flattering picture is proved to be untrue. The account of the Black Laughter in Russia contains some apt instruction for us, if we can bring ourselves to be attentive to it.

# WHITE LAUGHTER

§ 14. *White Laughter*.

THERE is nothing today for us to laugh about, it is true. Bernard Shaw and Company *laughed* all the time. A merry twinkle was never out of their eye. Happy sunny White children of long ago! But their laughter was the opposite of what ours should be. They laughed ever so genially over things that, unfortunately, we can no longer *afford* to laugh at: today we are all, actually or potentially, *Poor Whites*. The prosperity even of America is a very precarious thing, as most Americans today realize.

Few people, as yet, even, understand that we can no longer afford to laugh in that sense. Nine people out of ten live in the past: they are aware that 'things have changed,' but they do not realize very clearly in what specific way. They are creatures of habit: they go on laughing as formerly, at the same things, as though the same things were there, and as though the European were in the same place. This really tragic sloth, and unwillingness to admit anything unpleasant, of the Many, is our main difficulty in proposing a change of orientation for our satire, or indeed in proposing a realistic effort of any sort. *The Present can only be revealed to people when it has become Yesterday.* Another way of putting this is that people are historically-minded, and this, again and again, must be stressed. It is by taking advantage of this human peculiarity that the politician invariably operates, and brings off his most tragic *coups*. The *bovarysme* of man is as nothing compared to this trait (unless you take it as a depart-

269

ment of *bovarysme*)—namely, that Man is an animal that believes he is living in a different time to what in fact he is. So it is that a firm and concrete, totally unromantic, realization of the main features of the Present, gives the man possessing it enormous advantages over others. It is, as it were, the hypothetic ground of the lever of Archimedes, when he said of his lever, 'Give me somewhere to rest it, and I will move the world.'

Bernard Shaw and his light-hearted fabian chums laughed at their own kind. In those remote days their kind was all-powerful. That kind is *us*. The White is still, in appearance, where he was: but he is not powerful: he has no triumphant world, all of his own kind, behind him. We have all, less than a decade ago, issued from a war with each other—in which we *all* lost. We are surrounded by prophets announcing our doom. Our commerce, naturally, has languished and shrunk. It is a very different scene, in short, from that of merry, play-boy social-ism, mischievously disporting itself in the midst of that power and plenty of the Victorian Age.

But even that laughter, in its time, was foolish and ill-advised, as, earlier in the Nineteenth Century, were the romantic revolutionary tirades of Shelley and Byron. The Eminent Victorians, and their in-stitutions, could not, in their day, afford to be laughed at as they permitted everybody to do. The proof of the weakness of the racial policy of the White Overlord (simply taking him as an overlord and as-suming that it was his policy to remain that in some form or other, his lutheran conscience permitting) is to be read in the light of his present position.

# WHITE LAUGHTER

Today we should not give up our laughter: for the White Man knows how to laugh, and the Anglo-Saxon has a kind of genius for it. But we should develop another form of laughter. We should make a more practical use of this great force, and not treat it as an irresponsible, mischievous luxury. Other peoples, their habits, their faces, their institutions, are just as ridiculous as ours. It is a little *over*-christian to be this perpetual, 'dignified' butt! But it is no use at all for our laughter to be of that easy, 'kindly,' schoolboy variety, that merely endears the people laughed at to the lookers-on. *We* are not laughed at in that manner. There is nothing of the advertisement-value of that kind of laughter in the Black Laughter or Red Laughter directed at us.

So let us get a point into our new laughter, if we are going to have it at all. Do not let us fear to hurt people's feelings by our laughter, since we may depend on it they will not spare ours. Nothing can help us so much as to develop this type of laughter.

Let the usual *Black Laughter*, or *Red Laughter*, directed at us, go on: but let it become a thing of the past for us to remain as its amiable, accommodating, and self-abasing butts.

We can even dispense with the musical arpeggios of laughter itself: let us rather meet with the slightest smile all those things that so far we have received with delirious rapture—first, at all events, until we are sure of them. All this frantically advertised welter of ideas that pour over us from all sides, from nowhere, let us above all, at last meet *that* as it should be met. Do not let us spring up and pro-strate ourselves every half-minute, as the latest ambassador arrives with News from Nowhere, with an auctioneer's clatter. Let us remain seated, the feminine privilege: let us smile sceptically, also the feminine privilege: let us insist upon every feminine privilege: let us be faultlessly polite, or rather over-polite, crudely polite: let us show this political tout, dressed up as a wise man from the East, that we have expected him, that we should only have been surprised if he had not turned up: that we hope he soon will go. That is the only way to treat the Thousand and One Magi and Chaldeans who successively rattle our knocker.

# A FINAL PROPOSAL
## A MODEL 'MELTING-POT'

**T**HERE are, in the specifically *moral* nature of the situation in which we find ourselves, factors that I do not propose to investigate. There is the contradictory spectacle, which we can all observe, of our institutions, as they dehumanize themselves, clothing themselves more and more, and with a hideous pomposity, with the stuff of morals— that stuff of which the pagan world was healthily ignorant, in its physical expansiveness and instinct for a concrete truth, and which, for the greatest peoples of the East, has never existed except as a purely political systematization of something irretrievably inferior, a sentimental annexe of a metaphysical truth. It is natural that 'the Congo' should 'flood the Acropolis' (though I am not sure that I did not misunderstand the Princess) when we see the attitudes of Renaissance culture, as illustrated by the great french stylists, being subtly combined with the militant emotional gloom of the Salvation Army: when the Salvation Army marches weeping, in jazz-step, into the study of Montesquieu, then the crocodiles *are* on their way to Hellas.

What I shall especially neglect is to analyse the artificial character of this puritanic gloom, settling in a dense political smoke-screen about us, gushed from both official and unofficial reservoirs. I shall confine myself to remarking that the person who meets all these sham glooms with an anguished *De*

*Profundis*, instead of a laugh (however unpleasant), is scarcely wise, though he may be good. To see a vineyard in the sun surrounded by armed federal officers of the law, who prevent anybody from taking the grapes and making them into wine, is absurd, more than anything else. Foodstuffs rotting upon the quays while people are starving, is a fact that should be met, if at all, not by stylistic theologic melancholy, that seems obvious. Or again, the abstruse principles of the manufacture of paper-money, like the arbitrary non-manufacture of a healthy and pleasant wine, and all that results from one as from the other—of gloom and a sense of the *difficulty* of everything—this is not the material for profound heart-searching groans, although that is the correct unofficial response, it is true. But a reader of this book will be left with those sums or equations on his hands, to work out or not, as he may feel inclined. I have made it clear, I think, how the *ethical*, introduced into the physical problem of the Melting-pot, produces a gloomy and passionate infusion: that is all I set out to do. With a definite proposal, one that has been made often before by many people, I will bring this essay to a close.

In America the expression Melting-pot has been coined to describe the assimilation of european nationalities in the United States, and now of the negro population, ten million strong, which has begun in earnest. In Europe we have no such expression, for the excellent reason that there is no assimilation in progress. If the United States possessed fixed areas in which Danes, Spaniards, Germans, Negroes, Irish and so forth were segregated, as we are, each settled in certain states, with fortified frontiers, taught only their mother-tongue and unable to converse with the inhabitants of the next state, then there would be no Melting-pot there either. America without its Melting-pot would simply be another Europe, plus a Black Belt and a few Chinatowns.

There is a radical contradiction between the european and american way of regarding this problem. Perhaps because it is so much taken for granted, this difference passes for the most part unnoticed by us. Whereas the rulers of America are committed to fusion (however dissimilar the racial stocks) in one form or another, in Europe the question does not even arise. Since the French live upon one side of the Rhine and the Germans upon the other, or the English and the French upon opposite sides of the English Channel, there is no 'problem' as to their mixing: indeed the great majority of Germans or Frenchmen or Englishmen never see a member of the neighbour-nation except during such times as their respective governments decide appropriate for a mass-meeting, as it were, and they are despatched to kill one another with bomb and bayonet. Even then it is only the infantry who see members of the 'enemy' nation at all distinctly: and it is possible for an infantryman to pass many months in the Line without catching sight of more than a few of his european neighbours, and these mostly dead specimens, or even nothing more than their facetious skeletons.

Of these two attitudes—the melting and the non-

melting—the American appears to me by far the
better: I am heart and soul upon the side of the Melting-pot, *not* upon that of the Barbed Wire.   That is
why I have called this book 'The Ethics of the *Melting-pot*,' and not 'The Ethics of the Barbed Wire.'
But what a terribly sad thing it is to reflect that
literally millions of Basques, Finns, Scotsmen,
Danes, Normans, Prussians, Swiss, should be kept
rigidly apart while in Europe, by the intensive per-
petuation of purely historical frontiers (which the
Versailles Treaty has made even more numerous and
complicated than before), whereas if they emigrate
to America they are liable suddenly to be hectored
for an opposite reason—namely because they show
some slight compunction in coupling with a jet-
black Kaffir.   Personally I consider that they are
quite wrong in looking down upon the transplanted
Kaffir: but it is far more stupid of them (if, say, a
Swede) to look down upon a lovely Basque, or (if a
Bavarian) to look down upon an industrious Gascon-
esse.   Yet have they not always been taught to do
that, at least since the rise of the national idea in
Europe or since the time of the great religious
schisms?

My own view is that the Melting-pot should be set
up in Europe, upon the spot.   Instead of posters on
our walls which say 'Join the Royal Air Force and
See the World,' there should be posters (and offices
in every district to deal with applicants) saying,
'Marry a Swiss and See the World,' or, more jocularly,
'Get spliced to a Finn, and Get About.'

What can there be against it, except that it would
be impossible to have wars any more in Europe?   If

it is objected that there is no unifying principle in Europe to compare with *americanization*, it is necessary to recall that only five centuries ago the whole of Europe possessed one soul in a more fundamental way than America can be said to at this moment, and the actual appearance of its towns must have been at least as uniform as today (and that is very uniform), though in a more agreeable fashion. As to the individuals of the various races, there is no obstacle there. In the valleys of the Pyrenees, for instance, you meet with a great many people physically as like as two eggs to the inhabitant of Devonshire, Derby, Limerick, or Caithness: a swiss peasant woman is in character and physical appearance often so identical with a swedish, english, german, or french girl, that they might be twin sisters. This everyone must have remarked who has ever travelled to those countries. It has always been fratricidal that these people should be taught to disembowel, blind and poison each other on the score of their quite imaginary 'differences' of blood or mind, but today there is less excuse for it than ever before. So why not a *Melting-pot?*—instead of more and more intensive discouragement of such a fusion. Europe is not so very large: why should it not have one speech like China and acquire one government?

But feeling about Europe in that manner, and all too familiar with that situation, the spectacle of the rather feverish opposite to that attitude, wherever these same Europeans leave their countries and live in the proximity of people so different from themselves as the Negroes or the Chinese, cannot but occur to one as a very sudden and from some points of view

277

unsatisfactory reversal. On the one hand you have too absolute a segregation, on the other too absolute a freedom to mix. America is the child of Europe entirely, except for the Negroes and in Mexico and south of Panama the Indians, and the two problems should not be dissociated. What happens to Europe is of great importance to America, and vice versa—what happens to America, that other-Europe, must be of great moment to us.

This essay is much more to propose that we set up a Melting-pot in Europe—which would be as it were a Model Melting-pot, not at the boiling-point but cooking at a steady rate day in day out—than to venture any criticism of the principle underlying the american or african Melting-pot or, alternatively, Colour Line. Indeed a quite irrational attitude is often adopted by the American to miscegenation. Another factor of 'inferiority' feeling has its roots in a profound misunderstanding of the true situation. The American is apt to accept the false european attitude towards 'race,' as it is called. It is a common experience in talking to Americans to hear some magnificent human specimen (who is obviously the issue of say a first-class Swede and a magnificent Swissess, with a little Irish and a touch of Basque) refer to himself as a 'mongrel.' It is inconceivable, yet indeed that is how such a 'mixed' product is apt to look upon this superb marriage of Scandinavian, Goth and Celt—all stocks as closely related in blood—if it is 'blood' that is the trouble— as the brahmanic caste of India. Merely physically this epithet is given the lie: for all you have to do is to look at this sterling type of 'mixed' American to

278

admire the purity of line and fine adjustment achieved by the conjunction of these sister stocks.   Far from being a 'mongrel,' of course, he is a sort of super-European: the best of several closely allied stocks have met in him, in exactly the same way as was constantly happening in the noble european families —where the issue of a marriage between nobles, whether from England and Italy or Spain and Russia, did not constitute a 'half-breed,' but rather a more exalted feudal product, so subtly 'mixed.'

Some racial mixtures are not so fortunate as others, however, it is necessary to allow: the indian and spanish mixtures, in say Peru or Mexico, have not proved really very good.   The Barber of Seville that peeps through the Inca removes him from Mozart, and yet does not make a good Indian of him, though there are exceptions.   But practically all european intermarriage presents no problem at all, and is indeed politically much to be desired, as certain to abolish the fiction of our frontiers and the fiction of the 'necessity' of war.   The asiatic elements in Southern Spain, Italy and Russia aside, the European is as much of one blood as are the inhabitants of the British Isles, and in many instances more so—for instance the Bavarian and the lowland Scotch are man for man as nearly one race (to look at them, as well as in their character) as you could find anywhere at all.   If they spoke a common Ido the Austrian with his *Spielhahnfeder* and *Eichenlaub* stuck in his *Steierhut* would melt into the Crofter without noticing he had left his native village.

But (until they reach America, and all have to speak english, or, in Latin-America, spanish) the great difficulty is language. In discussing such a question as this we always get back to the problem of Babel. It is in the interest of the Melting-pot that every European should wish to learn Volapuc as I do, or to have some language picked for him that it shall be agreed all shall speak and that he can easily learn and speak—woo his possibly distant bride in, and talk over all those subjects of common interest with his brother at the other extremity of Europe, which since the decay of latin as a universal tongue no one has been able to do. I cannot imagine any person in Europe who, when the matter was presented to him in that light, would not plump for some Volapuc: but if there is anywhere a person who would not, how slender his reasons must be compared to those a Dutchman say in Africa could allege for refusing to mate his daughter with a Cape-Black or a settler from the Dekkan! And yet even the Dutchman would not be right, would he?—how much more wrong then would not the man in Europe be who stood out, for in fifty per cent. of the cases he would be vetoing a closer match than could be made even in the home-village at any given time—for I would guarantee to match a young man in a Devon village better in the Canton of Berne than would be possible probably, at any given moment, in his own english district.

On the other hand if the Dutchman in Africa had ten daughters and seized the other end of the stick (after a reading of Plomer) so fanatically as to pester them all to choose upon the spot a Black bridegroom, that would be a sentimental extreme that it would be perhaps allowable to deplore: if he should embellish his persuasiveness with highly-coloured abuse of all owners of a pale skin, then he would definitely become irritating and perhaps even absurd, and if his ten girls took him and flogged him no one could find it in his heart to blame them, though if called to a Grand Jury it would be necessary to send the whole of the ten girls to jail of course, for they should not, strictly speaking, flog their father, either, however misguided, as potentially his whiteness would be the symbol of their consanguinity and the ultimate reason for their objecting to the break-up of their pigment. This last illustration touches upon a complexity which (in rare instances, so far) qualifies the absolute simplicity of this question—the problem of the *gaga* Paleface Papa who reads Plomer or Du Bois. But—as I have prophesied—he will be dealt with by his children or grandchildren, when he disinherits them and leaves all his money to the female Kaffir cook.

What in these concluding pages it has been my intention to stress is that the fiery ethics of the Melting-pot are conjunctly european and protestant in origin more than anything else (though the gallic invention of the 'great nation' plays its part as well). The fanatical ill-temper and the black intolerance that accompany the discussion and propaganda for 'race-fusion' can be traced to those sources, when they cannot be directly traced to the equally intemperate ethical zeal of the 'radicalist' righteousness.

At this time the Anglo-Saxon is no longer paramount in North America: but his language is still the general speech, and american civilization is in its main principles anglo-saxon. The alternation of emotional indulgence in liberalist programmes (and anglo-saxon 'radicalism' is newer and more heated liberalism, merely) and unintelligent race-prejudice, with which distressing see-saw we are so familiar, is anglo-saxon, is it not? Neither the Spanish, Portuguese nor French as colonists have handled their respective Melting-pot in that manner. The latin tradition, more tolerant, catholic and mature, has not sentimentalized about the deeply-pigmented skin, nor fixed upon it, on the other hand, a stigma. You would not be so likely to get adepts of jazz in a Black Belt in a latin land, nor the ferocity of lynching neighboured by anti-White tracts, written by Whites, nor a universal thunder of psalms from Black and White throats mixed, and evangelist extremes of intolerance and hysterical expansion—it would be more likely you would find a firmer attitude, more satisfactory to both sides, far less superstitious, in the Latin.

Yet, although it is necessary to fix, for any such survey, the anglo-saxon responsibilities, they are not all anglo-saxon, and the nationalism of Europe as a whole is to blame, I think, both for the excesses of the 'Nordic Blondes' or what Mencken calls the 'Ofays,' where they occur, and for the excesses of their satirists and detractors. Must we not agree that it is the artificial principle of european *separatism* (of all the Irelands, Ulsters, Catalonias, Polands, Czecho-Slovakias and the rest) transplanted to America or Africa, that, there, is apt to issue in a quite new form in a hotbed of separatist, or of fusionist, passion—which in the near future may wreck those societies as it is wrecking ours?

## A MODEL 'MELTING-POT'

If (to show my enthusiasm for fusion) I may allow myself a strikingly *mixed* metaphor, it is at the fountain-head that we should establish our Melting-pot—an example to all other Melting-pots. And it is here in Europe that we should start a movement at once for the miscegenation of Europeans—with *each other*, that is—Asia and Africa could be considered later, no doubt, for incorporation in our Model Melting-pot.

I have dealt with this subject before, but in another connection, in *The Lion and the Fox* : I would refer the reader to pages 295-326 of that essay. There the problem of the Melting-pot as it applies—or rather as it does *not* apply—to England, was discussed at length, particularly as it concerns the 'Saxon' and the 'Celt.' The 'Celt,' I there demonstrated, was a complete myth: and I showed how, with a great deal of wit, Matthew Arnold, who was probably aware of the shadowy nature of his 'Celt,' staged an ironical drama for the John Bulls and Fenian Paddies of his time. I will quote a few lines from Chapter VI., Part IX., in which I lay bare the full working of Arnold's ironical vision. I say—

'From the treacherous polished surface of Arnold's prose (its body clouded for its reception) I will now expiscate that laughing idea which we have been preparing to examine. It is the idea of two island neighbours and strongly hallucinated brethren, the Irishman and the Englishman, the Celt and the Teuton (both in the baleful 'grip' of 'celtism,' which stands between them and success in science, or any exact, unemotional study), involved in a curious fratricidal strife and tangle of

romantic misunderstandings. . . . Arnold is not
himself' (I add) 'at all the dupe of the "celtic"
notion: his whole essay is written to expose it.
Yet he accepts the conventional nomenclature of
'Celt' for all that type of expression and sentiment that had been popularized under that name.'

And I then quote him, where he says, apropos of
this famous 'Celtism':
    'Nay, perhaps, if we are doomed to perish
(Heaven avert the omen!) we shall perish by our
Celtism, by our self-will and want of patience with
ideas, our inability to see the way the world is
going; and yet those very Celts, by our affinity
with whom we are perishing, will be hating and
upbraiding us all the time.'

It is generally forgotten that Ireland was colon-
ized, especially in the east, by the Norsemen, nor-
wegian being spoken in Dublin, as it was in Bristol,
until the fourteenth century.  That famous 'celtic'
literary buccaneer, Mr. Bernard Shaw, is no doubt
a typical Norseman, as to stock at least.  And in
the essay from which I have just quoted I illustrated
(page 322) the upshot of all this in the following
fashion, from an average experience of my own,
which I am sure many people could match.  Here
is what I wrote:—
    'During the martyrdom of the Mayor of Cork
I had several opportunities of seeing considerable numbers of irish people demonstrating among
the London crowds.  I was never able to dis-
cover which were Irish and which were English,

however. They looked to me exactly the same. With the best will in the world to discriminate the orderly groups of demonstrators from the orderly groups of spectators, and to satisfy the romantic proprieties on such an occasion, my eyes refused to effect the necessary separation, that the principle of "celtism" demanded, into chalk and cheese. I should have supposed that they were a lot of romantic english-people pretending to be irish-people, and demonstrating with the assistance of a few priests and pipers, if it had not been that they all looked extremely depressed, and english-people when they are giving romance the rein are always very elated.'

It is singular that from the time of Arnold's *Celtic Literature* to that of *The Lion and the Fox* there should have been nobody in England to detect this colossal anomaly—there where there have been so many people to foment, or (upon the other side) to take quite seriously, the Irish Separatist passion. The fact is that it has always paid the Irish individually too well, to allow them to laugh at it (though now it is all over they are beginning to do so, witness Mr. Bernard Shaw in his article in *Time and Tide*, Dec. 1928): and the english politician in every case found Ireland such an uncomfortable problem that he was in no mood to relish the farce that might lie hidden under these disturbances.

That will terminate for the present what I have to say upon this difficult subject. A Volapuc for Europe and an internationally organized 'Melting-pot,' a general international exchange of workers and of women or men, an official Marriage Bureau, with photographs and pedigrees and all those certificates that are indispensable in such a case—arrangements with the republics of America to adopt our particular Volapuc—that is the idea, in its brutal outline. I will not work it out further until I hear what response the public makes to my suggestions, not only because that would be otiose, seeing the passionate atmosphere of jingo ideology that prevails at the moment, but because I am not so well qualified as many other people to draw up a practical scheme. But I shall be extremely happy to get in touch with any experts who are so qualified, and to offer them what merely theoretic assistance lies in my power.

# APPENDIX

NOTE.—This review of Miss Mayo's *Mother India* appeared in *Enemy No. 2.* It is reprinted here without alteration, as an indirect contribution to the discussions conducted in *Paleface*.

# APPENDIX

## MOTHER INDIA

THIS very much discussed book breaks a *depth-record,* as it were: it unerringly sinks to a level of vulgar untruth that should make it a paragon of its kind. Miss Mayo is, therefore, to be congratulated: she has achieved what I feel she has intended; she has left an appreciably greater mess behind her in the world, or that part where she operates, than was there already, and has sent up an appreciable distance the international tension and fever. She has had the satisfaction of insulting three hundred million people: and should it be that three hundred million of her ancestors sustained insults, or one of her most prominent ancestors three hundred million insults, this should do something towards wiping that out. (Such fantastic assumptions come to your mind : for what can make a person want to write such a book?) There have already been mass meetings of protest in India. Her little book is assured of its place in the pantheon of Hate.

Its main argument leads the reader at once, with a firm matter-of-fact step, into the region of sex: and with a hand accustomed to the licences of the hospital, a few intimate physiological particulars are brusquely laid bare, just to put the reader in a good humour.

The argument is this: owing, says Miss Mayo, to their premature sex-life, all the inhabitants of India

T                                289

are 'degenerate'—quite the opposite of us. 'At about eight years old the Indian male child is apt to be hired out to prostitution,' she says. 'The little boy . . . is likely, if physically attractive, to be drafted for the satisfaction of grown men, or to be regularly attached to a temple, in the capacity of a prostitute. Neither parent, as a rule, sees any harm in this.' Indeed the indian mother, according to this lady, is addicted to practices all her own. 'So far are they from seeing good or evil, as we see good and evil, that the mother, high caste or low caste, will practise upon her children—the girl "to make her sleep well," the boy "to make him manly," an abuse which the boy, at least, is apt to continue daily for the rest of his life.' (The 'at least' is a curious clause.) Marriages between the immature is another feature of the picture. If, at eight years old, the boy is not 'attractive' presumably, his parents look round for a wife of his own age. So in that case between eight and fourteen he marries: but fourteen is late. Once married, being, of course, of an unbelievably degenerate stock, or else syphilitic, he is found to be barren. No one is surprised. Usually the child-wife, in that case, is sent to a neighbouring temple for the night, where a priest can be relied on not to dismiss her without a fair prospect of a child, if he knows his business and likes the look of the girl. For there are a few, a very few, undegenerate Indians: they become priests.

So it is with no surprise that you learn—or 'after the rough outline just given, small surprise will meet the statement that from one end of the land to the other the average male Hindu of thirty years . . .

is an old man: and that from seven to eight out of every ten such males between the ages of twenty-five and thirty are impotent.'

That is the sad tale of 'sex' that this writer, whose indignation and the form it has taken have sold a great many copies of her book, has to tell. That leprous thing—India—that provoked her to put all this down, she tells us, is such a gigantic menace to the United States that it would 'seem to deprive one of the right to indulge a personal reluctance to incur consequences.' So, deprived of all *rights*, with the air of a christian martyr, Miss Mayo goes manfully on, and throws Ganges mud at the great indian people, ridicules their religion (what is hers?), and quotes to support her statements the Abbé Dubois. The Abbé's book, as indicated by her in a footnote, is *Hindu Manners, Customs and Ceremonies*, Clarendon Press, 1924.

Of all the readers of *Mother India* how many are likely to know anything about the Abbé Dubois? One in a hundred may, but that is not probable. Yet it is, of course, a very well known and exceedingly interesting book, and most students of anthropology are familiar with it. Should Miss Mayo not point out, when she first quotes him in her account of her indian trip last year, that he died in 1848—instead of leaving it 'Clarendon Press, 1924,' and referring later on, in passing, to the fact that the evidence of the Abbé Dubois dates from 'the Nineteenth Century'? He is actually her main source of information: he is quoted on pages 31, 37, 73, 75, 119, 143, 165 and 204. No other authority is drawn upon to this extent. Some of the most 'sensational'

matter of her book comes out of this text-book of
the anthropology of British India. That, for example, is the case with the story about the Indian
child-wives who go to the temples, if barren, and
who are accommodated by the priests. The account given by the Abbé Dubois in *Hindu Manners
and Customs* is as follows: Miss Mayo does not quote
it, it is her custom to paraphrase, so as to make it
seem more actual, probably, and more like her own;
but, whatever the reason, it is a habit that breeds
confusion, unfortunate in the circumstances.

'Expert at reaping profit from the virtues as
well as the vices of their countrymen, the Brahmins see in these touching impulses of nature
merely a means of gaining wealth, and also at the
same time an opportunity of satisfying their
carnal lusts with impunity. There are few temples
where the presiding deity does not claim the power
of curing barrenness in women. . . . On their
arrival, the women hasten to disclose the object of
their pilgrimage to the Brahmins, the managers of
the temple. The latter advise them to pass the
night in the temple, where, they say, the great
Venkateswara, touched by their devotion, will
perhaps visit them in the spirit and accomplish
that which until then has been denied to them
through human power. I must draw a curtain
over the sequel of this deceitful suggestion. The
reader already guesses at it. The following morning these detestable hypocrites, pretending complete ignorance of what has passed, make due
enquiries into all details; and after having congratulated the women upon the reception they

met with from the god, receive the gifts with which they have provided themselves, and take leave of them. . . .' (*Hindu Manners*, etc., p. 594.)

It should be said that the well-known book of the Abbé Dubois is written in a very different tone as touching the indian people from that of Miss Mayo. But then, as Dr. Max Müller writes, the views of the Abbé Dubois were those of 'a scholar with sufficient knowledge, if not of Sanscrit, yet of Tamil, . . . to be able to enter into the views of the natives, to understand their manners and customs, and to make allowance for many of their superstitious opinions and practices, as mere corruptions of an originally far more rational and intelligent form of religion and philosophy.'

It is a quarrel between priests in the case of the Abbé Dubois. For was not this catholic priest in the Dekkan in order to get converts to Christianity? Naturally as a catholic priest he would not give a very glowing account of the Brahmin, his professional rival. Nor would it be at all likely that his account of the indian cults would be exactly propaganda for them, nor that he would compare them favourably with his own 'shop.' But in his treatment of the indian people there is no trace of the Mayo attitude.

In a prefatory note to *Hindu Manners and Customs*, Dr. Max Müller writes as follows:—

'It is difficult to believe that the Abbé Dubois, the author of *Mœurs, Institutions et Cérémonies des peuples de l'Inde*, died in only 1848. By his position as a scholar and as a student of Indian subjects, he really belongs to a period previous to the revival of Sanscrit studies in India. . . . I had no idea, when in 1846 I was attending in Paris the lectures of Eugène Burnouf at the *Collège de France*, that the old Abbé was still living and in full activity as *Directeur des Missions Etrangères*, and I doubt whether even Burnouf himself was aware of his existence in Paris. The Abbé belongs really to the eighteenth century, but as there is much to be learnt even from such as Roberto de' Nobili, who went to India in 1606 . . . so again the eighteenth century was by no means devoid of eminent students of Sanscrit, of Indian religion, and Indian subjects in general. It is true that in our days their observations and researches possess chiefly a historical interest. . . .'

This note of Dr. Max Müller's was not written yesterday; but for him, even, the *Hindu Manners, Customs and Ceremonies* 'possess chiefly a historical interest.'

Under these circumstances, and since no one could pretend that *Mother India* was intended for anything but a large popular Public very unlikely even to have heard of the Abbé Dubois, or at all likely to refer to his work, would it not have been more honest, in quoting the Abbé Dubois, to explain all this to the reader, instead of merely giving the reference, with the name of the Clarendon Press, and the date *1924*? But apart from that, was it honest at all to mingle the 'eighteenth century' information of this authority with gossip of today, and a few facts hastily gathered in a short tour?

Again there is the fact that the information taken from the eighteenth century account of the Abbé Dubois is not necessarily quoted in his words.   It is (pp. 36-37, *Mother India*) mixed up with material from *Young India, Sept. 2, 1926,* and that of other unspecified sources, and so recounted by the author as though all part of one story, in the result making the eighteenth century generalizations of the Abbé Dubois appear something that had happened yesterday.

There is no indication at all that its writer is anything but a very clever, able and practised person; she knows quite well that what she gives is not evidence : that it is presented in such a way as to be violently offensive on every ground to the Hindu (she favours strangely the Mohammadan):  she cannot fail to see that in an insidious manner it puts the British Government of India in the position of a machiavellian power, leaving the unfortunate Indian alone in his apparently unexampled depravity and squalor (all the men sexually impotent and broken at twenty-five years old—the average age of demise 23, etc. etc.), whereas she, no doubt, has more than enough political intelligence to be aware that should the English leave India tomorrow the Soviet would quietly walk in, if they are not practically there already;  and a little compassion for the Indian (which she does not possess—nothing but the affectation of the fury of a kind of mad sanitary inspector) would save her from contemplating that particular change of masters for even such reptiles, 'slaves,' perverted heathens, morons and masturbators, as she complacently describes:  she knows that her inflammatory gibes about 'slave psychology' addressed to the indian people is the material of 'radical' oratory or of nationalist spread-eagleism such as no european public would swallow today, since they have found out that they are not, themselves, so peculiarly 'free,' and that as to 'slave-psychology' *people who live in glass-houses*, and so on: and, finally, when she claims that the music of the spinning wheel of Gandhi has been a main inspiration to her in writing her book, she pollutes one of the only saintly figures in the world; and it is to be hoped that he will use all the lustrational resources of his caste-training to cleanse himself of any traces left by the passage of Miss Mayo: also in connection with Gandhi, she is not so naïve as not to know that her super-american gospel of dogmatic modernist reform (or *is* it american, or rather should Americans in general be held responsible for their Mayos? I believe not) can scarcely be said to have anything to do with what Gandhi teaches.

What particular demon actuates Miss Mayo? I may go into that when I come to use her book, along with many others, as evidence in later parts of my *Paleface*. But, now, I think, in imitation of the Abbé Dubois, I will at this point 'draw a curtain' over Miss Mayo—not over her 'daring' or 'outspoken' bits about sex, heaven preserve us (Abbé Dubois is much more amusing, if that is what you want, and there's much more of it), but—just over Miss Mayo.

But there is another thing that Miss Mayo knows —not quite to draw to the curtain. Miss Mayo knows that if an indian lady journalist, for instance, hurried to America on such a mission as Miss Mayo's, she could very easily draw an equally untruthful picture. She knows this as well as I know similarly that a visit to England or Germany could be made into a *Mother England* or *Mother Germany*. Indeed no day passes but we are able in Europe to observe this in practice: I refer to the accounts the European is fed with about *Mother America*, accounts that are intended to make his flesh creep or his blood boil. No picture done in that way *can* be true, of course: and I am certainly the last person to lend any credence to the stories of the *Mother America* type. Miss Mayo, I am very sure, has nothing to do with anything that we should legitimately call 'America.' The indian lady visitor to the United States, let us suppose, has arrived. She 'courteously' requests to be 'shown over,' and in her book she can say how very 'courteous,' at least (that looks well, it shows how fair and unbiassed you are), everybody was (how very *stupidly* courteous to such a person she may privately reflect): and she could (very easily) have a remarkably 'highly-placed diplomatist' or 'a great inventor' perhaps (that would look well) always at her elbow, just as Miss Mayo always has a *particularly* 'high-caste Brahmin' at her elbow, to inform against *other* high-caste Brahmins: the indian lady visitor or inquisitor, the 'restless analyst' from the East, could quote extensively from some american equivalent of the *Loom of Youth,* and tell the horrified Indian Public how in all the schools and universities of the United States homosexuality was rampant: then she could tell the usual stories of pregnant high-school girls—reveal whole classes carried away in one brake to the Lying-

in Hospital: she could state *as a fact* that all american men were sexually impotent at thirty (hence the
Broadway girl-shows), and that self-abuse was intense and universal throughout the 48 States of the
Union: she could describe the death-rate per day in
an american city by violent crime, quote Mencken
for bits about the monstrosities of Prohibition: and
she could wind up by saying that America is 'a
physical menace' (cf. p. 23, *Mother India*) to the
Hindu.

'Under present conditions of human activity,
whereby, *whether we will or no,* the roads that join
us to every part of the world continually shorten
and multiply, it would appear that some knowledge of main facts concerning so big and to-day
so near a neighbour should be a part of our intelligence and self-protection.'   (*Mother India*, p. 20.)

The above italics are mine.

Or the indian lady investigator might take another
line.   'The average male Hindu of thirty years . . .
is an old man,' says Miss Mayo.   But the indian
visitor to the United States might describe herself
as astounded to find that at thirty years old the
White Man seemed no older than 'our Indians' at
eight, and, indeed, that that was the case at almost
any age: she could remark thereupon that she
doubted, so childish were they (almost as though on
purpose, she might suggest), whether these 'boy-
men' had ever exercised their sexual nature at all,
or ever, properly speaking, reached puberty; and,
indeed, it was her belief that they never did, that
was what *she* thought about it, and that she sus-

pected them of pretending to be pederasts, very often, only to cover this sexual apathy, and so as to retain a sort of false, prolonged, childish immaturity, and in order also to evade (much stiffening and ruffling of Madras-suffragist indignation, here!)—criminally to evade their sexual duties; that as to the american mothers, far from sitting by their daughters' bedsides, and 'helping them to get to sleep' in the indian fashion, instead, these mothers put on flesh-coloured tights and went and danced all night, while their husbands stole out, gun in hand, and went lynching Negroes in the next block.

All this the indian lady journalist could write to her terrified, indignant, delighted countrymen and countrywomen. She could point out that now at any moment Mr. Levine might be expected to 'hop' over to Mother India—or Miss Mayo, again, by way of the air, for that matter—and heaven knows what germs he (or she) would not bring from such a country as the United States! She might suggest that Gandhi be sent to see what could be done to instil a certain sense of womanhood into these lost populations. Perhaps President Coolidge could be persuaded to spin for a few hours every day. But at least Gandhi—or perhaps the League of Nations? —might dissuade the United States males from abusing themselves, every day, at least.

And then, of course, she could quote Prescott's *Conquest of Mexico* to give an idea of the sort of blood-sacrifices currently perpetrated by the Americans. This she could easily mix up with the Ku Klux Klan, and say that they disembowelled fifty Negroes a day in any fair-sized american city.

This book she would call (in Tamil) *Hail Columbia, Happy Land.*

This is a sort of book, at all events, that you can't have enough of, both ways, and all ways. It promotes that excellent feeling of brotherly love between nations and races that is so very useful and comfortable for all of us.

# INDEX

301

# INDEX